An Orchestrated Mistake

Shane O'Dell

Nibiru Publishing

An Orchestrated Mistake. Copyright 2021 by Shane O'Dell. All rights reserved. No part of this book may be used or reproduced in any manner whatsoever without written permission except in the case of brief quotations embodied in critical articles and reviews. For information, email shane@anorchestratedmistake.com.

Library of Congress Cataloging-in-Publication Data has been applied for.

ISBN: 978-1-7775962-0-0

Cover Design: Sandika S. Sathsara

To order copies of *An Orchestrated Mistake* or to contact Shane O'Dell, please visit www.anorchestratedmistake.com.

Dedication

This book is dedicated to all those who stood by me.

Thank you.

Contents

Chapter One	1
Chapter Two	18
Chapter Three	38
Chapter Four	56
Chapter Five	76
Chapter Six	87
Chapter Seven	103
Chapter Eight	129
Chapter Nine	139
Chapter Ten	158
Chapter Eleven	182
Chapter Twelve	202
Chapter Thirteen	226
Chapter Fourteen	248
Chapter Fifteen	264
Chapter Sixteen	286
Chapter Seventeen	308
Chapter Eighteen	330
Chapter Nineteen	353

Once upon a time, there was a fool so arrogant he believed the laws in the court of health did not apply to him.

This is the story of an escape from a life sentence.

CHAPTER ONE

I never needed an alarm clock to wake up. My cravings for a cigarette would always trigger that. Reaching out for the ashtray on the nightstand before I was fully conscious, I'd often send it crashing to the floor, the smell of the rising plume of ash signaling the beginning of another day for me, Nicholas Alexander.

"Shit," I mumbled, peering over the edge of the bed before reaching down, fingering through the shards of broken glass and pulling out the remnants of last night's cigarette before clamping it between my teeth and rolling out of bed.

I stopped in the kitchen to get the pot of coffee out of the fridge and poured myself a cup, adding the last dregs from the milk carton before continuing to the bathroom. There, I took the unlit butt out of my mouth long enough to brush my teeth before returning it to its rightful home between my lips.

Opening the bathroom mirror, I looked for my razor and spotted my old glucose meter on the top shelf, looking like an old, abandoned radiator in a junkyard. Wondering if the thing still worked, I fumbled through a drawer, found some old test strips, and shoved one in. Stabbing my finger with a tired lance, I drew a drop of blood, touched it to the strip, and waited for the verdict. Not even a number appeared. It just read: 'HI.'

"Whatever," I scoffed before lighting the butt and slapping shaving cream on my face.

I got dressed for work in my best Mets t-shirt and pair of blue jeans I'd purchased for a couple of bucks from the wardrobe department during the wrap of our last film. I stood in my bedroom, gulping down the last of my cold coffee, eyeing the ashes and broken glass ashtray beside my bed. *I really must clean that up when I get home tonight*, I thought. *If not tonight, then definitely by next weekend.* And so another workweek had begun.

If I walked to the subway at the right pace, I'd have just enough time to have an entire cigarette, grab a coffee and paper at the corner bodega, and then dash up the stairs to the station platform.

Riding the subway into Manhattan from my apartment in Brooklyn took the better part of an hour, but once seated, I wasted no time opening my paper to the only two sections worth reading. The first was *The Boondocks* comic strip. Nothing amused me more than reading about ten-year-old Huey Freeman sticking it to the man. I've been trying for forty-four years to stick it to the man, but all it ever got me was an audit. After my daily dose of *The Boondocks,* I'd locate the other section that gave me hope: the sports page. I am always optimistic I would relish my team's victory, but they imploded in the late stages of the game as usual. I am greeted with the usual disappointment my team is once again on the outside looking in mere weeks after training camp. I swear if people didn't read the damn paper before work, they'd be in much better moods by the time they got there.

No matter how much time I give myself to commute somewhere in New York, the MTA always finds a way to have me running late. Changing subways at Penn Station, I dash through the morning throngs of commuters, zigzagging between cops, Wall Street types, and families from the Midwest standing on the station platform with their mouths agape trying to make sense of it all. I don't try to make sense of anything anymore. I much prefer to just focus on my work. That way, I don't have to listen to the uncertainty in my head.

I'd barely taken any time off from work since moving to New York from Vancouver nine years ago. In fact, since arriving in the Big Apple, I had barely been outside of the five boroughs. Unless, of course, you want to count the time I made a wrong turn in a camera truck and ended up in Weehawken, New Jersey. I think you have to stumble around a place for more than five minutes before you can claim to have visited there, and time spent waiting in line at a fast-food drive-thru doesn't count.

An Orchestrated Mistake

I guess I'm guilty of not having much balance in my life. Especially during those last few years in New York. How can you tell when work has become an unbalanced obligation if you're working at something you love? I'm far too busy wrestling with life's illusions to answer that.

I popped up out of the subway at 23rd & 7th Avenue. There, Sonus's electric guitar immediately assaulted my ears. Sonus is the Latin word for noise, but before you mistake me for a wimpy chain-smoking intellectual, you should probably know that the only other Latin term I know is *Tempus Fugit*, or 'time flies.' Anyway, Sonus, this sixty-something fellow, is there on the sidewalk every morning banging away on his electric guitar. No rhythm, no melody, just noise. I rarely, if ever, saw anyone throw any money into his open guitar case. No one ever stopped to listen. Mostly they were just hurrying. After all, most New Yorkers seem mandated to hurry. I just figured they were hurrying to get away from Sonus. On occasion, I'd toss a buck or two into his guitar case, but I think I was just paying him to stop that awful noise. He never did. Sonus would just smile and nod, then continue banging on that abused electric guitar as I'd hurry my way down 23rd toward 6th Avenue to get my breakfast before my head exploded.

"Hey, buddy," the old-timer in his food cart would call out to me as I got close. "The usual?"

"Yeah, but I'm hungry this morning. Can you give me that chocolate donut too?" I asked, pointing to one behind the glass. "Yeah, the one with the sprinkles," I added as he reached for the donut.

"Two Sweet'n Low, half-and-half," he confirmed, dropping the donut in a bag and pouring a coffee.

"You know it."

"I do!"

An Orchestrated Mistake

I'd been stopping at the Puerto Rican old timer's food cart since we moved our offices up from the Meatpacking District to Chelsea a few years ago. Every morning, I got the same thing: two eggs and cheese on a croissant with ketchup and pepper and a large coffee with two Sweet'n Lows and half-and-half. I liked just showing up at the cart without engaging in the idle chit-chat that usually goes with placing an order. Idle chit-chat is life's speed bumps. It's not that I like going to any restaurant or vendor where they're so familiar with me they know me by name. I'd hate that too, as then I'd have to engage in that idle chit-chat. No, I like to patronize a place where I'm just familiar enough for them to know what to offer me when I arrive. To them, my name is 'Buddy' or 'Dude' or 'Fella.' I'll even accept 'Sir' if I'm not feeling too ancient. I love anonymity. It's probably why I was a goalie in hockey as a kid. I got to wear a mask.

With my order in a bag safely tucked under my arm, I darted against the light across 6th Avenue while lighting another cigarette and inhaling my donut. The fading car horns behind me indicated the danger had passed, and I completed another safe crossing, so I'd amble down 22nd Street toward my office, happily munching and inhaling.

"Hola!" Laura would announce, entering the office with a single dog leash draped over her shoulders. Looking up from my desk, I'd acknowledge her as two sets of paws scrambled for traction on the hardwood floor.

"Insane bunnies," I said, watching Lulu and Zombie fly toward Laura's office. Grinning, Blake would enter right after the dogs, carrying the second leash.

"Yeah, they're crazy," Blake would proclaim, stopping with Laura to admire the morning ritual. They'd chuckle, looking at me to confirm I was enjoying the moment before continuing to their offices.

Once Laura and Blake disappeared, I'd immediately start preparing for my breakfast guests by tearing up the egg croissant into bite-size pieces. Lulu, the black lab, was always the first to arrive, followed by Zombie, who was a cute little black and white mix. They'd both take their seats beside my desk, tails wagging, and like true New York dogs, pleading with their big brown eyes for me to hurry.

"You both know this has to stop, don't you?" I asked to a set of wagging tails in overdrive. Laura didn't like me feeding the dogs. I don't think it was so much because it promoted begging or something; these two were way past begging rehab. I think it was more because Laura never really trusted I was buying anything that was truly edible, whether for the dogs or me. For me, I just can't say 'no' to big brown eyes and wagging tails. Besides, I rarely ate breakfast. The odd donut was enough for me. My standard fare was a coffee and a cigarette, so what would I do with my breakfast croissant every morning? I suppose I could have stopped buying it, but how will my Puerto Rican friend put his grandkids through college? Maybe more importantly, what are Lulu and Zombie going to think when they show up for breakfast and breakfast didn't show up? No, until Lulu and Zombie tell me they'd rather just have a cigarette and a coffee, I'll keep buying two eggs with cheese on a croissant.

After the breakfast conspiracy had been gobbled down and my guests had scampered off, Blake walked over holding a script. "Nick, I read the script you gave me."

"Whaddya think?" I asked, looking up from my computer.

"Not bad. It definitely has some laughs."

"I thought so too," I replied, refraining from telling Blake that while reading it on the subway, I laughed so hard Diet Coke shot out my nose. "It needs work," I continued. "But I do think there's a fun story there."

"Yeah. I think Laura wants to read it," Blake said, flipping through the pages. "A friend of yours wrote it?"

"Yeah. He gave it to me to see what I thought. Made me laugh a few times, so I wanted to see what you thought."

"I like it. If ya don't need it back, let me pass it to Laura."

"Sure." I shrugged. "I don't need it."

I knew Blake would get a bang out of my friend's script; that's why I gave it to him. It's just quirky enough to appeal to his sense of humor. I was the production manager on the first full-length film Blake directed. That feature is a sophisticated thriller set on New York's Mulberry Street and is where Zombie inherited her name. Laura produced, Blake wrote and directed, and I managed production. After first reading the script and seeing the budget, I thought they were joking when they told me they were committed to shooting it. It was a full-length feature with crowd scenes, helicopters, tons of makeup, and special effects, and the budget was twenty bucks and a six-pack.

"You're joking, right?" I said to Laura, looking up from the last page of the budget.

"No." She laughed. "Make it happen, Alexander."

And we did. Not only did we make the film happen, it went on to win numerous awards on the festival circuit, becoming a hit with both audiences and critics, and eventually sold, going on to a distribution deal. We had a blast making that film, and for me, it epitomized what independent filmmaking is all about—bringing an entertaining story to the screen in an unconventional way. It was the reason I moved to New York. Well, one of the reasons.

Later that morning, I sauntered over to Heather's desk. Heather headed up our development department at Three Walls Productions, our independent film company. Heather also dabbled in real estate on the side. I loved Heather because she reminded me of one of those dotty Englishwomen my mother used to watch on British sitcoms. You know, the one who is just a little too preoccupied with where they are to realize that they've already been there. A wonderful quality if you think about it. No matter how many times they've seen it or experienced it, everything is done with such a high level of concentration it's like they're experiencing it for the first time.

"Heather," I said, sauntering over.

"Yes, Nicholas."

"You have to save me."

"Why? What's happened, Nicholas?" she asked without looking up from her computer.

"If you don't have any apartment listings, I'm going to have to stay with my sister out on Long Island until I can find a place."

"What's wrong with that? Might be fun."

"No, it won't. I stayed with her for the first six months when I moved to New York."

"Then it will be like old times."

"I hated it. You don't know my sister. You don't know my brother-in-law. The man's an idiot."

"It'll just be temporary, Nicholas. You'll get a chance to bond with your nieces."

"The man regurgitates the six o'clock news and passes it off as original thought."

"Where have you been looking?" Heather asked, looking up for the first time.

"Brooklyn, Queens. This weekend I went up to see a place in the Bronx."

"And nothing?"

"Nothing I could afford that I would call home. The house I'm in now has sold. I told my landlord that I'd be out of the basement suite in two months. It's the end of two months."

"Nicholas, maybe you should consider getting a roommate until you can find a nice place on your own."

"Heather, my days of having a roommate are long gone. That's all I need is to come home and find my roommate has eaten my leftovers."

"Nicholas," Heather replied, shaking her head and looking back down at her computer. "You don't even cook, so there is no fear of anyone eating a leftover."

"Yes, there is. I have leftovers. They'll eat my leftover Chinese takeout."

"Nicholas," Heather replied with her British accent dripping. "No one with any self-respect would dare touch, never mind eat, anything you would pass off as a leftover."

"Well, I still don't want a roommate."

"I'll keep an eye out, but I'm not making any promises."

"Thanks, but please try," I said, turning back to my desk.

"Alexander!" Laura shouted, coming out of her office. "I noticed Madeline isn't here this morning."

"And she won't be," I replied, taking a seat behind my desk.

"You fired her?!" Laura asked incredulously.

"Well, isn't that what everybody wanted?"

"Yeah! But we didn't think you'd actually have the balls to do it!"

"Well, surprise."

"I'm impressed," Laura said. "Maybe you'll be a producer yet."

An Orchestrated Mistake

"I told her Friday after work. I still feel terrible. How can you fire an intern?"

"Nicholas, she was awful, and she was annoying everyone."

"She wasn't even getting paid," I mumbled.

"Well, at least she is no longer not getting paid here," Laura mused.

"Who's not getting paid here?" Andre asked as he entered the office.

"Madeline," Laura said. "Nicholas fired her."

"Really?" Andre questioned, looking at me with an arched eyebrow.

"I know! Can you believe it?" Laura chimed.

"No. That's great." Andre smirked. "I knew you'd eventually get tough, Nick," he added, continuing to his office.

Andre and Laura are the executive producers and founders of Three Walls Productions, a company they formed years ago. The two of them make quite a dynamic team, complementing each other's attributes exceedingly well. Both possess the talent and skill to make projects happen and even look like movie producers cast by central casting. Andre is sophisticatedly handsome and dresses with his European flair. Laura, who started her career in the music industry, looks like an ex-rock n' roller turned glamorous movie producer. Together, their films have won numerous awards around the world. How Schmucky the Clown from Canada ended up in their New York office, I'm sure, has left the artistic gods shaking their heads.

"So, what happened?" Laura asked. "You just fired Madeline here after work? How did I miss that?"

"No, I took her out after work."

"You took her out to fire her?"

"Yes."

"Where did you take her?"

"For pizza and lemonade."

"Pizza and lemonade?" Laura questioned, laughing. "Is that what they do in Canada to fire someone? Take them for pizza and lemonade?"

"No," I responded flatly. "They take them to Tim Horton's."

"Hey, Heather!" Laura shouted across the office, laughing. "Nicholas fired Madeline on Friday, and he took her for pizza and lemonade to do it!"

"Oh! I'm sorry you had to fire her, Nicholas," Heather said, walking over. "But she really was annoying."

"I don't know why I had to be the one to fire her," I complained.

"Because you're supposed to be the office manager." Laura laughed.

I suppose Laura was right. Managing the office was one of my job descriptions, whether we were in production or out. Working at a small independent film company is not unlike working at a small-town radio station. Everyone has to play a little music and read the news.

"So how did she take it? Did she cry?" Heather asked.

"Better question is, did Nicholas cry?" Laura chuckled.

"No, I didn't cry. And yes, Heather, once she realized she was being let go, she did cry."

"Aww. That's so sad," Heather said.

An Orchestrated Mistake

"Not half as sad as if Nicholas cried." Laura grinned. "What did you say, Nicholas?" In an accent that couldn't have been more Canadian had it been dipped in maple syrup and wrapped in Canadian bacon, "I'm so sooorry, but geewillikers, Madeline. I'm really sooorry, but I think I'm going to have to let you go. Gosh darn, Madeline, I sure hope you like that we're ooout and abooot for pizza and lemonade." Laura and Heather were both roaring with laughter.

"It wasn't like that," I grumbled. "Yes, she was upset, but by the end of our pizza, I had her laughing and feeling great about herself. She perked right up after I told her I'd write her a letter of recommendation."

"What will you say?" Laura asked. "Madeline has an incredible ability to disrupt and annoy an entire office?"

"No. She has some good qualities. I'll think of something."

"You're a patient man, Nicholas Alexander," Laura said, turning to walk back into her office. "Save us all a place in Heaven!"

"Laura!" Heather called out, walking back to her desk. "If you ever want to fire me, will you have Nicholas do it so he can take me for pizza and lemonade?" The laughter in the office was thunderous.

I hated letting Madeline go, but not because, as Laura believed to be my natural, apologetic, reconciliatory, Canadian nature, but because I believe in dreams, and I'd hate for Madeline to stop believing in hers.

All aspects of the entertainment industry are very subjective, so people often naively assume they can step right into the profession without giving much thought to developing the discipline of the craft. I'll just sit down and write a book or a screenplay or become a singer or painter without putting in the years, sometimes decades of rejection it takes to develop that artistic muscle.

An Orchestrated Mistake

I've spent the better part of twenty-five years in the business in one capacity or another and like to believe I was being true to some grand narrative swirling around in my head when in reality, I was probably staggering around the empty spaces between my thoughts. It's not enough to have a dream. You have to believe it and live in it every day. Believing in our dreams is what keeps us going, perhaps more so in entertainment because of the nature of the profession. I'd hate to be the one responsible for silencing a dream, especially with something as benign as pizza and lemonade.

It was with my dream tucked deep in my pocket that I came to New York almost ten years ago. The music in my head was no longer loud enough in Vancouver, and my passions no longer held any rhythm. Without that magic, my dream of becoming a writer/producer of books, plays, and film had become an abandoned caricature on the conveyor belt of life. The experience I'd attained in Vancouver had become nothing more than idle wisdom since I no longer applied it to enrich and advance my dream.

I had moderate success as an actor in Vancouver, but I wasn't satisfied repeating lines that had already been written. I wanted to write my own. In Vancouver, I had written and co-produced one play which was well received. I'd also written half a dozen unproduced screenplays and made two attempts to write a book. Both times the latter never got much past page sixty before frustration set in and I would abandon the project. The dream of pursuing my authentic self had me departing for New York with my play safely tucked under my arm. What I didn't realize as I jetted to New York on a one-way ticket was that I was giving up repeating lines that had already been written to work behind the scenes on projects that had already been written. After arriving in New York, I was just too busy trying to survive in show business to devote any real time to create new and original stories. I became obsessed with looking at other people's material as the ticket to my artistic freedom rather than creating my own.

An Orchestrated Mistake

Blake's movie aside, after several years, I found a script I was passionate about. However, when the project I was hoping to produce, *Number 44*, completely fell apart, I pretty much stopped looking. After *44* tanked, I no longer eagerly attended script development meetings. Unless I was doing a favor for a friend, I didn't even read a script. I ran the office for Three Walls Productions and would float from production to production. When *Number 44* crashed, so went the belief in my dream, even though I knew instinctively I needed to create my own story. But a story about what? I had no idea.

Number 44 was the powerful true story of Ernie Davis. Davis was the first black man to win the Heisman Trophy in 1961, but this wasn't a story about American football; it was about passion and dreams. It was the story of a young Black man leaping over the racial barriers during the civil rights movement. Ernie triumphed in spite of life's obstacles because he never wavered in his belief in the human spirit. Ernie Davis was not just another Black American pioneer during a tumultuous time in human history. He was a leader who led by example, and his strength of character helped move forward the human yardsticks. President John F. Kennedy met him after he won the Heisman Trophy and later sent him a telegraph at the celebrations in Ernie's hometown of Elmira, New York, that read in part, "It's a privilege for me to address you tonight as an outstanding American and as a worthy example of our youth. I salute you."

During the script development, I had the chance to speak with Ernie's mother, Marie, who was then in her 80s. Marie told me about Ernie returning home during the summer from Syracuse University and how the children of Elmira would join him as he ran through the streets of the small town almost two decades before that iconic moment in *Rocky* when children joined Stallone through the streets of Philadelphia. Marie Davis still lived in the same house Ernie bought for her with the money he received from the Cleveland Browns when he was the first black man to be drafted first overall by the NFL team.

An Orchestrated Mistake

The stories this soft-spoken humble woman told me about her son exemplified what it meant to look inside yourself, draw on the strength of your human spirit, and commit to pursuing a dream. Ernie had far too many achievements in his short life to list here because tragically, his life was cut short at the age of twenty-three when he was diagnosed with acute monocytic leukemia. He died eleven months after being drafted by the Browns and never played a regular-season game in a Browns' uniform. Both the House and the Senate of the United States eulogized him, and over ten thousand mourners came out to pay their respects at his wake in Elmira. His life has been the subject of countless articles, books, and documentaries, but I was stunned when a young black director in Los Angeles told me over the phone there had never been a narrative script written about his life. Until now.

"You've written a script?" I gasped over the phone.

"Yeah," he responded in his Midwestern drawl.

"Send it to me!"

I knew the story was great, but would his script live up to the story? Sadly, it didn't, but there was enough there to make me believe this writer/director was the talent to make this project happen. Unfortunately, I wasn't able to convince Laura and Andre to take on the project. So, the writer and I went it alone. We spent the better part of two years in countless late-night phone calls discussing and developing the script, and those conversations are some of the most satisfying and rewarding moments of my career. We both knew that if this film was going to be successful, it had to be more than just about football. It had to be about the connection Ernie had with the human spirit within his many admirers. Men at the time wanted to be Ernie Davis, women had wanted to marry him, and we needed to show that the passion and courage he lived by throughout his young life would transcend his tragic death.

We had finally brought the script close to where it needed to be. We had even hired a casting director to send the script out for

An Orchestrated Mistake

actor attachments when I received the most deflating phone call from a producer friend. Universal Studios had gone through a stream of writers, but they finally had a script about Ernie Davis they wanted to shoot. Dennis Quaid was attached to play the coach of Syracuse, and they were to begin filming in a few short months with a budget of $40 million. There was no way we would be ready to begin shooting in a few short months, and if I thought I was devastated by that phone call, I was incensed when I got hold of the script Universal intended to shoot. They were using Ernie Davis's story to make yet another movie about American football!

In our script, *Number 44*, football was the vehicle used to tell the inspiring story of Ernie Davis. In Universal's *The Express*, Davis was the conduit to tell the story of a black man winning the Heisman Trophy and the game of football. Two starkly different points of view on the same story. There wasn't room for a second film on Ernie Davis, and even if there was, I'd never be able to raise the financing after I was sure *The Express* would bomb at the box office.

After years of quietly working on a script I wanted to produce, I had failed as a producer to bring a project I was passionate about to the screen. In failing to convince the film company I was working for to take the project on, I had failed the writer/director, and I felt I had failed the memory of Ernie Davis. I was crushed.

The Express opened to mediocre reviews and did poorly at the box office, as I knew it would, but I found no solace in the film's failure. An opportunity had been squandered for the triumphant yet tragic telling of a real American hero.

I wasn't surprised Hollywood had failed to grasp the essence of the story in the making of *The Express*. Years earlier, in an attempt to become a writer/producer, I had pitched a Hollywood studio on a script I had written about substance abuse in professional sports. After reading the script, an executive called me in and said, "Like the writing, kid, but nobody is going to believe these guys are taking drugs! They're professional athletes, for Christ's sake! What else ya got?" A few months later, I gave another studio a script I had written that revolved around a conflict in the Middle East. There, the female studio executive said to me, "I like the female lead, but nobody cares about the Middle East anymore. It's old news. What else ya got?" Those experiences made me realize I wasn't cut out for the studio system, but perhaps I would be more suited for the world of independent film. I left L.A. and returned to Vancouver, toiling away in and out of the business for another ten years before realizing I would never develop an affinity for mountain biking in the rain. I purchased a one-way ticket to New York and the world of Independent film.

****

After almost ten years in the New York film world, I'd had a lot of fun and gained a lot of experience, but *Number 44* was my only serious attempt at becoming a film producer. Ignoring my authentic self pushed my life out of balance and demonstrated to me that the act of not trying is far more painful than the experience of failure. Anything worth doing well eventually will draw blood.

Like *Number 44*, the script my friend gave me that I passed to Blake needed some work. Unlike *44*, it was a silly comedy, but I did see a place for it up on the screen. There is no emotional commitment or complex plot; it's a movie to strictly entertain. One of those movies you walk out of afterward, turn to your companion and ask, "So where do you want to go eat?" Some movies are just about the food afterwards.

My friend's script, *Thaddeus,* was just the vehicle I needed to get balance back in my life. This time, however, I wanted the backing of the company I worked for. I wanted the backing of Three Walls Productions. I didn't want to be *44*'d again. I wasn't going to be 'unofficially' producing a project after hours. I wanted the resources of Three Walls to help bring this script to the screen. This time I wasn't going to approach Three Walls head-

An Orchestrated Mistake

on as I did before. If they were going to option the script, they'd have to come to that decision on their own. This time, I wasn't giving them the opportunity to say no. This time, I would get them to say yes.

I saw the way to achieve this was through Blake. I trusted Blake and his judgment of material. If Blake didn't like it, I knew it was all going to be moot, but if Blake liked *Thaddeus*, I knew there was a good chance Laura would want to read it and perhaps like it too. If Laura liked it, then there was a good chance Andre would want to read it. If both Laura and Andre liked the script, then I knew there was a reasonable possibility of them wanting to option it, and if that happened, I would have the weight of Three Walls Productions to help propel this project to the screen.

Thaddeus wasn't the kind of script I had in mind when I'd moved to New York, but I had learned many lessons while developing *Number 44*, and it was time to put those lessons to work on *Thaddeus*. However, *Thaddeus* had more important lessons to teach me. Lessons beyond filmmaking. Maybe *Thaddeus* had something to teach me about life. Something that went far beyond pizza and lemonade.

CHAPTER TWO

I have a theory that New Yorkers only get into relationships to share the rent. Since my last relationship mercifully flew south in the first winter of the last millennium, I'd been bearing the monthly burden on my own in Brooklyn for quite some time. I'd thought about getting back in the relationship game, if for no other reason than to cut my monthly expenses. Still, every time I got close, my potential soulmate would discover something annoying about me, like the science projects I tend to leave in the fridge or my lack of interest in all chores domestic. For me, that point of annoyance would begin much earlier, like when I presented them with their own set of keys. Moving in with a significant other usually marked the final death throes of my relationships, thus proving that a relationship for me could never rise above the status of a mistress and that home truly is a maze of my solitude.

Knowing and accepting this about myself made the acceptance of Deirdre's (my eldest sister) suggestion to move in with her and her family until I found a place all the more dumbfounding. It really should be against the law to live with a blood relative once you've reached the age of eighteen, and if you break this law, it should be punishable by one year's communal living with a house full of relatives. It should be written in our national constitutions or something.

"Come on, it'll be fun," Deirdre told me one day over the phone. "Jay does shiftwork, and besides, there'll be real food in the fridge." That wasn't a selling point. My sister's culinary skills aren't much better than my own. One year she invited me out for Christmas dinner and served up hot dogs. Really, could you imagine inviting someone out for Christmas dinner and then producing a wiener? In Deirdre's defense, they were turkey dogs, but still, I guess I should have expected it. Jay is a part-time Jew, and Deirdre is a one-holiday-a-year Christian, so they never know whether to put up a tree or burn one down with a Menorah at Christmas.

An Orchestrated Mistake

"Nicholas, we both know you are not taking any time off work to look for a place, so stop pretending and move in with us. It'll give you a chance to spend some time with your nieces that you never see."

"I see Molly and Shayna," I protested. "I took them to that fair with Jay a few weeks ago."

"Nicholas, that was like six months ago, and you had to come home early because Shayna threw up on the tilt-a-whirl."

"Well, she ate too much cotton candy."

"You gave it to her! Never mind, just move in with us."

"Fine," I said, knowing that I'd run out of time to find a place. "But I'm looking for an apartment every weekend!"

I don't know why I was so picky about where I lived. It's not like I spent much time there or fixed the place up to make it feel like home. The only picture I ever hung up on a wall was of two wolf pups howling in the twilight while their mother looks on. Home was wherever I hung those wolves.

My first Saturday at my sister's place, she came into the kitchen in the morning asking, "Where's the pot of coffee?"

"In the fridge," I replied without looking up from *The Boondocks*.

"Why the hell is it in there?" Deirdre demanded, opening the fridge.

"I like cold coffee," I told her. Cold coffee is a taste I acquired at work because I never got around to drinking my coffee while it was hot.

"I hate cold coffee," Deirdre complained.

"So put it in the microwave."

"I wouldn't have to if you just made it fresh this morning."

"Then I wouldn't like it," I said, looking up.

"Oh, great. So now we need two coffee makers?"

"Probably." I shrugged, draining my cup. "I'm going outside for a cigarette."

"You eat breakfast?" Deirdre asked.

"I did."

"What did you have?"

"I found the girl's stash of Pop-Tarts."

"Nicholas!"

"Next time, get the chocolate ones with sprinkles."

"Those are for the girls! And you shouldn't be eating them anyway!" Deirdre snapped.

"One or two won't kill me," I said, opening the kitchen door. "I'll be out here smoking if you want to join me."

My sister was right. Chocolate Pop-Tarts are probably not the healthiest choice for breakfast if you're diabetically challenged, but then again, coffee and a cigarette probably weren't much better. I'd been putting sticks of dynamite in my mouth for years now and haven't blown up yet. At forty-four, I figured the fuse was still pretty long. While others took time off from life with a cold or the flu, I could work eighteen-plus hours day after day with nary a sniffle. I wasn't worried about diabetes. It's not like I could feel it or see it. When the doctor had told me back in Vancouver at the age of thirty-one I was a diabetic, I wasn't even sure what the hell he was talking about.

"Diabetic?" I questioned when he told me.

"Yes. You were pre-diabetic two years ago. Your previous doctor didn't tell you?"

"No. She was about to retire and never said a word. Don't you have to be fat to be diabetic?" I asked.

"No. Your family have a history of diabetes?"

"No idea," I responded.

That night I had called my mother and told her I was diagnosed with diabetes.

"Rubbish!" she replied. "You're not fat."

"Apparently, it can be genetic or something," I told her. "Anyone in our family ever had diabetes?"

"Certainly not!" my mother had shot back. "You're certainly not a diabetic!"

"Tell that to the doctor," I said. "Just seems to me like bad planning to be a diabetic when you have a sweet tooth."

My mother's response wasn't the only thing that frustrated my doctor. He was reasonably sure I had adult-onset diabetes, Type II, not juvenile diabetes, or Type I, but what really clogged his engine was he also deemed me an uncooperative patient. I don't know why he would have thought that. I took the diabetes clinic course at St. Paul's Hospital as he asked me, and my attendance record was stellar. So what if the nurses giving the course might have complained I just sat in the back doodling and didn't make an effort to participate. Or that during our brisk twenty-minute walks, I just ambled at the back, returning business calls on my cell. I'm just saying that might have been what the nurses reported. In my defense, I should say I was relatively young back then, so I still believed I was invincible.

Shortly after I slept-walked through the clinic, the sky gods again tried to perform an intervention. Heading over to Vancouver Island on the ferry, I looked over at the empty seat next to me, and staring up at me was a newspaper headline, *Diabetes a Leading Cause of Death in Canada*. I flipped the paper over and headed out on deck to enjoy the view of the passing Gulf Islands. "Really makes you glad to be alive, doesn't it?" said an elderly man joining me at the railing.

"Yeah," I said, taking a deep breath of ocean air. "It's beautiful."

"I'm heading over for my friend's funeral," the old man added after a moment.

"Oh, I'm sorry."

"Nothing to be sorry about. Just as well he died. He didn't have much of a life. Lost both his legs."

"Lost them in the war, did he?" I asked, thinking the fellow old enough to be a World War Two vet.

"Hell no!" was his stark reply. "Came out of that without a scratch! That damn diabetes took 'em! Yup, that's what killed him! If I ever get that Goddamn disease, just shoot me!"

"Oh," I responded, staring down at the churning Pacific Ocean. I pulled out a cigarette as I contemplated if drowning was as painless as they say.

One of the few things mentioned at the diabetes clinic that stuck with me was when flying it is important to inform the airline you're a diabetic. I wasn't sure why, but if it meant getting an extra bag of peanuts or better snacks, I was all for it. I had informed Air Canada when I purchased my ticket from Vancouver to Toronto. During the meal service, a male flight attendant came swishing down the aisle holding a tray above his head shrieking, "Mr. Alexander! Mr. Alexander, identify yourself, please! Diabetic meal for Mr. Alexander!" I looked up from my book, stunned, and let the attendant swish by as heads swiveled to get a look at this diabetic. When Richard Simmons sashayed up the aisle a second time, calling out with more energy, "Mr. Alexander!

Diabetic meal! Identify yourself, please!" I sheepishly raised my hand, bringing the attendant prancing right over to me. "You Mr. Alexander?!"

"Yes." I nodded.

"You diabetic?"

"Yes," I mumbled to the back of the seat in front of me.

"Good! Then here's your diabetic meal!" he announced to the cabin.

Seeing the embarrassment on my face, the woman next to me patted my arm. "It's okay," she said. "I'm actually a nurse. I treat diabetics."

"Perfect," I grumbled, slumping in my seat. "Guess I won't be eating those M&M's in my carry-on." Turning my attention out the window, it crossed my mind to jump out over Saskatchewan.

Almost two years after being diagnosed in Vancouver, things came to a head with my doctor in his office after a blood test. "You've got to get the sugars down!" he scolded me.

"They are down," I shot back.

"Whose results are you looking at? Because they're certainly not yours! I've been telling you, if you don't start taking this seriously, it's going to jump up and knock you on your fucking ass!"

"Wow!" I said, stunned.

"Yes! Wow!"

"I mean, wow! I've never heard a doctor drop the F-bomb before."

An Orchestrated Mistake

"You know what?!" he shouted, throwing his hands in the air. "I'm done. I'm finished. I'm tired of your smart-ass quips. I'm tired of you not taking this seriously. I'm just not fighting you anymore. Do what you want! Why the fuck should I care when you obviously don't?"

"I do care," I replied, shifting in my chair. "You told me I could control it through diet and exercise."

"And you're not doing either!" he shouted.

"I am!"

"When?" he asked, glaring at me.

"I walk to Starbucks."

The doctor clenched his jaw so tight his tendons in his jaw were twitching. "And you give me a food chart like this?!" he snarled, picking a sheet of paper off his desk. "I asked you to keep a record of your food!"

"I did."

"Breakfast Monday," he said, reading from the sheet. "Snickers and a cigarette."

"Monday I was in a hurry."

"Tuesday. Carnation Instant Breakfast. In another hurry?"

I tried to remember.

"Wednesday you must have been in a real hurry because you only had a coffee and a cigarette. And why the hell are you putting your smoking habits on a food chart?"

"Sometimes a cigarette is breakfast," I replied, watching him wince. "So I'm not a breakfast person."

"Okay," the doctor snarled sarcastically. "Then let's see what you had for supper."

An Orchestrated Mistake

"Probably not a good idea," I mumbled.

"Monday Quarter Pounder, fries, and a Diet Coke. Oh, things are looking up. Diet? Were they all out of regular Coke? Tuesday, pizza. Wednesday is good. I believe you actually cooked a meal. Macaroni and cheese!"

"I'm honest," I said. The doctor glared at me like a bull about to charge. "Look, I get your point."

"No, you don't," he barked. "In two years you haven't done anything that I've asked you. In fact, you've done the opposite. You're eating habits are worse. You're smoking more."

"I feel fine."

"Today! But in ten years, when this lifestyle catches up to you, how are you going to feel?"

"I'll burn that bridge when I get to it," I said, trying to lighten the atmosphere. "Look, I'll fix things, but right now I just don't have time to deal with all this. Eating is just something I do to keep my hands busy during a meeting."

"You know what?" the doctor said as he walked to open his door. "Here's your file. I can't help you. I've done all I can. Good luck."

Until then, I didn't know that doctors could dump patients—well, at least I had never heard of a doctor dumping a patient. It was, after all, Canada, the land of the easy-going, a thousand apologies, and socialized medicine.

It was shortly after getting dumped by my doctor that my mother lost her thirteen-year battle with leukemia, my third acting agent dumped me, deeming me too difficult to work with, and a dinner theatre I had been developing for four years flew south, I knew the writing was on the wall. You might say I was having a bit of a bad run, but when I came home late one night to find the stray cat I had adopted rolling around on my bedroom floor from

An Orchestrated Mistake

a stroke, I knew it was time to blow Vancouver and be true to myself.

Sure glad it only takes the subtle signs in life to get my attention. I could easily argue which event it was that finally triggered that damn canary to sing, but on February first, I finally heard the tune. By March first, at the age of thirty-four, I had sold or given away everything I owned, packed my play, and boarded a plane to New York with two suitcases full of cracked dreams and high expectations. I was going to finally live the Ray Bradbury quote I had so often paraphrased: *Jump off the cliff of life and build your wings on the way down.*

Other than Deirdre and her husband, Jay, I knew no one in New York. If I thought fifteen years or so experience in entertainment in Canada would count for anything, I was more delusional than a political candidate during an election. I couldn't wait to get out of my sister's place after arriving—mainly because their marriage was so toxic, and, of course, I was over eighteen and living with relatives.

I must have sent out over five hundred resumes in that first few months in New York. I never heard anything back except from one producer who saw I was living in the same town he grew up in on Long Island. He just wanted to reminisce about his childhood.

When I explained I wasn't from Long Island but Canada, he claimed not to understand hockey but was partial to Canadian bacon and promptly announced he was late for a meeting. I knew moving to New York would be like starting over, but I had no idea I would have to begin at ground zero.

"You realize this is an unpaid position?" the production coordinator of an Independent film said to me over the phone.

"You'll be a production intern, so there isn't any money."

"I know," I said. "But your ad says you'll pay transportation costs."

An Orchestrated Mistake

Working on everything from films to documentaries to music videos, I crossed paths with Three Walls Productions a few times, but back then, Three Walls only had two full-time employees, Laura and Andre. They would crew-up and hire when they went into production, but then pretty much everyone would move on to the next project after wrap. On occasion, Three Walls would hire office staff to work when they were between projects.

Heidi, a young German girl, worked part-time in Three Walls Productions' office, but as a freelance production manager, she too would often be hired away, but not before calling me to come and fill in. There were times Heidi and I would work together in the office, this usually revolving around the distribution of a film. Laughter often echoed inside at Three Walls, and it was often at the expense of my Canadianisms or Heidi's understanding of English as her second language.

One day while we both worked on delivering the elements for a film, Heidi looked over at me and asked, "Nicholas, what's a boner?"

"What?" I choked.

"A boner. The French distributor is describing a scene where they talk about a boner. So, what's a boner?"

I gaped out the office window as if I'd find the words I was searching for doing the backstroke up the Hudson.

"They want the trailer where they talk about a boner," Heidi prompted.

"I know, I know, Heidi. I'm just trying…"

"Yeah, Alexander!" Laura laughed, stepping out of her office. "Explain to Heidi what a boner is."

"I know, Laura," I replied. "I'm thinking."

"You have to think what a boner is?" Laura teased.

An Orchestrated Mistake

"Yes. No, I mean."

"Heidi has no clue what you mean," Laura chided. "Look, he's turning red!"

My frown at Laura softened when I turned back to Heidi and saw her staring wide-eyed at me expectantly.

"It's when a guy gets, well, you know," I said, slowly raising my index finger.

Heidi's eyes widened, and whistling, she said, "Got it!"

Laura burst into hysterics, returning to her office while Heidi and I stared down at our desks in utter silence.

"Let's go smoke," Heidi finally said, standing up.

"Right," I replied.

About a year and a half into my New York film career, Heidi called me at home in Brooklyn to ask me if I would come into work at Three Walls the next day.

"I can't, Heidi," I told her over the phone. "I've been offered my first gig out of town. I'll be working on a film in Miami for a few months," I said, throwing my cleanest dirty clothes into a duffle bag. "My flight leaves tomorrow morning." Heidi wished me luck but called back twenty minutes later.

"Nicholas, I just spoke with Laura in London. She doesn't want you to go to Miami."

"Heidi, I have to," I said, searching through a pile of dirty clothes for a missing sock. "I've already accepted the offer. I have my ticket."

"I told Laura that," Heidi replied. "She told me to tell you that if you stay, she'll make it worth your while."

An Orchestrated Mistake

"What does that mean?" I asked, pleased that I'd found the missing sock.

"She wants to offer you a full-time job. She said she'll speak to you as soon as she gets back."

"Full time?" I questioned.

"Yes. I can't do it, and she and Andre really need someone. You interested?"

Why wouldn't I be interested in working full-time with two of the top Independent producers in New York? "I guess I'm not going to Miami," I told Heidi.

"Good. I'll call Laura."

"Sure," I said, staring at my overstuffed duffle bag. "It's kind of a bummer, though," I added.

"What?" Heidi asked. "You're not going to Miami?"

"No," I said. "Now I have to do laundry."

Accepting the full-time position at Three Walls Productions meant I could no longer run off to auditions or jump the subway to bang off a quick radio commercial. That point was hammered home to me when I left the office on my lunch hour to do a thirty-second radio ad for Clorox Bleach. I was supposed to be in and out of the studio in fifteen minutes, tops, but the client listening in from San Francisco was having a problem with one of the actor's accents. Since there were only two of us in the studio, and I was the only Canadian, I naturally assumed it was me they were complaining about.

"We need you to sound more like Nicholas," the director finally said to the young girl playing my wife. "Try and sound like him, you know, like you're from the Midwest." After several more takes, the director was getting frustrated and asked the young actress where she was from. "California," she had replied.

"Well, you're not sounding very American," he shot back over the headsets. "Try to mimic Nicholas's accent if you can. Nicholas, where are you from?"

"Canada."

When I finally got back to Three Walls, I apologized profusely to Heidi for being so long. "No problem," Heidi had replied, but I could hear the tension in her voice.

"It was supposed to be a quick gig," I said. "In and out. I'm sorry."

"I said it's fine," Heidi snapped.

"Well, that was my last acting gig," I announced to Heidi. The very sound of that pronouncement left me stunned.

"Okay, fine," Heidi agreed.

"No, I mean it. That was it. I'm quitting acting."

"It's up to you."

"I'll call my agent tomorrow to tell him."

"Okay."

"I don't know what I was thinking. You can't work full-time and run around to auditions. That's just insane."

"I get it, Nicholas! You're quitting! We'll go smoke later and talk about it."

"No. I'm good. I don't need to talk about it. I've made up my mind."

"Oh my God! Let's go smoke!"

"Right!"

An Orchestrated Mistake

I did call my agent the next day to tell him, and after he suggested we get together to talk about it, I told him there's nothing to talk about. My mind was made up. It wasn't really, but I didn't want to give him the opportunity to talk me out of my decision. I loved acting. It was a wonderful opportunity to crawl into a character's skin and escape my own. I did see, however, Three Walls as a more direct career path to my endgame: becoming a writer/producer.

****

"Hola!" Laura said, coming through the office front door. Lulu and Zombie came barreling in behind her, followed by Blake, who acknowledged me with a nod. "Hey, Nick." Moments later, the two four-legged bandits returned for their breakfast, beginning the morning routine.

"What's this?" Laura asked after I stepped into her office and placed an invoice on her desk.

"It's from *Saints*," I said, referring to our latest film. "I told you about it. First, we thought this was paid, and then it turns out it wasn't. Then the camera department said they never ordered the lens, but it turned out they did, but never used it and forgot to send it back, so we got charged for it. It's that invoice."

"Right," Laura said, staring at the invoice. "But I still thought we paid it."

"We did," I told her. "These are the late charges."

"Unbelievable," Laura said, signing. "Andre," she added, calling across the office, "can you believe we're still paying invoices on *Guide to Recognizing Your Saints*?"

"Unbelievable," Andre uttered without looking up from his laptop.

"Alexander!" Laura called out before I could exit their office. "You're looking awfully guilty." I followed Laura's gaze to Lulu standing in the doorway beside me, licking her chops. "I think she's been into your garbage again." Laura laughed.

"Oh," I said, glaring at Lulu.

"I read your friend's script, *Thaddeus*, over the weekend," Laura said, frowning at Zombie, who trotted in chewing like she had a mouthful of peanut butter. "Looks like they've both been into your garbage, Alexander," Laura mused.

"Nothing in my garbage," I replied, annoyed that the two dogs were exposing our breakfast conspiracy.

"So, I liked the script," Laura said, looking in Zombie's mouth.

"It's quite silly."

"Yeah, it's pretty silly," I echoed. "But that's Mike. He's pretty dark and silly. When you meet him, you don't want to shake his hand. You want to roll your eyes."

"It's definitely from your garbage, Alexander," Laura said, pulling a chewed sandwich wrapper out of Zombie's mouth. "It has ketchup on it." I glared at Zombie. "I laughed out loud a few times," Laura said.

"It's a parody of the TV show *CSI*," I told Laura.

"I got that," she said.

"One of the top-rated shows on television. It's like *CSI* meets *Airplane* or *Naked Gun*. Two franchises that cleaned up at the box office."

Looking up, Andre questioned, "Who cleaned up at the box office?"

"*Airplane. Naked Gun*," I told Andre.

"Yes," he said, looking back down at his computer.

An Orchestrated Mistake

"Mike's written outlines for two more scripts after this one. I don't know. Maybe *Thaddeus* could be a franchise," I told Laura loud enough to get Andre's attention.

"Who's Mike?" Andre asked.

"Nicholas's friend," Laura replied. "He wrote a script called *Thaddeus*. It's quite funny."

"You read it?" Andre asked Laura.

"This weekend. I laughed quite a few times. You should read it, Andre."

"Nicholas, your sister is on line two," Heather said, poking her head in the office.

"Thanks, Heather." Family's timing is impeccable.

"You should read it, Andre," Laura suggested, holding out the script for me to pass to Andre's desk. "It's silly, but I think you might like it."

"Worst case scenario," I said, taking the script, "you'll have a few laughs. Best case scenario? Three Walls will have found a franchise film," I said, placing the script on Andre's desk.

"What's up?" I asked, returning to my desk and picking up line two.

"You must be busy," Deirdre said.

"A little. Just trying to get Mike's script optioned. So, what's up?"

"Oh," Deirdre said like she understood. "Well, I have great news too."

"You're finally leaving Jay?"

"Funny. No, I got you an appointment to see my doctor tomorrow."

"What?"

"Dr. Kaye, my doctor. He can see you tomorrow morning."

"I'm working tomorrow."

"Take the morning off."

"No."

"Nicholas, have you looked in a mirror lately? You're not going to be producing anything if you don't see a doctor."

"I'll find my own doctor," I said curtly.

"And get dumped again!" she scolded.

I hadn't told my sister that I had been dumped in Canada a decade earlier. She was referring to my latest doctor in New York, who had said pretty much the same thing to me as my doctor in Canada before showing me the door. I understood why the doctor in Vancouver dumped me. I was wasting the taxpayer's money. But in New York, I was paying all medical bills—they weren't cheap. I hadn't been feeling great the last two years. My energy was really low. My ability to remember details and focus seemed crippled. I knew I was struggling even just to concentrate, and I would need a lot more than I had if I were going to produce *Thaddeus*.

"All right! I'll go! I'll go see your damn doctor!"

"You will?"

"Yes."

"Great. Tell Laura you'll take the day off, and I'll drive you for any tests Kaye orders."

"No. He gets an hour, and you can dump me at the train station."

"You really are a jerk."

"I know."

My sister knew my track record with doctors, and like in Vancouver, she knew a New York doctor had also dumped me. I'm sure she thought it would take a top-rope battle royal to convince me to see Kaye, and I would have thought that too, but things had changed. For the last couple of years, I'd been feeling nowhere near a hundred percent, and I'd have to be if Four Walls optioned *Thaddeus* and Andre and Laura gave me the chance to produce. I knew it was a long shot, but I had to be ready. So, seeing Doctor Kaye wasn't an option. I couldn't get this close to a lifelong dream only to have it derailed by something that, in most cases, is manageable: health.

An Orchestrated Mistake

CHAPTER THREE

There are a few things I've always known about myself. One is I don't enjoy first-world celebrations of any kind: Christmas, birthdays, Easter, etc. I have no time for them. Unless you're a child or living in abject poverty, you don't need a gift from anyone. Buy your own damn gift. The second thing I know about myself is that I'm a total social introvert. I mastered at a young age to sound like I'm divulging a lot, when in fact, I've said nothing revealing about my true self. This skill I learned and perfected from my mother. If she were reading this today, I know what she'd say: "I don't care that you've written a memoir, but do you have to make it so damn personal?!" And the last thing I've more recently learned is that orchestrated mistakes have always governed my life.

I didn't set out to get into the entertainment industry. I'm not one of those people who can say, *I always knew I was going to be...* I thought if anyone paid me anything just to do something, it would be a miracle. I always loved stories, but then again, it wasn't like I was reading or watching the classics. I grew up dissecting *The Rockford Files* like it was *Pride & Prejudice*. However, my mother did expose me to the lives and stories of Dickens, Wilde, and my favorite, Twain. However, as a youth, I was more interested in protecting a net on a sheet of ice than being curled up watching or reading a classic.

Long after I should have hung up my goalie skates, I was still trying out for and being cut by Junior A hockey teams. The only reason I continued to play was that it afforded me the opportunity to wear that mask. So, just after getting cut from yet another team, I met and befriended the fellow that did the play-by-play broadcasts for the Junior A league. He told me he wasn't thrilled with his current cohort doing the color commentary and asked if I'd be interested in joining his broadcast. I figured I knew hockey, had an interest in broadcasting, so I accepted his offer. After the hockey season, the station kept me on to do the sports. As dumb luck would have it, I happened to be at the station when the evening jock got into a heated argument with the program

An Orchestrated Mistake

director and was promptly fired. Being the only other on-air talent around at the time, I instantly went from the sports booth to the DJ booth. It was only supposed to be temporary, but since I was a master at running my mouth and saying nothing, I was a natural and stayed on for almost a year. Incidentally, it was during this time I first tried a cigarette. The afternoon drive jock would leave his smokes in the booth, and I picked them up, thinking they would make my voice sound more mature. Well, that and I enjoyed the buzz from the nicotine that made listening to Buck Owens more tolerable. Within a year of working the airwaves, Johnny Paycheck's 'Take This Job and Shove It' was at the top of my playlist. If I had to mention the station, weather, and time once more, I would find myself tap-dancing on the railing of some downtown bridge.

I had taken acting classes in high school, though not because of my love of the arts, but for the fact it wasn't physics or calculus. Now believing I had real acting experience, I called the first acting agent I found in the phone book. I exaggerated my theater experience to get the meeting, and once again, the universe intervened. Before I met with the agent, she received a call to find a stand-in for Eric Roberts on the film *Star 80*. In I walked after she hung up, the right height, hair color, and build. I had the job before I sat down. I phoned the radio station and quit the following Monday, so I started my film career without knowing a thing, least of all, what a stand-in was. To paraphrase Ray Bradbury again, I was jumping off the cliff of life and building my wings on the way down.

"I'm supposed to report to the director," I said when I arrived at our location on the first day. "I wrote his name down, but now I can't find it," I added, searching my pockets.

"Would it be Bob Fosse?" the second assistant director, David, said with a sardonic tone.

"Yeah! That's him! I'm supposed to report to Bob Fosse. Which one is he?" I asked, looking around the apartment that was our location.

An Orchestrated Mistake

"And you are?"

"Nicholas. Nicholas Alexander. I'm the stand-in for Eric Roberts."

"I see."

Leaning in conspiratorially, I said, "You know I'm also not sure which one he is either. Maybe you could point him out too?"

"Why don't you follow me," David said, leading me to an empty bedroom. "Wait here. Someone will be with you shortly."

This showbiz thing was turning out to be a snap. At nineteen, I had had my own radio show, and now I was on the set of a real Hollywood movie. I'm sure this Bob fellow will show up any minute to give me my lines, and a star will be born.

"Hello," a voice said behind me as I gazed out the window at the mountains of Vancouver.

"Hi," I said, spinning around. The first thing I noticed about this fifty-ish man was the cigarette suspended in the left corner of his mouth. The yellow nicotine stain down the left side of his salt & pepper goatee was evidence that a cigarette had dangled in this location many times before.

I watched him as he walked around the room, dropping to one knee to look through his viewfinder that had been tied by a string around his neck.

"Can you get down in front of the window and do a few push-ups for me, please?" he asked.

"Me?" I asked as if there were others in the room.

"Please."

I got down and did a few push-ups while the man looked at me through his viewfinder. After about ten push-ups, I bounced up. "There," I said.

An Orchestrated Mistake

"No, no. Keep going, please," he said, still looking through his finder.

I got down again and fired off about thirty more, grateful that the failings of the junior hockey camps were still only in my recent past. After about thirty more, though, I felt finished and collapsed to the floor. I was thankful I had given up cigarettes days before I left the station. It wasn't like I saw the error of my ways, however. I started up again during a self-destructive phase years later.

"Keep going," he said, looking through his viewfinder.

Listen, buddy, I thought to myself, *if I could keep going, I'd probably still be playing hockey.* "Really?" I asked. "You want me to do more?"

"Please. I'll tell you when to stop."

I started doing more push-ups, and it wasn't long before sweat began to form and drip into one eye, causing it to sting. I closed my stinging eye when the man yelled, "Sven! Sven! In here!" I glanced over with my one good eye just as a man in his sixties entered the room. He, too, sported a beard, but without the nicotine stains, and he too stared through his viewfinder at me doing push-ups.

"Tell me what you think?" the first man asked, down on one knee.

"Yes. Yes," Sven mumbled.

"Or do you think it will be a better shot from over here?" the first man asked.

Sven went over to where he was and knelt beside him. "Yes. Yes, maybe," Sven said.

My arms were morphing into soggy spaghetti at this point, and I didn't know how much longer I could keep up these one-eyed push-ups. "Good?" I groaned.

An Orchestrated Mistake

"Yes," I heard Sven mumble, and I collapsed to the floor in a pool of sweat. "No! No! I need you to keep going, please!" Sven said.

The two men got into some sort of discussion about camera angles. I couldn't tell because now sweat filled my ear passages. Finally, the two men said, "Thank you," and left the room. I collapsed to the floor in an ocean of sweat and total exhaustion.

"Hey!" David said, poking his head in the room. I didn't have the strength to lift my head, so I just looked at him with my one good eye. He smirked. "That was Bob Fosse."

For the next seven weeks, I got to work closely with two entertainment legends, director Bob Fosse and cinematographer Sven Nykvist. What an education it was to work closely with these two multi-talented and Academy Award-winning masters. However, it was a casual lunchtime conversation with Wolfgang, one of the producers, which set me on my career path.

"You want to be an actor?" Wolfgang asked.

"I'm not sure. Bob suggested I go to theater school if I'm serious about acting."

"He's right."

"He suggested a few different schools but told me to talk to Eric. Eric suggested the American Academy of Dramatic Arts."

"It's a good school."

"I don't know. It's actually your job that really interests me," I told Wolfgang. "You seem to be working with everyone."

"True."

I had noticed Wolfgang in discussions with various departments during the filming, but what really stood out was he seemed to have Fosse's vision of the big picture and was keenly aware of how to achieve it. I would inch my way closer anytime I heard Wolfgang, or anyone for the matter, discussing the story or the script. Whenever those conversations took place, I was mesmerized. One afternoon, I was so intrigued by Wolfgang's conversation I didn't hear Fosse calling for me from the set. Wolfgang heard Bob calling and stopped and stared at me. "What are you waiting for? Go! Go!"

"So, is there a school for producers?" I asked Wolfgang.

"Not really." He laughed. "Experience. Life is your school."

"So, how did you become a producer?"

"How do you achieve anything?" Wolfgang said. "Study your craft."

In essence, he told me the job of a producer is to understand the elements of filmmaking and bring them together with the director's vision to make a moving picture.

"Work your way up from a production assistant. Or maybe," Wolfgang said, pointing towards Eric at the next table, "like Bob said, become an actor and study life. Either way, it doesn't happen overnight."

I took all three men's advice. Fosse's to go to theatre school, Eric's to attend the American Academy of Dramatic Arts, and Wolfgang's to become a full-time observer of life.

After graduating from the American Academy of Dramatic Arts in Los Angeles, I returned to Vancouver and became a journeyman actor. This gave me the chance to put on another mask. It was also getting the opportunity to interpret a character within a story that I enjoyed. Before I was deemed too challenging to work with by Vancouver casting directors, I did okay as an actor, prompting one theater critic to write following my performance as a mentally challenged character, "…either Alexander is a brilliant actor, or he is really like that." I'm still not quite sure how to interpret that review.

An Orchestrated Mistake

****

"Nicholas! Hustle your scrawny ass!" Deirdre yelled over the car horn. My sister has about as much patience as a banker for the infirm.

Jumping in the front seat, I told her, "Relax, will ya? We have plenty of time. Let's grab a coffee at Dunkin Donuts."

"Nicholaaas," Deirdre replied in that sing-songy way that doesn't quite mean no. "I told you I don't want to be late. And I know you, you'll get a donut," my sister lamented.

"What do you take me for? I'm a diabetic on my way to the doctor for a check-up. I'm not insane. Come on, it'll be my treat."

Ten minutes later, my sister and I were pulling out of Dunkin Donuts, coffees in hand. I reached inside the bag and pulled out a Boston Crème donut.

"Jesus, Nicholas!" My sister admonished me and promptly drove over the curb. "Are you kidding me?" she shrieked as we both hit zero gravity.

"What are you doing?" I asked my sister after she followed me into the doctor's examining room.

"I'm coming in with you," she said, taking a seat in the corner.

"Why?"

"I don't trust you to tell the truth."

"What truth?" I questioned.

"That you're a crap-eating, chain-smoking diabetic who's so full of himself he won't listen to anyone, and if he doesn't get his shit together soon, he'll probably never see his nieces graduate."

"You eat crap, and you smoke," I parried.

"I'm not the one seeing the doctor," Deirdre replied with a smug grin. "I'm also not diabetic."

"Today," I shot back.

"Did you bring your file from your previous doctor?" Dr. Kaye asked after greeting me.

"Tell Dr. Kaye what you did with the file," Deirdre suggested.

"I don't have it," I said, glaring at my sister.

"He threw it out, Dr. Kaye," my sister tattled. "Dumped it right in the garbage after the doctor threw him out."

"Do you mind?" I scolded Deirdre. Turning back to Dr. Kaye. "I threw it out."

"I'll order some tests," Kaye said. "Any idea what your A1C was?" he asked, referring to my average blood sugars for the last three months.

I shrugged.

"He hasn't a clue," Deirdre chimed in. "Ask him what his sugars were this morning. He can't tell you that either. They're probably through the roof after that chocolate donut."

"Does she have to be in here?" I asked Kaye.

"I would rather hear things from your brother," Kaye said to Deirdre. "Maybe you should just wait outside."

"He's not going to tell you the truth, Dr. Kaye. He's smarmy. I wouldn't trust a word he said."

"That's fine. Blood tests don't lie," Kaye said, motioning my sister towards the door. "One hundred and thirty-six pounds," Kaye said when I stepped off the scale. "So let me ask you again. Are you on or off insulin?"

An Orchestrated Mistake

"Off," I replied. "But I'm supposed to be on, but I don't really take it. Well, sometimes I do…when I remember. So, I guess technically I'm on insulin, but in reality, I'm not."

Kaye involuntarily winced. "I'm afraid to ask how long this has been going on."

"I guess about two years," I said. "Since I was hospitalized after they threatened to cut off my leg."

"What???"

"The last doctor panicked when he saw some kind of viral infection in my left leg. Said if I didn't get to the hospital and get it treated, I could lose it."

"So you went, I assume?" Kaye said, eyeing my left leg.

"Eventually." I shrugged. "I felt it was much to do about nothing. I was in the hospital for six days and ended up with a $32,000 medical bill. For that kind of money, I could have flown to Monaco, played blackjack, and doubled down and lost every hand for a week and still spent less."

"But you wouldn't have your leg," Kaye pointed out.

"True." I shrugged. "But I would have had a better time."

It crossed my mind to tell Kaye the story of the surgeon pitching me a screenplay he had written on the operating table, but Kaye was already looking a little shell-shocked from my visit. That pitch was insane, though. While I was frozen from the waist down, naked and spread eagle on the operating table, the surgeon took that moment to ask me where I worked, and when I said, "Three Walls Productions," he stopped cutting and looked up. "Three Walls, Three Walls," he repeated. "Where have I heard that name?" he asked the flock of interns witnessing the operation.

"It's a film company," I said, my eyes glued to his bloody scalpel.

An Orchestrated Mistake

"Yes! That's right!" he said, poking the air with the scalpel. "You work for a film company?"

"Yes."

"Interesting," he said, making another incision at my groin. "My brother and I wrote a screenplay. Would you like to hear it?" he asked.

"Oh," I groaned. "I guess." What could I say? My blood was dripping off his scalpel that was inches away from my balls. Like I was going to say no? A chorus of cheers went up from the interns, and the surgeon launched into his insanely boring pitch. Anytime I thought he was about to finish, some lame intern would ask, "And then what happens?" and the surgeon would get more animated with the scalpel-like he was conducting a two-hundred-piece orchestra.

I caught the eye of the nurse who was monitoring my vitals. "Doctor!" she said, reminding him he was in the middle of surgery.

"Yes, yes," the surgeon said. "So would you like to read it?" he finally asked.

Again, he's got me splayed naked with a bloody scalpel poised between my legs. What the hell could I say? "Love to," I mumbled to another congratulatory cheer from the interns.

The script was just as lousy as his pitch, so when I was released from the hospital, I gave him the Hollywood 'slow no.' I didn't say anything, and his script disappeared into the entertainment world's black hole. Welcome to show business, Doctor.

*****

"How much do you smoke?" Dr. Kaye asked.

"That's sort of like the insulin," I said. "It depends. When we're not in production, about a pack a day. When we're in production, about two packs a day. Three if we're shooting outside on location."

"Ever thought of quitting?" Kaye asked.

"All the time."

"And?"

"And I light a cigarette to think about it."

"Well, I'm going to ask that you think about it a little harder. I'm also asking you to take your insulin regularly, and we'll adjust the dose after your blood work comes back." Kaye noticed I was suppressing an eye roll. "I'm telling you, Nicholas, you better get your diabetes under control, or you're in for a heap of trouble."

"I hear ya," I said, glad to be leaving Kaye's office.

"And knock off the chocolate donuts!" Kaye shouted. But it was too late. I'd already closed the door.

The problem I seem to have with doctors is they're always asking you to modify or change your behavior. It must be frustrating for them to go to work every day and have their advice completely ignored. They must teach a course at medical school that prepares them for this. I'm sure it's called *Howling at the Moon 101*.

****

"I didn't think that when you said you had Mets tickets they'd be atop of Kilimanjaro," I groused a few days later, climbing the stadium stairs.

"Produce my movie," Mike instructed from behind, "and you can buy your own skybox. Maybe two. One for you and one for a friend. If you have one."

"Shaw," I said without turning around.

An Orchestrated Mistake

"What?"

"If you have a friend," I said. "You stole that line from George Bernard Shaw. He said that to Churchill."

"I'm a word artist," Mike confessed. "We create. We don't steal anything."

"Nothing that you can't eat or shove in your pockets," I said, stopping to catch my breath. "And maybe I don't want to produce your script."

"Of course you do," Mike replied, leaning on the railing beside me. "It'll give you a chance to work with a real word artist. You'll be working with me."

"If there was ever a reason to pass on a script," I moaned to the heavens.

"Hey, you pass on *Thaddeus*," Mike declared, "then you can just get used to these stairs."

"Maybe I'll find a real word artist who's written a script of social significance. A script that will enlighten and entertain."

"Enlighten and entertain," Mike scoffed. "Nobody wants to be enlightened and entertained. They're watching *Ice Road Truckers* on the History Channel. You're also forgetting the golden rule of show business: It's always about me!"

"You know," I said, continuing up the stairs, "I can never decide what's more endearing, your Napoleonic complex or your ego."

"Fuck off. And keep climbing."

I hadn't told Mike I'd informally submitted his script to Three Walls Productions. Since *44*, there was just too much self-doubt weaving through my veins to determine if I wanted to produce his screenplay. I also wasn't sure if I was the right person to champion this kind of material. *Thaddeus* was a comedy—not even

An Orchestrated Mistake

a real comedy in the sense of the word, but a spoof, so it was at the polar opposite end of the movie spectrum to *Number 44*. I was doing everything I could to get *Thaddeus* optioned. I didn't want to be told no and *44*'d for a second time. By not telling Mike, was I playing it safe, protecting myself from getting stung again? I think I was, but I wasn't sure I had the energy to produce a movie. It takes a lot of energy to work with a writer and coax a script to the screen. It can take years, and I didn't know if I was up for that task. What I was doing, whether it was consciously or subconsciously, was orchestrating events and conversations to get to yes and then trust the movie gods to figure out if I was destined to be its producer.

There was another problem confronting me in getting the script optioned. Mike is in the Writer's Guild, and I knew there was no way Three Walls was in a position to pay the $50,000 minimum the Guild would demand for the option. Three Walls is a small Independent film company, not some big Hollywood studio with deep pockets. Mike's background is in Hollywood, so I couldn't see him agreeing to the money of an Independent film. I needed to engage him in a conversation to find out where he stood on the issue of money. I thought there might be one angle that would be worth exploring, and I did have something going in my favor. Mike was a little hungrier for work since he had left Hollywood. The altitude of those Mets tickets was proof of that.

Looking around us after we took our seats, I said, "There are still a couple of rows behind us. You could have saved yourself a couple more bucks."

"If I knew I was bringing you, I would have," Mike said as he took a bite of his hotdog.

"They're like ants!" I announced, looking down on the field. "Are they even using a baseball? They could be miming the game for all we know."

A visiting Milwaukee player's bat cracked, and Mike and I watched the ball sail into the stands for a home run. "Even if they were miming," Mike said, "it'd still be over by the first inning."

An Orchestrated Mistake

Later during the game, Mike returned to our seats with a new round of refreshments. "You're going next time," he grumbled, handing me a beer and a hotdog.

"I won't want anything else," I said, ignoring Mike's glare. To try and lighten his mood and take both our minds off what was happening on the field, I brought up the script. "You given any thought about who should play Thaddeus?" I asked.

"I heard Tom Cruise is looking for a comedy," Mike said. "If that means you have to join Scientology, so be it."

"You'll never get Cruise for Independent film money. He's too Hollywood."

"I'm Hollywood."

"Ex-Hollywood," I reminded Mike, nodding to our nosebleed seating.

"If you want Three Walls to produce, you're going to have to take a pay cut. At least in the beginning."

"How much of a pay cut?" Mike questioned, trying to get mustard off his shirt.

"A big one." I shrugged. "Three Walls is not a Hollywood studio that throws money at writers for options."

"I'll accept scale," Mike announced.

"I think it will have to be less than scale."

"Less than scale?"

"Much less, or there is no way Three Walls will option it."

"I'm in the Union," Mike protested. "They have to at least pay Union minimum."

"There are ways around that," I said. "*Thaddeus* has studio written all over it anyway, so why do you want Three Walls to produce it?"

"One, because I'm not in Hollywood and don't have an agent anymore. And two, because if I sold it to some studio, I'd be out of the equation and they'd just fuck it up. Like they did *House Guest*," Mike said, referring to the studio film he co-wrote. "If anyone is going to fuck up my movies from now on, it might as well be my friends. Then I'll have the right to crash on their couch and drink all their booze."

"Like you care if you have the right."

"What do you think Three Walls will pay?"

"I don't know that they'll pay anything," I said. "I haven't given it to them, and as I said, *Thaddeus* has studio written all over it. We do smaller Independent films. *Thaddeus* might not be right for Three Walls," I said with a shrug.

Mike fixed his gaze back down to the field. "Then fuck Three Walls. We can produce it and sell it ourselves."

"No way," I shot back. "I'd be in way over my head without Laura and Andre. I couldn't do it."

"So, what's your plan then?" Mike asked. "Are you going to give them the script or not?"

"No point, really. What if they liked it and wanted to option it? You won't like what they offer."

"How do you know?" Mike asked. "Throw something at me you realistically think they'd offer."

"Okay," I said, taking a sip of beer. "A dollar."

"A buck?" Mike asked incredulously. "You can't be serious? A dollar for the option?"

An Orchestrated Mistake

"Yes."

"I said realistic."

"That is."

"That's not realistic. It's a fucking joke."

"Told ya you wouldn't like it."

"I don't just not like it. I fucking hate it! A buck for my script?" Mike challenged, turning to face me.

"Yes."

Mike stared back down at the field as a Mets player was tagged out stealing a base. "I don't know what's more depressing, your offer or this fucking game. Fuck Three Walls. Even if they want it, I'm not giving it to them for a buck."

"Maybe there could be other incentives."

"Like what?"

"Maybe a deal could work something like this," I suggested. "You sell us a two-year option to *Thaddeus* for a dollar."

"I hate it already," Mike snapped.

"Hear me out. We then have two years to raise the financing, and once we do, you're paid the first half of scale, or twenty-five grand, and the second half is due on the first day of shooting. So, you've got your full $50,000 for the option before we've rolled one frame of film. Plus, at the point of production," I added before Mike could interrupt, "your predetermined writer's fees kick in for the sale of the script."

"Hmmm, maybe," Mike said. "But how do you get around the Union?"

"Easy. We make you a producer on the film. Now, you get a producer's fee on top of everything, and you're involved in making the film. And the best part is if the film bombs at the box office, I don't have to let you crash on my couch because you helped fuck it up."

"We word artists never fuck up movies. We leave that to the producers."

"And this time, you'll be one of them," I said.

"So, Three Walls gets my script for two years for a buck?"

"That's right."

"And if they don't raise the money to get it to production, then I don't get paid?"

"Right again," I said.

"So, then I've essentially tied up my script and wasted two years?"

"Not essentially. You have. We all have, but that's the risk. But consider Three Walls Productions' track record. We got two Academy Award nominations. Andre and Laura won producers of the year at the Independent Spirit Awards. We get films made."

Mike took a slug of his drink and looked down at the field. I could tell he was on the fence, and I needed something to push him off.

"Here's something else you should consider," I said. "You need an agent, and we've worked with all the big agencies. CAA, ICM, United Artists—pick one, and we've probably got a connection there. We'll introduce you to a few agents to help jumpstart your career. It's also easier to land an agent when you've already got an offer in your pocket."

"I get all this plus a dollar?" Mike asked with an air of acrimony.

An Orchestrated Mistake

"Hey, if you think you can do better on your own, I say go for it."

Mike looked at me like he was going to regurgitate a vital organ before he let out a painful groan. "A dollar for two years?" he asked again.

"Yup."

Mike looked down at the field and then turned back to me. "If I only get a dollar, you're only getting fifty cents," he said, extending his right hand.

"Agreed," I said, shaking his hand.

Mike shook and turned towards the field before adding, "That's fifty cents Canadian."

The blow of another Mets ignominious defeat was softened by the agreement in principle that Mike and I had reached on *Thaddeus*. Of course, the agreement hinged on whether Andre liked the script or not and if he and Laura felt it was worth their time and expense to develop. Even if they got the option for a dollar, it still costs thousands and can take years to develop a script. And would they like it enough for that kind of expense and time commitment? More importantly for me was that *Thaddeus* was a big ambitious venture, and there's no guarantee that they'll bring me on to such a project as a producer. They might be more comfortable keeping me in my familiar role as a production manager or coordinator. I wouldn't have been thrilled to be overlooked as a producer, but I would have understood their decision not to trust things to a producing novice. Especially one that can barely climb the stairs at a baseball stadium, never mind climbing to the summit of a feature film. Leaving the stadium that afternoon, I felt my life had been inching towards this moment, and I had pushed the events around *Thaddeus* as best I could. It would now be up to the universal movie gods to determine if *Thaddeus* would fly, and if so, what my role would be.

An Orchestrated Mistake

CHAPTER FOUR

"Two hamburger everything plus mustard!" the Bangladeshi manager shouted upon spotting me enter Papayas take-out restaurant. I'd been going to Papayas for lunch at 23rd & 7th several times a month since we moved our offices to Chelsea. My experience at Papayas is not unlike my relationship with the Puerto Rican street vendor in the morning. I'm just familiar enough for him to know what to offer me when I arrive, but not familiar enough for him to engage in anything beyond, 'Hey buddy, how are you?' It's perfect.

It's not that the food is so amazing at this little place that it keeps me coming back; in fact, I'm sure there are more than a few New Yorkers who hold their nose as they pass by. What keeps me coming back is that I never have to wait, no matter how busy the place gets. The manager always seems to spot me entering and shout my order to the cooks.

The special is always two hamburgers with everything plus mustard. I didn't know why it was two hamburgers, one would suffice, but I supposed the second burger was offered in case you missed how disgusting the first one was you could confirm it with a second.

The burgers usually come with a wilting piece of lettuce, a tomato harvested in the last millennium, mayonnaise, ketchup, and of course, mustard. I say *usually* because there is never a one-hundred percent guarantee what you'll find residing between those two soggy buns. Once I found a raw French fry trying to make a break for freedom. I ate him anyway. If you request cheese, it's a bit of a crapshoot as to whether or not a slice of processed cheese will appear. I never order cheese because I don't believe in paying for something I'm not guaranteed. I will say, though, when you do get cheese, it effectively seals in the grease. For a distinguished palate like my own, these burgers are disgustingly delicious. Here's a little tip for you, though. If you find yourself in New York and you decide you want to have the quintessential New York experience and try these take-out burgers, it's vital you say 'plus mustard' when placing your order. If you don't, it will create so much confusion there's a good chance you just might end up receiving a hotdog.

I never cared for mustard on my burger. Mustard seemed to overwhelm the taste of all the other condiments working so hard to make the burger palatable. I used to tell my Bangladeshi friend religiously, "Please don't put any mustard on my burger. No mustard!"

"No mustard??" he'd question in falsetto.

"That's right," I'd tell him. "No mustard."

"No mustard on both hamburger?"

"No mustard on both burgers."

"Okay." He'd shrug. "Two hamburger everything no mustard!" he'd holler at the cooks with contempt.

After breaking the Papaya's commandment, *Thou shalt have mustard on thy burger,* I found the burger could be missing anything. The tomato, mayonnaise, ketchup, or even that wilting piece of lettuce, but once finding the meat had gone AWOL, I gave up and started ordering my burgers just the way my Bangladeshi friend likes to serve them—with everything plus mustard. The cooks had been nailing my order ever since. For me, mustard on my burger has become an acquired taste.

"Two hamburger everything plus mustard!" he yelled to the cooks over that busy Thursday lunchtime crowd. A few minutes later, he's holding up a brown bag. "Two hamburger everything plus mustard!" he hollered, and I worked my way to the counter through the throng of impatient New Yorkers. "How you, my friend?" he asked when I got to the counter.

"I've climbed to the top of the world," I told him.

"That's nice. I give you large diet soda today," he replied as he handed me my order.

He's not really interested in how I am. I'm nothing more than a quick six bucks plus tip, and in fairness, that's true of all food establishments. They could care less about how we actually are, and for us, it's all about the lip service we receive anyway. We tip according to polite lip service. I could have told him, 'I've just been diagnosed with terminal cancer, the bank repossessed my home, and my cat died,' and he'd still say, 'That's nice. I give you large diet soda today.' And what's also true is I'd still fork over a nice tip.

"See you next week," I said, giving him my money.

"I be here," he responded. "Especially for you."

Sure you will, I thought and pushed my way to the exit past the glinted glares of the queue I had jumped. That's how you tell how choked a New Yorker is, by the frost in their glare. I returned to the office, and right on cue, the four-legged bandits trotted out to greet me. They always seemed to know when I was returning with food. Others in the office would return with food, but the bandits never seemed interested to greet them. I, on the other hand, always seemed to be eating with an audience. I'm not sure how I feel about having the same culinary taste as a couple of dogs. I guess it could be worse. At least they weren't mooching my cigarettes—yet.

I tore off a couple of bites for my guests and took a bite myself while I checked my email. There was an email from a young New York director who had asked me recently to produce her short film. I wasn't sure I had wanted to, but when I read her script and then met with her to discuss the story, I just couldn't say no. Rachel's script was intelligent and moving, and most importantly, I could see she had vision, was driven, and passionate about her material. I had told her I didn't have the time or the resources to raise the money for a short film, but if she found the money for the modest budget, I would produce her film. Her email was to let me know she had found the money. I wrote her back immediately to tell her I was on board to produce, and we should meet next week to hammer out our plans. It wasn't the Holy Grail of a full-length feature, but many of the intrinsic challenges of producing a script are still there whether the project is large or small. I had enjoyed the couple of brief script meetings Rachel and I had, and while I had the time, I was only too happy for the opportunity to test my producing muscles.

"Nicholas, can you step in for a minute?" Andre buzzed over my intercom.

"Sure," I said, breaking off two more bites for each wagging tail.

"What's up?" I said, stepping into Laura and Andre's office.

"Mike's a friend of yours?" Andre asked.

"Yeah," I answered, catching Laura swallow a smirk from behind her computer. "We've suffered through a few Mets seasons together," I continued. "You know, misery likes company and all. Or in Mike's case, misery needs an audience."

"What can you tell me about his work?"

"He co-wrote the movie *House Guest*. He was a TV writer and showrunner in L.A. I've read a few of his spec film scripts. A couple of them aren't bad."

"And *Thaddeus*?"

"I think it's just silly enough to work."

"We do too…" Andre said, nodding towards Laura. "Think you could work with Mike?"

"Yeah, I could," I said, wondering if patience is actually found through meditation.

"We're concerned that given Mike's background, he won't accept an option on our terms," Andre said, clasping his hands behind his head as he leaned back in his chair.

"I wouldn't worry about that," I said. "I think I could convince him."

"You think so?"

"Sure," I said with a shrug. "I don't think it will be a problem."

"Then speak to Mike," Andre said. A huge grin broke out across Andre's face before he added, "And you're the point producer on *Thaddeus*."

I thought Andre's line of questioning might be moving towards Three Walls optioning Mike's script. Even though I had worked and positioned myself to be a producer on the project, I was still completely stunned speechless when he announced I'd be producing.

The sound of Laura laughing while she clapped her hands together pulled me out of a daze. I looked between Andre and Laura and could see and feel the genuine joy these two were experiencing by sharing this news with me.

"Ya?" Andre questioned his new producer, who was still standing stunned in the middle of their office.

"Yes, yes!" I said. "I'll call Mike right now," I added, backing out of the office. "Thank you."

I floated back to my desk with the same ecstasy that pumped through my veins after getting my first laugh as an actor on stage. I could still hear Andre and Laura chuckling when I sat down at my desk, took a deep breath, and punched in Mike's number with a shaky index finger.

"DiGaetano," I said when Mike picked up.

"What do you want? I'm very busy," Mike quipped when he heard my voice.

An Orchestrated Mistake

"Put down the Doritos and wine and listen to me," I replied. "Remember the other week at the Mets game?"

"I'm still depressed."

"Well, don't be. Laura and Andre want to option your script. You remember the option scenario we discussed?"

"Why do you think I'm depressed?"

"Well, don't jump until I get your signature," I said.

I went over the general terms again with Mike, and we agreed we'd meet on the weekend to discuss the script and compare our lists of talent to consider. If I thought there would be any celebratory high fives through the phone with Mike, I was mistaken. "Okay," Mike said before hanging up. "I guess this means you won't have to go back to Canada to hunt moose."

It has taken me forty-four years, but I finally reached the base of the summit, and the view was spectacular. I wasn't a writer/producer yet, but I had nailed half the dream. Only once *Thaddeus* and Rachel's film were safely playing on the screen could I officially plant my flag on Producer's Peak. Nevertheless, I was going to enjoy the steep learning curve for the final push to produce a feature film. With the tools I already had in place and Laura and Andre's guidance, my job was to listen, learn, and execute the lessons in order to produce these films. Any self-doubts or anxiety I was feeling about my ability to produce the projects or whether I even had the stamina for such undertakings was washed away by the infusion of pure creative adrenaline. I'd figure out what I wanted to write once those two films hit the screen.

The rest of that Thursday and all day Friday, I spent working my wish list of talent for *Thaddeus*, and when I wasn't doing that or script notes, I was in Laura's office peppering her with questions about the budget and schedule.

An Orchestrated Mistake

That Saturday, I took the train to midtown to meet Mike at a diner. "You look puzzled," I said to him after he looked over my talent lists.

"Not at all," Mike replied while fingering his French fries. "I was just wondering when people suffering from bulimia decide it's time to stop, do they simply throw up their hands?"

"You're twisted," I managed to get out before choking on a mouthful of coffee. "I can't believe I've agreed to work with you."

"Yeah, but you did agree," Mike quipped. "We have a contract."

"Not yet," I reminded him.

"We will have a contract, and then you'll be stuck with me."

"A contract is just confetti before the tear," I shot back.

"I'm claiming that," Mike said, writing it down.

"It's yours. So, who do you like on the list for Thaddeus?" I asked.

"Some I like, others I think you're way off."

"Who's way off?"

"Steve Carell for one," Mike said, looking at the list.

"Steve Carell would be a great Thaddeus," I said. "He has that anger thing happening, just like Thaddeus."

"He's too old."

"He's barely in his forties! He's like my age."

"You're too old."

"Forties is not too old."

An Orchestrated Mistake

"He looks too old," Mike said.

"All right, we'll come back to Carell," I said, shaking my head. "So, who on the list do you like?"

"Neal Patrick Harris."

"He's not on the list," I said, grabbing the sheet out of Mike's hand.

"Well, he should be."

"Neal Patrick Harris doesn't look like a cantankerous middle-aged cop," I said.

"I don't see Thaddeus as a cantankerous middle-aged cop," Mike said as he took the list back.

"Neither do I."

"Steve Carell?" Mike retorted.

"Steve Carell looks a hell of a lot more like a Thaddeus than Neal Patrick Harris," I parried. Mike looked like he was about to defend his choice, so I cut him off. I had forgotten that a producer needs to be able to do the two-step around an artist's ego.

"Let's forget Steve and Neal," I said. "Tell me who on the list you actually *do* like?"

Taking off his glasses, Mike studied the sheet of paper. "Matthew Broderick," he finally announced.

"You have no clue who should be playing Thaddeus," I bemoaned.

"Matthew's older than Steve."

"He doesn't look older."

"Well, he is."

"You put him on the list," Mike said.

"I know, but Steve Carell is more of a Thaddeus than Matthew."

"Then why did you put Matthew on the list?"

"Because I think he's a good actor and a realistic possibility."

"He is," Mike agreed. "Right after Neal Patrick Harris."

"Let's come back to Thaddeus," I said, frustrated. "What about the female lead? Sherry...what's her name."

"Netherland," Mike prompted.

"Right. What about her?"

"Sarah Silverman is a solid choice."

"Finally, someone we can agree on."

"Yeah. Amy Poehler works as well," Mike said, studying the list. "Amy would be good for the Heidi Gross character too."

"Yeah, I like Amy," I told Mike. "I've worked with her before. I drove her to set once when I was a production assistant."

"Then call her up," Mike suggested sarcastically. "By showbiz standards, you're practically family."

"I got us lost in Brooklyn," I mumbled.

"Then forget it," Mike quipped. "She probably still has nightmares."

Mike and I went back and forth over our choices for the cast and a director for the better part of that Saturday afternoon. Josh Brolin, Ben Affleck, Matt Damon, and Ryan Reynolds finally topped our wish list for Thaddeus. Okay, I know we were a bit optimistic, but that's why it's called a wish list. You start with the

An Orchestrated Mistake

A-listers and hope by the time your film is cast, you haven't had to cast the Maytag repairman. We both begrudgingly included each other's choice of Neal and Steve.

I spent the rest of the weekend on my sister's back porch drinking coffee, smoking cigarettes, and making detailed script notes. Making script notes is easy, but getting writers to agree to them, that's like mating elephants.

"I have some script notes," I told Mike Sunday night over the phone. "We should meet later this week to go over them."

"Fine," Mike said. "I've already cut seven minutes out of the script. I just hope they aren't the best seven minutes."

"I hope so too."

"When we get together and I ignore your notes, don't take it personally," Mike advised. "Remember the first rule of show business. It's always about me."

"I forgot how exhausting it is working with writers." I sighed.

"I'm not just a writer," Mike shot back. "I'm a word artist."

"Whatever you are, you better be damn funny or we're both not getting paid."

"If someone you don't think is funny thinks something you said is funny, is it really funny?"

"I need to go," I said, suddenly exhausted. "I'll call you later in the week."

"I might be in Florida later this week," Mike announced. "An eighty-four-year-old woman just won the hundred-million-dollar Powerball. I'll be down there trying to convince her she's my grandmother."

"We should have optioned a drama," I said before hanging up.

An Orchestrated Mistake

I woke up early for work that Monday morning feeling a little tired, but not really surprised because I had chosen to work all weekend. There was the usual assault on my ears by Sonus when I popped up from the subway, heading to the rendezvous with my Puerto Rican friend for Lulu and Zombie's breakfast. It was a typical unremarkable Monday morning in terms of all my familiar routines, except for one. I would be engrossed all day with laying the groundwork for the two films I was expected to produce.

By two in the afternoon, I realized I hadn't left my desk, not even for an obligatory cigarette, and even though I wasn't feeling particularly hungry, I thought I should at least run to Papaya's to grab a couple of burgers.

I pushed the button for the elevator and immediately began to pace impatiently in the third-floor lobby. I waited for what seemed an eternity and knew right away those damn Shambhala folks heading up to the sixth floor to meditate were monopolizing the elevators. Why would anyone open up a meditation center in a busy Manhattan office building? As I paced frantically in front of the elevators, I wondered who the hell has the time to meditate anyway. This is New York.

Usually, when I had to wait for the elevators, I'd charge down the stairs, but today for some reason, I seemed more content to just manically pace.

Finally, the elevator arrived, the doors opened, and I took one step in, prepared to give any lurking Zen-seekers the infamous New Yorker frosty glare when my life's orbit shifted in an instant.

As I stepped through the elevator doors, I was instantly my six-year-old self sinking helplessly below the surface of Shuswap Lake in B.C., looking up at the shimmering sun through the water as I sank. I was helpless. I couldn't breathe. I could only hear my nine-year-old sister Deirdre's muffled screams from shore as I struggled to return to the surface. My sister's screams were directed at the older boy who took me out on the lake on his inner tube and then pushed me off. Looking up through the water as I descended, the rippling sun began to fade as my feet scrambled for a solid surface.

My legs no longer supported me. They became two broken matchsticks beneath me the moment I stepped onto the elevator. I fell helplessly towards the back of the elevator. As I extended my hand to break my fall, my body twisted and I caught a glimpse of someone, a woman perhaps, shrieking. Looking upward as I was falling, the clouded bright lights of the elevator dominated my vision as my body twisted further and slammed into the back of the elevator with a deafening thud. Staring up at the lights, the cloudiness got thicker as euphoric energy permeated my body as my senses numbed. Like descending into the lake, I was acutely aware of all the clouded sights and muffled sounds that enveloped me.

The need to survive is strong. My feet began kicking as hard as my six-year-old legs willed them, and I felt myself ascend towards the surface of the lake. The sun got brighter and the shrieking louder as I rose, but it wasn't bright enough or loud enough to sustain life. I could see my hands at the end of my outstretched arms reaching for the sun and thought if I could just reach the sun, I could pull myself up to the surface. Staring up through the water at the shimmering sun, I realized my legs didn't have the strength to return me to the surface, and once again, the sun began to fade as I began to sink. Resigning myself to the stillness and peace as I floated down, I felt a boy's hand grasp my arm and violently yank me to the surface. Life rushed into my lungs as the lake released me, and feeling the warmth of the sun, I heard my sister's screams, "Get him! Get him!" as the boy pulled me back onto his floating tube.

I was slumped against the back wall of the elevator, my legs like two strands of crumpled rope beneath me, and no herculean effort was enough to position them in their rightful place. I needed help. Struggling to stand, the woman grabbed hold of my arms, and with the support of the back wall, she lifted me to my feet. "Wah wah, wah," she said, sounding like the teacher in *Charlie Brown*. My legs struggled to hold my weight, but with the woman's help and the support of the wall, I was standing—just barely. I stared at her. Her long black hair framed a white, featureless face. She said something. I haven't a clue what it was. There was a peaceful sensation surrounding my confusion and terror. I tried to step forward but lost my balance and fell back against the wall. "Wah wah," she said.

"I, I, I tripped," I think I said, but have no idea because my voice was just as distorted and confusing as hers. Holding my arm, the woman replied, "Wah wah."

I tried again. "I tripped," I think I repeated. She stared at me, but I couldn't make out the expression on her face, nor could I tell what expression was on my own. I remained leaning against the back wall of the elevator while it descended. The woman was still talking to me, but I had no idea what she was saying.

When the elevator doors finally opened, my Canadian instincts took over and I gestured with a rubber arm for her to exit first. She hesitated, began to exit, and looked back as I pushed off the wall, but I only managed two shaky steps before stumbling forward to the elevator doors.

"Wah, okay?" she asked. I heard that she said 'okay.'

"Fffine." I nodded. "Go ahead." I leaned against the elevator door and pretended to be looking for something in my right pocket, but my right hand couldn't find the inside of my pocket.

"You okay?" she asked again, walking back to me.

"Yeeeah. I, I'm grrreat!" I said like a stoned Tony the Tiger.

"You don't seem great."

"Stumbled," I said with a lame shrug.

"You're sure?"

"Just nneed mmy keys," I said, pointing to my right pocket. She stared at my right pocket. "Really," I added. She nodded and slowly turned to exit but only made it to the lobby doors before turning around again to give me the once over. "Really," I said, forcing a smile. Unconvinced, she returned the smile and exited.

Glad to no longer be under her watchful gaze and relieved to have the lobby to myself, I knew I too had to exit. The problem was I couldn't logically process what I needed to do. My instinct was to return to the relative safety of my office, but I was afraid I'd run into Laura or one of my coworkers and they'd instantly start questioning my behavior—a behavior that was frightening and one that I didn't have any answers for. I also wasn't sure if my world had finished spiraling out of control. And if whatever just happened in the elevator occurred in front of Laura or anyone else, they'd undoubtedly have me on my way to the hospital. A hospital I could not afford. Uncertain what to do, and with only fractured thoughts, I did the only logical thing I could do. I carried on outside as if nothing happened.

Steadying myself with the wall, I inched my way through the lobby like I was walking the deck of a ship in the middle of a typhoon. My heart was hammering through my chest when I finally made it outside and staggered out onto the sidewalk, falling back against the building for support.

Pressed against the building, I wanted to keep moving to prove to myself nothing had happened, but even I, the delusional king that I am, knew something in my brain had seriously shifted out of alignment. I knew I needed a hospital, but the thought of another $32,000 medical bill kept me pressed motionless against the side of the building. I hoped whatever had broken in my brain would repair itself in time, or perhaps at any moment, I would hear a director yell, "Cut! That's a wrap!" But this was not a movie nor a dream. This was reality.

I'm sure I looked like any other stunned office worker escaping their prison to grab a swig of fresh air to the passerby. I couldn't make out the details of their faces or pull complete sentences as they passed by, and this only accelerated my heart rate and added to the confusion that was becoming internal panic.

An Orchestrated Mistake

My thoughts were fractured, scrambled, and had developed a stutter and seemed to be no longer capable of completing themselves before racing on. I needed to slow down, not panic, and think through what was happening before all rational thought slid over the horizon.

I then did something I'd done for the last fourteen years whenever I wanted just to quiet my mind and think. I fumbled for my right pocket, my hand making it inside on the third attempt, and I was able to pull out my pack of Winston cigarettes.

My world still shaking, and not quite sure if the earthquake was over, I fumbled for a cigarette and then grappled to find my mouth. Finally holding the cigarette between what I discovered was my now numb lips, I held the lighter with both hands and guided the shaking flame under the cigarette.

The long pull I took invoked a violent coughing fit. Applying delusional logic, I thought that I would have plausible deniability to what I knew was taking place if I could continue to smoke.

I was having a stroke. But how is a stroke possible? I'm only forty-four, and even I'm not dumb enough to tempt fate by lighting a cigarette during a stroke. That would just be insane. So, this can't be a stroke.

Leaning on the building while puffing on my cigarette, I knew I needed to do a systems check. Figure out what was working and what had taken a hit. My cigarette was now finding my mouth with regularity, so I took this as a positive sign. I was pulling words and phrases from conversations from those who passed by, and I could now make out the details of their faces. I tried to step away from the building, but my arm immediately shot back for support. Okay, so my balance is a little off, but I'm sure it will return as soon as I finish this cigarette.

While I was preoccupied trying to stand on my own without the support of the building, the cigarette in my left hand burnt down, and I didn't notice the cherry was burning my hand until I looked at it. I dropped the cigarette to the sidewalk and tried to step on it with my left foot. I missed the cigarette butt completely. Continuing to lean on the building, I lifted my left foot and again tried to bring it down on the butt but came down wide. I tried again and missed the mark for the third time. I turned to lean on the building to use my right foot, but just lifting my right leg slightly had me wobbling. I turned back to my left, stared down at the elusive butt, and failed my fourth attempt. Leaning into the building with my shoulder, I took hold of my thigh with both hands and guided my left foot down on the extinguished butt. All doubt was removed as to whether I had a stroke. I knew then I had. Stunned by the effort and concentration it had taken, anger and frustration rumbled through my body, and I lifted my left leg again with both hands and slammed it down on top of the butt. Anger at myself began to swell as I raised my left leg with my hands and slammed it down a fourth and fifth time, then a sixth and seventh, like a demonic petulant child.

The disappointment and rage that consumed me was directed only at myself, and out of breath and leaning against the building, I was surprised to feel the moisture of frustration streaming down my cheeks. The evidence was all around me. I had had a stroke the moment those elevator doors opened.

I needed to do something, but the only thing I could think of now was getting back to my office. I slid my way back along the walls through the lobby to the elevators, and after several attempts, was able to press the call button. I swayed slightly as I waited, and when the elevator came, I staggered back like a drunk as the people exited. After I staggered onto the elevator, the doors began to close and I heard a man yell, "Hold the elevator!" I tried to hit the *open door* button but hit close instead, and the doors slammed shut in the man's face. "Prick!" I heard him yell as he slammed his fists on the closed doors. I was able to get back to my desk undetected, and I thought if anyone questioned my slow, awkward movements, I'd blame it on a bout of food poisoning. Everyone would believe that. I noticed I had a message on my phone and picked up the receiver with my left hand but couldn't control my right to punch in the code. My right arm seemed incapable of accurately guiding my right index finger over the correct buttons. I tried a second time, and just like my early attempts to step on the cigarette, I couldn't do it. Replacing the handset, I stared at my right hand. I tried to touch the tip of each finger to my thumb, but I couldn't do it either. I tried with my left hand, and even though it was numb, I could spastically accomplish finger to thumb. I tried snapping my fingers—no measured snap from either hand. I tried tapping my feet under my desk, and even by middle-aged white guy standards, there was no rhythm at all.

Picking up a pen, I tried to sign my name on a piece of paper. I couldn't do it. My signature was just a few squiggly lines. My second attempt was worse than my first.

"Nicholas!" Mira, our latest office intern, called out. "You need to sign Andre's birthday card," she instructed, walking over and placing the card in front of me. I looked at the card and glanced up to Mira, who'd taken a step back waiting for me to sign. I picked up the card with my left hand.

"Cute card," I mumbled, putting it down.

"Well, sign it, Nicholas. You're the last one."

"I will. Why don't you leave it with me, and I'll think of something to write?"

"How about 'Happy Birthday!'" Mira suggested sarcastically.

"Andre's out of town," I said. "Just leave it and I'll sign it later."

"Nicholas, you're the last one. Just sign the card."

"Why don't you sign it for me," I awkwardly suggested to the young intern.

"Why would I sign it?"

I hadn't an answer. I shrugged. Mira looked down at me and frowned. She picked up the pen to put it in my right hand, where she noticed my hand was trembling. "Nicholas, what's going on?" she asked with a nervous giggle. Her eyes darted to mine, and the fear that must have been in my eyes now registered as tears in her own.

"What are you two conspiring?" Laura laughed, crossing towards my desk. My heart rate went from a canter to a full gallop.

"Nicholas can't sign Andre's card," Mira blurted out.

Looking down at me, Laura was absorbed by the aura of fear that surrounded my desk. Her eyes shot from Mira to the pen to my own.

"What the hell is going on, Alexander?"

I stared at Laura, and lying to her for the first time, I said, "I honestly don't know."

Her jovial mood was now gone. Mira hadn't said 'won't' sign the card. She had said, 'can't,' and this had both women waiting for an explanation.

"Nicholas, what's going on?" Laura asked again, stepping closer.

"I can sign the card." I chuckled.

"Then sign it."

"I can. It's just right now my right hand is playing tricks on me." Laura leaned across my desk, and I knew I would have to give a better explanation than that. I pulled my eyes away from Laura's relentless gaze and noticed Mira's quivering bottom lip. How can I tell them what just happened when I'm not even sure myself? I knew if I gave Laura the details, she'd call 911 and have me on my way to Beth Israel or some other hospital I couldn't afford. "I must have banged it when I came in," I finally said. "I'm fine, really." The glare from both women told me they weren't buying it. "I think I'm a little tired today, too," I added.

"You look tired," Laura said after a moment.

"Yeah, I'm just tired," I said, picking up Andre's card and signing it with what I hoped at least resembled my signature.

"You should see your doctor," Laura instructed.

"He's out on Long Island," I said. "I'll see him first thing tomorrow." Laura took in what I said and looked over at Mira, who was still chewing her bottom lip. "Really," I said. "I'll see him tomorrow."

"Let me get my keys," Laura said. "I'm driving you to Penn."

I continued my sales pitch to Laura that I was okay on the drive up to Penn Station. She voiced her concern about how I handle my diabetes, and when she said I could be susceptible to a stroke, I almost started dry heaving out onto 8th Avenue. I waited until she pulled away from the curb before attempting to struggle through the throngs of New York commuters.

It took all my strength and concentration to make my way down to the tracks at Penn Station. Without proper balance, I was bounced around like a pinball by the crowds, and the long escalators down gave me such a devastating case of vertigo I was forced to ride the escalator while sitting down. When the train arrived, I let the wall of humanity push me into the train and was relieved to have scored a window seat before the train began moving. I tried again to do my thumb to fingers routine and tap my feet but gave up quickly in frustration.

Once the train was out of the midtown tunnel, I fumbled for my cell phone and punched my sister's numbers. "Hey, it's me," I said when my sister picked up. "I'm on the train home. Can you pick me up at the station in an hour?"

"Wow, you'll be home early. That's a first. What happened? First week as a producer, and you're already fired?" Deirdre laughed.

"See you in an hour," I said, ignoring her humor. "And can you make an appointment with your doctor for me?"

"Sure, what's wrong?"

"Nothing," I said, failing once again to touch the tip of my fingers to my right thumb. "Tomorrow morning, first thing would be great."

"Sure. Are you okay? Nicholas? Hello?"

"Yeah, I'm fine. I'll see you in an hour," I said, hanging up.

Replacing my phone in my shirt pocket, the image of Mira's fearful tears rushed into my mind. Letting my head rest against the window, I can't be sure whether it was the disappointment, anger, or even fear that induced moisture in my own eyes. I stared out the window as the rocking train jostled my body as the blurry borough of Queens rolled by.

CHAPTER FIVE

I knew the last thing I should have been doing given the day's events was sitting on my sister's picnic table by the back porch at 2am sipping beer and smoking cigarettes, but I was. I wanted to ensure I'd sleep the moment I hit the pillow. I had no interest in lying in bed gazing at the ceiling asking myself, *What if?* What if I hadn't believed that the laws of health didn't apply to me? That moment had long passed, and now I was just craving copious amounts of hops and nicotine to numb and quiet my soul.

I had tried to sleep earlier in the afternoon after my sister had picked me up and I had briefed her with a sanitized version of the day's occurrence, but by then I was far beyond sleep. I discovered you can't sleep when you're in shock. Instead, I spent the rest of the afternoon confirming what had happened by trying to tap my feet and sign my name with my niece's red crayon on the back picnic table. Pounding the evidence of my new health crisis into my psyche seemed much more productive and appropriate than rest.

When I finally did pull myself up the stairs in the middle of the night, the two tall Budweiser's proved not enough, and all I could do was doze until my alarm went off, exposing the theory of *you'll feel better in the morning* as a fraud. I hadn't felt this lousy since my first hangover at sixteen.

I grabbed my jeans off the back of a chair but was unable to step into them as I had done just twenty-four hours before. I could no longer balance on one leg long enough to pull them on and instead fell back on the bed and pulled them on like a teenage girl dressing for a party. I struggled with my socks before making the mistake of reaching for a buttoned shirt. "Jesus!" I howled, fighting with the buttons. A top-rope battle royal was taking place between my fingers and the buttonholes, and when I finally did get the shirt done up, I noticed in the full-length mirror that I had done up the shirt lopsided. "Awww! Come on!" I complained, fumbling again with the buttons. I ripped open the shirt out of frustration, sending a stream of buttons tinkering to the floor.

An Orchestrated Mistake

"Perfect!" I shouted, looking at myself panting in the mirror. Standing there in just my Levis, I looked like an emaciated raccoon. I'd never noticed I had ribs before, and why hadn't I noticed that dark circles were orbiting my eyes? The image staring back at me in the mirror wasn't me, but it did reflect exactly how I felt: like death. I grabbed a t-shirt, pulled it on, and, taking a stair at a time while clinging to the railing with both hands, made my way down to the kitchen.

"I hear you're having a good morning," Deirdre teased as I entered the kitchen.

"Fabulous." I scowled.

"This will cheer you up," she said, handing me a coffee. "It's cold. I made it last night. How do you feel?"

"Like a grenade went off inside my head." I nodded, taking the coffee.

"Kind of looks like you dove on one too," my sister chided.

"Encouraging. I'm going out back for a smoke."

"You're kidding? You're going to smoke?"

"Why not?" I said. "I've already pulled the pin."

I stared at the paper from the night before with my clumsy attempts at my signature. I ignored my ineptness, lighting a cigarette after taking a seat, but the sight of my failures in red crayon further battered my psyche. I flipped the paper over but was only greeted with more failed images.

****

"Thwap, thwap, thwap," echoed in my sister's and my ears as we walked down the hall of the medical building to Kaye's office. My left shoe was slapping down uncontrollably on the tiled floor with each step. My glare towards my sister announced I didn't want to hear any comments on this obnoxious sound. Mercifully, Deirdre withdrew into her thoughts.

"You look like hell," Kaye said, closing the examining room door.

"Years of medical school, and that's your diagnosis?" I quipped.

"Let me take a closer look," Kaye said, turning my head from side to side between his hands. "Yep. That's hell," he deadpanned. "Why don't you tell me what's going on?" he asked, stepping back.

It did cross my mind to give Kaye the watered-down version of events that I had perfected in the last eighteen hours, but even I knew, delusional as I was, I needed to be straight up with Kaye. "I stepped onto the elevator around two yesterday and just fell over," I told him. "It was like a bad film with an unfocused camera, bad sound, and I...I..." Emotions welled up inside, completely catching me off guard. "It wasn't fun," I added quickly, taking a deep breath.

"Push down as hard as you can on my hands," Kaye said, extending his arms. I pushed down as hard as I could, continuing to tell my story, but there was some fractured disconnect to my thoughts, preventing me from articulating in my usual manner. I could see the story, even see most of the words, but I couldn't find the path to access them. Some moments it seemed like there were just empty canyons where a word was supposed to be. It was like portions of my vocabulary were moved to an undisclosed location and I couldn't find them. I knew I was making sense, but I felt uncomfortable, fractured, and so very disconnected for someone who has made a career out of communicating.

"Slow down," Kaye said. "Just breathe, and just with your eyes, follow the tip of my finger."

"I don't feel like me," I said to Kaye, following his finger. "I mean not just physically, but emotionally. It's like I might explode."

"What do you mean you might explode?"

"I...I...I don't know what I mean," I finally said.

"Why don't you hop off the table and walk heel to toe without looking down," Kaye said. "Pick a spot on the wall and focus on that."

I put my right heel to my left toe and immediately stumbled.

"Wait, wait," I protested. "I wasn't ready. Let me try again." I didn't fare any better on my second attempt. "Let me try once more," I said. "I think I picked the wrong spot," I added, pointing to the wall.

After stumbling a third time, Kaye asked sarcastically, "Did you pick the right spot that time?"

Kaye finished his examination and told me to put my shoes and shirt back on and meet him in his office. "I'll get your sister," he said as he opened the door.

"Really?" I asked. "You really think she needs to be there?"

"I think she needs to hear this."

"How did it go?" My sister whispered like we were at a state funeral as she took a seat beside me in Kaye's office.

"Fine," I whispered. "I start training for the marathon tomorrow."

Kaye forcefully closed his office door and had barely taken his seat before he snarled, "You know you've had a stroke!" I caught my sister's head snap towards me in the corner of my eye. "You're done with smoking!! You're done!!" Kaye declared. "You should be in a hospital!!" he continued as his body shook with rage. "You're lucky you're even moving!! I should send you to the hospital now!!"

"I can't afford…"

"Insurance or no insurance, it's where you belong!!" Kaye wailed.

"I'm okay," I murmured.

"You're not okay," he snapped. "Do you even grasp what took place yesterday?" I shrugged but nodded 'yes.' "I don't think you do! You could have fallen in that elevator and never gotten up! Ever!"

I never once really thought during the stroke that I was going to die. Then again, I'm sure a heroin addict doesn't believe that they'll overdose either. I had to admire Kaye's flair for the dramatic. He definitely had my sister's attention, but as soon as he launched into a lecture on diabetes, my eyes instinctively glassed over, and I started going over casting ideas for *Thaddeus*.

"You listening to what I'm telling you?" Kaye snapped at the end of his monologue.

"Sure."

Kaye shook his head and began writing on a notepad. "Here's a number for a clinic to get an MRI. I want this done today!" he said, glaring at me.

"Can I do it tomorrow?" I asked. "I was thinking of going back to work today."

"Today!" Kaye barked. "I want the MRI and the blood tests done today!"

"So, I'll be back to work tomorrow?" I asked, taking the slip of paper.

An Orchestrated Mistake

Kaye gritted his teeth and stared at the floor like he was counting to ten. "Without proper treatment," he said, looking up, "and knowing you as I do, I'd say you may never go back."

"What?!"

"You willing to admit yourself into a hospital and get proper treatment?" I shook my head 'no.' "Admit yourself to a rehab clinic?" I shrugged my shoulders. "Then I'd say your chances of some sort of recovery are nil. So, I haven't a clue when you'll be back to work."

"I've never seen Kaye so angry," Deirdre said back in the car. "He was really pissed," she added as she put the car in reverse.

"He probably needed to blow off some steam," I commented, pulling out my Winston's. "He seems like one of those wound-up kind of guys."

"Are you kidding me!?" Deirdre bellowed, slamming on the brakes.

"What?"

"You're having a cigarette? Did you hear anything Kaye said?"

"Yes. I heard what he said."

Ignoring Deirdre's glare, I lit my cigarette. "Un-fucking-believable!" she snarled. Not wanting to get into an argument, I turned on the radio, and Journey's song "Be Good to Yourself" blared through the speakers. Serendipity can be a bitch. "Don't say a word," I commanded. "Just drive," I added, shutting off the radio.

"I need the phone," I told my sister as we walked through the front door of her house. "I need to tell the office I won't be in until tomorrow."

"Work can wait," Deirdre said. "I'm calling the clinic."

"Fine. I'll get my cell," I grumbled, pulling myself up the stairs.

I couldn't get a signal up in my room, and coming back down the stairs, clutching the railing, I took a stair at a time, but when my patience ran out, I took the last two stairs together and crashed with a thud onto the hardwood floor.

"Jesus, Nicholas!" Deirdre yelped, rushing into the room. "Just wait! You can have the phone in a minute."

"I'm fine," I said, pushing her hand away. "I've got my own phone," I added, pulling myself up with the railing.

"Un-fucking believable." Deirdre scowled, walking away.

Waiting for Laura to pick up, while sitting at the back picnic table, I noticed the paper with my scrawling hieroglyphics had blown to the ground. I bent down to pick it up and, losing my balance, almost fell over but recovered, falling back onto the bench just as Laura came on the line.

"Alexander?"

"Laura!" I said. "Well, you were right. It was a stroke."

"Where are you?"

"My sister's. I'm going for an MRI this afternoon and blood tests. I guess that's supposed to tell us more."

"Why aren't you in the hospital?" Laura asked.

"I don't need a hospital."

"Nicholas, you've had a stroke. Your doctor didn't think you should be in the hospital?" Laura asked incredulously.

"He thought about it, but he didn't insist or anything."

"He didn't?"

An Orchestrated Mistake

"Not really," I replied.

"Don't you think you should be in a hospital?"

"No," I said as medical bills danced in my head.

Laura and I went back and forth on this before she reluctantly gave up and asked me what I planned to do about my recovery.

"Not sure yet," I told her, picking up the red crayon. "I'll go for the MRI this afternoon and probably take the rest of the day off. But I'll be in first thing tomorrow." The stunned silence was thunderous. "Hello? Laura?"

"Nicholas, if you come in tomorrow, you're fired," Laura announced.

"What?" I asked, sitting up at the picnic table.

"If you come into work tomorrow, you're fired," Laura repeated.

Laura's statement had blindsided me. I didn't expect that kind of reaction to my news. I couldn't say a word even if I could find one.

"Did you hear me?" Laura asked.

"Yes. But I can't take time off work," I choked. "I need to produce *Thaddeus*."

"*Thaddeus* will be here when you get back," Laura said in an almost paternal tone. "Right now, you need to work on yourself."

"When can I come back to work?" I asked, wounded.

"When you've recovered," Laura said. "And, Nicholas, don't even think about coming back until then."

My conversation with Laura left me stunned, deflated, and further depressed. I'd only ever self-identified with my career, and without my work, I was afraid I'd become a meaningless shadow in a vacant mirror. For me, my career had trumped everything—health, relationships, and even love. My career is the only thing I felt connected to. It had been years of hit and miss, and when I finally got a legitimate chance of attaining my life's dream, it's threatened in the instant it took an elevator door to open. Sitting there at the picnic table contemplating Laura's words, I picked up the red crayon again and tried signing my name, but only produced a squiggly line before I tossed the crayon back down.

I didn't want the irony of every song on the radio reflecting my mood, so I asked my sister to leave the radio off as we drove to the clinic for the MRI. As we neared the clinic, Deirdre finally asked, "What did Laura have to say?"

"Nothing," I mumbled.

"Nothing? You did tell her you had a stroke?"

"Yes."

"And she said nothing? She must have said something."

Watching the town of Freeport pass by, I grumbled, "She said I'd be fired if I went into work tomorrow."

"Oh. Well, good." Daggers in my eyes aimed for my sister's temple. "Well, you weren't seriously thinking of going to work tomorrow, were you?" Deirdre asked.

"I'm breathing. I'm walking. Why not?"

"Jesus, Nicholas! I'm glad Laura threatened to fire you!"

I released the daggers.

Long after everyone had gone to bed, I sat at the picnic table smoking cigarettes while contemplating the last thirty-six hours. The MRI earlier that afternoon had only confirmed what Kaye had told me in his office, that I had indeed suffered a stroke.

An Orchestrated Mistake

"I really shouldn't say anything," the technician had said. "It really should come from your doctor, but I think you should go to a hospital. You're susceptible to a whole slew of complications—heart attack, seizures—lots of things can go wrong after a stroke."

"Many things have gone wrong already," I told him as I shuffled out of the room. "The only thing a hospital can give me now is another bill and perhaps a second stroke."

I'm not sure what should have rated higher on the moron meter that night, my concerns about medical bills or continuing to inhale copious amounts of cigarettes. Since I was doing both, I wondered whether I was wishing for a second stroke to finish the job. The first stroke had only left me damaged. Beyond the physical damage, I was deeply concerned about my emotional state of mind. My thoughts seemed to stutter, and fractured images came to mind. I was emotionally vulnerable and felt the need to withdraw from reality. I had prided myself in not having such feelings. I hadn't felt vulnerable since my first love ripped my heart out, put her spiked heel through it, and handed it back to me for lunch. I despise being vulnerable.

I knew exactly how I had let this happen. The more I got away with deferring responsibility for my health, the more I pushed the envelope. And the more I got away with, the more I believed I was invincible.

Replaying my self-destruction over and over in my head wasn't going to help me move forward. I needed a plan, and the plan I thought of that night was to get a second opinion. For something as serious as a stroke, I surely wasn't going to rely on the word of one doctor and an MRI, was I? Perhaps what had happened was that I had had some kind of freak seizure. A seizure whose effects will dissipate over time, maybe even by tomorrow. And if they haven't, I'll seek out a second opinion.

Thrilled with my plan, I saw the paper under a vase with all my awkward attempts at my signature. I was sure at that moment that by tomorrow I wouldn't even need a second opinion, as the effects of the seizure, or whatever it was, would have passed. They probably were already beginning to pass. To prove this to myself, I slid the paper out in front of me, picked up the red crayon, took a long pull of my cigarette, and while exhaling, signed my name. Before me in red crayon was maybe the letter 'N,' or perhaps it was a picture of a coiled rope followed by a flat line. Whatever the scrawl was, it didn't come close to resembling my signature. I stared at the image for several moments, and with each blink, the water in my eyes brought it in and out of focus. I realized I was staring at my second opinion.

    I put my cigarette out in the ashtray and stood up, leaning on the table for support. I could no longer deny my new reality, and I also knew I had to do something about it. Turning, I walked back into the house. Just inside the kitchen door was a wastebasket, and reaching into my shirt pocket, I pulled out the remainder of my Winston's and dropped them into the trash. Using the kitchen counter and the walls to steady myself, I made my way through the house to the bottom of the stairs, turned off the lights, and in the darkness, placed both hands on the railing of the staircase and slowly began to pull myself up.

CHAPTER SIX

I'm not a particularly tough guy. In fact, it could be quite easily argued I'm a bit of a wuss, but what I do have is a very high tolerance for discomfort. I won't say pain. Pain is surviving day to day in the third world. That's real pain. What I experience from time to time is discomfort, and before I moved to New York, I was pretty good at avoiding it.

Growing up on the West Coast of Canada, I spent almost fifteen years as a goaltender with hockey pucks fired at my head and taking some pretty unorthodox risks as many young people do, but I walked away with nary a scratch.

Life in Canada was pretty much discomfort-free, but after spending what seemed like twenty minutes in New York, the light deflectors fell off a camera, cracking my nose, spewing blood everywhere, and gifting me for the first time, not one, but two black eyes. After wrapping the shoot, I stopped by the Blarney Stone in Midtown Manhattan for a drink looking like Rocky Balboa. As I saddled up to the bar, the bartender asked me, "Whiskey, to get your mind off the wife?" Having a busted nose and two black eyes presented me with some discomfort, but it wasn't enough to send me to the hospital or even prevent me from heading into work the next morning.

Not even the stroke would have kept me away from work for more than twenty-four hours. No, for that I needed the threat of termination. I again asked myself, *How do you recognize that your life is completely out of balance when you're doing something you genuinely love?* Wish I knew. I should also add that in addition to having a high tolerance for discomfort, I'm also pretty damn stubborn, and that, along with my delusional stupidity, is a very dangerous combination.

I'm still not sure which had me feeling more miserable and depressed in those days after the stroke, the effects of the stroke or being told I had to stay home and recover. I hadn't spent any significant time away from the office since my week in Beth Israel

An Orchestrated Mistake

Hospital following the leg incident. After that fiasco, I swore I'd take better care of myself. I even went so far as to book a two-week vacation to California to see my middle sister, Sonya, but after contracting shingles upon my release from the hospital, I spent the two weeks on my back in my Brooklyn apartment eating ravioli out of a can and watching reruns of *Judge Judy*. So much for finding balance in my life.

After Kaye confirmed the stroke with the MRI, he reluctantly sent me home instead of to a hospital, but not before another diatribe on the effects of diabetes and handing me a fistful of prescriptions, none of which would produce the desired outcome I so badly craved.

"It's ridiculous that Kaye insists I come here every two days," I complained to my sister over my thumping left leg as we exited Kaye's office. "It's not like anything is going to change in two days!"

"Maybe he just wants to make sure you're still alive." Deirdre smirked.

As much as those first days were difficult, I'm sure they were just as difficult for my sister. Not just because Deirdre was driving my grumbling self all over Long Island to medical appointments and pharmacies, but also because she had to put up with me clogging up the flow to the river of life in her home.

Sleep heals the body, but I wasn't sleeping. I just couldn't seem to shut off my fractured thoughts. At night, while deciding the ceiling needed a new coat of paint, my mind would race from *Thaddeus* to Rachel's project—to anything but my broken body.

At the first stirrings of life, I'd grab my housecoat, thump my way down the stairs, and stand in the middle of the kitchen, forcing those on a tight schedule to run around me as they prepared for their day. I soon discovered as I stood there that getting kids fed and off to school in the mornings is much like the negotiations between an agent and producer. It's very tense, it can happen at a very high volume, and it often takes a miracle to get the job done. It wasn't enough for me to be just a physical presence jamming up the kitchen. I also had to be an annoyance by commenting on everything.

"You really think the girls should be eating Cap'n Crunch?" I asked my sister as she poured out bowls for Molly, nine, and Shayna, seven.

"They like it," Deirdre replied.

"So. It's still not good for them. Why not get them something healthier?"

"You didn't seem to mind eating their Pop-Tarts."

"I'm an adult. I also have the option of making healthy choices."

"Oh please!" Deirdre chided. "Like you ever did!"

"Well, I could have. I'm just saying maybe you should offer them some yogurt and fruit instead. Or make them some bacon and eggs or something."

"I don't have time in the morning."

"Well, you could get up earlier," I suggested. The sound I heard was my sister's false teeth grinding. "I just don't think you should be feeding them all that sugar."

"Uncle Nicholas," Molly said, bringing a spoonful of Cap'n Crunch to her mouth.

"Yes, Molly."

"Buzz off!" she ordered, inhaling her cereal.

After the kids had left for school, my sister would disappear to do her household chores. I'd take that as my cue to head out to the backyard to do my version of rehabilitation therapy. This consisted of going down the two steps from the porch to the lawn and back up again. I'd do this until I was bored, which maybe took a minute and a half, and then I'd sit at the picnic table and practice my signature with the red crayon.

After my therapy, I'd go inside and head up to my room to stare at my computer while waiting for emails to arrive from work. Sadly, the only emails I'd receive were health inquires. Any email I was expecting telling me how the world of New York Independent film ceased to function without me just never materialized. After that disappointment, I'd roam the house looking for my sister, who I'd usually find on her knees laboring away at some chore like scrubbing a toilet. I'd think this was the ideal time to enlighten her on the Illuminati's role in the pernicious banking system, so I'd launch into a lecture while leaning against the bathroom door.

"Are you listening?" I'd ask after the only audible reply from her was a grunt or a groan while she scrubbed.

"YES!" she'd snap through a clenched jaw.

"No, you're not," I'd respond. "You're not interested, I can tell. So, when you finish up in here, what are you making us for lunch?" It would be at that point I'd think it best I wander off to let my sister cool off.

One of the things I wasn't looking forward to, but I knew I had to do, was phone Mike to tell him I'd had a stroke. I waited a couple of days, probably in the hopes that I'd make some miraculous recovery, but when that didn't happen, I knew I had to make the call. If I thought I was going to get any concern and compassion from Mike, I needn't have worried.

"*Thaddeus* was a stroke of genius," Mike said after I explained what happened. "That was all the strokes we needed."

"Well, we got another one," I said.

"Now we need a stroke of luck."

An Orchestrated Mistake

"No, we don't. I just have a few physical challenges, but other than that, nothing's changed."

"Sure it has," Mike replied. "You're fucked, I'm depressed, what a fucking team. It's in the Writer's Guild contract that all writers are depressed, so I don't have a choice in the matter. Now we'll have to add more anti-depressants to our budget, but in case anybody asks, we'll list them under duct tape."

"Nobody needs anti-depressants."

"That's easy for you to say. The producer holding your future didn't just have a stroke!"

"No, he didn't. I did."

"I'm fucked!"

"Don't worry, Mike," I said sarcastically. "I'll recover and produce your script."

"You better," Mike admonished. "Or I'll be forced to work with the producers of *Kitchen Nightmares*." It was comforting to feel that Mike had actually stepped outside of himself and expressed genuine concern and compassion for a fellow human being. I'll have to remember to thank him for his selfless support should I ever have to make an acceptance speech.

What I told Mike about the stroke only causing me a few minor challenges wasn't exactly true. Emotional anomalies were appearing that I couldn't understand or comprehend. The first one to get my attention happened while I was up in my room watching the Mets highlight reel on TV. When Jose Reyes hit a home run, the crowd at the New York stadium roared in a mad frenzy, and as the camera panned around the stadium at this euphoric insanity, I was completely caught off guard by my reaction. The sight of all those cheering New York fans had tears rolling down my cheeks. Watching all those happy fans had caused an emotional earthquake inside, and I couldn't swallow hard enough to keep it all down. This left me not just emotional but stunned.

I wanted to put this down to a bizarre, isolated incident, but later, watching Ranger's hockey fans jubilant at their home team scoring, another emotional wave had me reaching for a box of Kleenex.

Since the stroke, my emotions were never very far from the surface, but now the sight of happiness had me tasting them, and the worst part was I was powerless to control them. I had spent the better part of my life avoiding my emotions, instead choosing to live by Mother's mantra, *Just never bare your soul,'* so this new phenomenon had more than my attention. It had me scared. Is this what it's like when you're losing your mind? You can't control your emotions and weep at the sight of pure joy? I didn't like not being in charge of my emotions, and I thought, *If there is a sky god, please don't let me cross paths with a child playing with a small puppy!*

I also had an anger that was simmering just below the surface. This anger was revealed during my frustrations while attempting familiar tasks, like the button incident up in my room. I would also overheat while writing an email when words I traditionally could spell would now be misspelled and I no longer had the ability to correct them without spellcheck. I took to writing everything, including emails, in Word so the program could correct everything for me before I sent it. I'm sure my sister heard me many times howling at my computer when I couldn't figure out how a word was spelled.

It wasn't just the spelling. It was the meaning of words, too, and that frustrated me. Words I had known and used now had definitions that escaped me. I would stare at a word on the page or my computer, mumbling to myself I knew the meaning, but I had no clue.

Sitting at the picnic table one day, I came across the word *dubious*. I stared at this word for a long time. I knew what it meant and knew I had even used it before, but I could no longer recall its meaning. I tried to get the meaning from the context of the sentence, but that didn't offer up any clues. When I began shaking with frustration and anger, I finally gave up and went inside in search of my sister. I found her sitting in the den with a cigarette dangling out of her mouth while she worked on her computer.

"What does dubious mean?" I asked, leaning against the door.

"Um. Doubting," Deirdre said without looking up. "Why?"

"No reason," I said, rereading the sentence to see if it now made sense. Deirdre typed away fanatically on the computer as smoke billowed up into her eyes.

"Didn't feel like putting your teeth in this morning?" I asked in a more sardonic tone than I intended. She just grunted. "What are you working on?" I asked.

"The website for my new business," she replied, taking a deep drag of her cigarette.

"Internet business?" I questioned. She nodded 'yes.' "What's it called?" Deirdre stopped typing and squinted up at me through a blue haze. Without her teeth in, it looked like she was eating her nose. "Well?" I asked.

"Go healthy dot com," she said through the smoke.

"You're kidding?"

"Nope."

"So, you might say your business is off to a dubious start?"

"Funny," she replied, gumming her cigarette.

I finally stubbornly relented, and the online thesaurus and Google became my friends. Not just in spelling and comprehension, but they also helped me find the right words if I was struggling when writing. Reading a book was a whole different challenge.

An Orchestrated Mistake

"I thought you said you were coming out here to practice the stairs," Deirdre said one day, stepping out onto the back porch.

"I did," I replied. "I'm resting."

"You've been out here all of two minutes."

"Three, and I'm tired."

I was tired, but it wasn't just the physical. It was also the emotional exhaustion from the realization my life had been reduced to practicing stairs and writing my signature in a red crayon.

"Well, I've found something for you to try," Deirdre said.

"Whatever it is, I'm not interested," I replied.

"You haven't even heard what I'm going to suggest!"

"I don't need to. If you're suggesting it, it's probably bat-shit crazy and will cost me a fortune." I swear when P.T Barnum looked into the future he saw the birth of my oldest sister before he uttered the phrase, *'There's a sucker born every minute.'*

"I know what you're thinking," Deirdre said. "But this isn't like that. This woman heals with her hands."

"As opposed to what? Her elbows?"

"She uses the energy from her hands. It's called Reiki. She heals with energy by moving her hands all over your body but never actually touches you."

"If she's moving her hands all over me, I want her touching me, preferably with a happy ending."

"Jesus, Nicholas!"

"Well, it sounds like just another one of your crazy ideas, so forget it, I'm not interested."

An Orchestrated Mistake

"How do you know you're not interested? You don't even know what Reiki is. This could really help you."

"I doubt it."

"It's not like you're trying anything on your own."

"Sure I am."

"I'd hardly call pulling yourself up and down two stairs for three minutes a day effective therapy."

"It's something, and it doesn't cost me a thing."

"I'll pay for the Reiki," Deirdre said. "Just try it. It couldn't hurt, and you don't need to do anything but just lie there. It totally appeals to your sense of sloth."

I had to admit my sister was right. Not having to exert any effort did sort of appeal to my sense of effective therapy, and since I was utterly bored with my inane routines and I wasn't paying for it, I agreed to give 'Miss Healing Hands' a try.

The moment I laid eyes on Miss Healing Hands, I wanted to burst out laughing. There was something about this well-nourished hippie that just made me want to howl. When I reached to shake her pudgy little hand, she completely ignored it and pulled me in tighter than a stranger should, whispering in my ear, "I know!" What the hell did she know? That I'd become so thin my briefs now needed suspenders? I get very nervous when strangers whisper things in my ear. I looked over towards my sister for a possible rescue, but that wasn't happening. Great, I was on my own with a whispering flower child.

Healing Hands directed me into a room at the back of her home that looked more like a New Age brothel than a room for healing. It was complete with hanging crystals, massage table, and a couch that looked like it had been killed in action during the 1960s sexual revolution.

An Orchestrated Mistake

"Sit," she said in her breathy whisper. While I decided whether or not to sit on the couch, she touched my shoulder, causing me to leap into the dangling crystals. "Relax," she whispered, rubbing my back. "Everything is going to be fine. Sit," she said again, guiding me onto the couch and taking a seat beside me. This woman was far too touchy, even by showbiz standards, and as she explained to me what Reiki was, I slowly worked my way to the opposite end of the couch. I felt safer being out of reach.

Explaining Reiki, she told me I might get emotional and possibly burst into tears. "This is normal," she whispered. Unless she planned on showing me a highlight reel of the Mets scoring, I thought the chances of me bursting into tears were nil. This poor old broad would be lucky if I felt anything, and when she asked me if I had any questions, I couldn't resist asking her, "Do I need to do a Gregorian chant?"

"No," she whispered. "There must be silence." I nodded in agreement and bit hard on the inside of my mouth.

The only time I heard her use her actual vocal cords during our one-hour session was when she shrieked after I almost took a header getting up on her damn therapy table. "Oh, God! Don't do that!" she yelped, clutching her chest.

As Healing Hands hovered over me, she told me to *feel* the energy, but the only thing I felt was like a horse's ass for even agreeing to try this. When she whispered again I should "Feel the energy," the line 'I feel nothing' from the musical *Chorus Line* popped into my head, and I started to laugh. "That's right," she whispered. "Let it out." This sent me into bigger fits of hysterics. "That's okay," she continued. "Most people cry, but you're laughing. That's all right. It's your truth. Let your truth out." My truth now had me laughing so hard I was crying.

After my session, I came out into the waiting area, where my sister looked up from playing with her phone. "How was it?" she asked.

An Orchestrated Mistake

Before I could answer, Healing Hands chimed in. "I think it went well. He had quite a unique experience."

"Yes, unique," I echoed, motioning my sister towards the door.

"So, Nicholas, should we set up another session for you?" Healing Hands asked.

"I've got your card," I said, picking one up off the coffee table.

Outside, Deirdre asked as we were getting in the car, "So you liked it? Do you think it was worth it?"

"How much did you pay?" I asked as I slid into the passenger seat.

"Sixty."

Taking my finger out of my mouth and examining it for blood, I said, "I'm glad it was your sixty."

So, Reiki wasn't going to be part of my recovery plan, but then again, I didn't have much of a plan. I just hoped the good fortune that had been present in my life up to those elevator doors would once again find me. I'm sure Reiki works for some folks, but for me, the whole experience reminded me of being on mushrooms—but unlike mushrooms, it wasn't an experience I wanted to repeat.

It had been a little over ten days since my phone call with Laura, and while I was understandably no closer to feeling better, I felt I was becoming more disconnected and despondent to all the happenings around me. Responding to email inquiries about my health did not provide the artistic oxygen I so desperately craved. Even though I knew my friends, coworkers, and family were there, I felt isolated, alone, and trapped in a broken body with the noise of fractured thoughts. The unpredictable mood swings had my psyche working overtime to stay balanced, and I was leaning heavily on my mother's mantra, *'Just never bare your soul.*' I needed to get back to work in the worst way, to do something, anything that would give me the opportunity to focus on a story—any story other than my own. I needed to emotionally pull it together before I considered tap dancing off the railings of the Brooklyn Bridge. Naturally, I contemplated calling Mike to discuss *Thaddeus*, but I wasn't in the mood to listen to him pontificate about the multiple universes that revolved around him.

I hadn't spoken with Rachel since shortly before the stroke, and her script and temperament were exactly what I needed.

"I thought about calling your cell," Rachel said after greeting me. "But when your office said you were out for a while, I thought you might be on vacation."

"More of an unwanted vacation," I replied, giving Rachel the condensed version of my elevator ride.

"Oh my God!" she squealed. "Are you okay?"

"I'm fine," I replied. "I'm sorry I fell off the radar, but I'll be back to work soon. I still want to produce your film, but we're going to have to push back the shoot."

"Yes! Of course! I want you to produce! Don't worry about the shoot. I want you better! Take as much time as you need!"

"You mean you're not interested in hiring the producers of *Kitchen Nightmares*?"

"Who?"

"Forget it."

"Have you ever thought about acupuncture?" Rachel asked.

"Like instead of Reiki?"

An Orchestrated Mistake

"No, no, it's nothing like Reiki. Would you try it? I know this great doctor in Chinatown, and I bet he could help you. I've been wanting to see him again. We could meet there this Saturday."

"Well, I don't know…"

"Say yes! We'll go for lunch and after go over my tweaks to the script. That is if you're up to it."

I definitely wasn't up for getting poked with needles, but if that's what I had to do to take a script meeting, I would do it.

"Shoot me the address," I said.

When I agreed to meet Rachel, it never occurred to me that my body wouldn't be up for what my spirit demanded. I also never considered that just the commute into the city would have me greeting the darker side of misery.

The population of Manhattan had tripled in the eleven days since I'd last been into the city, and all of them were loitering that Saturday in Penn Station. The crowds were knocking me around like a juiced pinball, and I no longer trusted myself to walk along the platform's edge to avoid the dense mob. When I did lose patience and ventured towards the edge, a fellow clipped me with his suitcase, almost toppling me down onto the tracks.

It took two hands to slowly pull myself up the stairs to the subway platform, and once there, I fell back against the wall, exhausted and overwhelmed.

I let several trains go by, hoping that the crowds would thin so I could easily step and board, but of course, as more trains arrived and left, so did more passengers. I wasn't quick or strong enough to push my way on before the doors closed and the train disappeared down the tunnel.

When I finally boarded a southbound #1 train, I was pushed into the middle of the car, unable to reach through the crowds to hold on to anything. I was forced to widen my stance, but it wasn't enough for me to maintain my balance, and when the train

An Orchestrated Mistake

lurched, I fell on seated passengers who parted and let me hit the floor. Dazed and humiliated, I reached through the forest of legs for the pole and pulled myself up, but a commuter who thought they would be helpful pushed me up from behind and sent me crashing into more passengers on the other side of the pole. "Have another drink!" a man blurted out, and I had no sooner thought, *That's the best line you can come up with?* When he added, "Asshole!" I shot back with the best line I could think of, "Thanks."

After 'Toad's Wild Ride,' I had to scale the north face of Everest from the subway platform up to Canal Street. Halfway up the stairs, I did something I had never done when climbing a staircase—I had to stop and catch my breath. I held on with two hands while passengers bumped past me, and after a few minutes, the blue sky from the top of the stairs beckoned me on.

The crowds up on Canal Street were denser than those at Penn Station, and I ricocheted my way through them for several blocks until I found the acupuncturist's office. Exhausted, I leaned on the building before finally opening the door, and when I did, my jaw dropped. There before me was the longest staircase up to the second floor in not just New York but North America. If I had the energy, I would have just turned around and gone home, but instead, I took a deep breath and began pulling myself up one stair at a time.

Rachel spotted me the moment I stepped inside the waiting room. "I was getting nervous you weren't coming," she said, greeting me with a hug. "Did you have any problems?"

"No, of course not," I said, collapsing into a chair.

Rachel and I chatted very briefly about our lives before I was called and led into a room by a nurse. She helped me up on a table, telling me to lie down, that the doctor would be in shortly. As soon as my head hit the pillow, I began drifting in and out of consciousness, and when the elderly Chinese doctor came in, I could barely lift my head to greet him. He explained a little about acupuncture and what he intended to do, but his accent was so thick and I was so exhausted I didn't understand a word he said. "Begin," I finally urged him, motioning my hand over my body.

Again, I'm sure acupuncture works for some people, but I didn't feel a thing, and for a hundred bucks I want to feel something—preferably something with a light buzz. After my session, the doctor told me I would need at least three treatments a week for the next several months, but the thought of negotiating my way to the clinic three times a week had me thinking, *Just shake his hand, smile and nod, and back out of the room.*

"Well, what do you think?" Rachel asked when I got back in the waiting room.

"Like I'm about to spring a leak," I replied, motioning her towards the door.

"He's so good," Rachel cooed as I opened the door. "My session was unbelievable!"

I took a deep breath, staring down that long staircase, and grabbed the railing with both hands. "You're right," I said. "It's just unbelievable."

Rachel helped me navigate my way through the crowds on Canal to the restaurant, and it was a huge relief to have no further physical demands placed on me other than to sit. The moment after we were seated, Rachel pulled out her script with the new changes and handed it to me. It was as if my body instantly began recharging the moment my hands touched the paper. "So let me show you where I've made some changes. The first one is on page two…"

For two hours, I forgot I had had a stroke. Rachel and I went through her script, and the conversation moved easily from story to cameras to locations. I was back playing on my home field, and it sure felt good.

Protecting my psyche from another beating, I decided to walk back to Penn Station rather than brave the subway again. As I strolled, occasionally stopping to stare through shop windows, it became obvious to me the stroke hadn't just damaged me physically, but it had also crippled my soul with feelings of inadequacy. Right or wrong, I knew exactly what I had to do.

Getting home, I went straight up to my room, flipped open my laptop, and wrote an email to Laura and Andre.

Hey Guys! I'm feeling so much better! I'm back to my old self, and I'm ready to get back to work on Monday. I know what you're thinking, that it might be too soon. But really it isn't, I'm fine. I'll see you Monday! Nicholas.

CHAPTER SEVEN

It wasn't just the distortion from Sonus's guitar that greeted me as I climbed the subway stairs at 23rd & 7th Avenue, but also a rogue wave of self-doubt which hit me as I stopped halfway up. Puffing while on the stairwell, I was seriously questioning my wisdom to return to work only two weeks after the stroke, and this wasn't the first time that Monday I doubted my decision.

Getting dressed earlier that morning had seemed like it had taken three days, burned all my reserve energy, and by the time I had finished tying my shoes, the only thing I wanted to do was crawl back into bed. My sister drove me to the train, but it seemed that everything took ten times the energy and forever to accomplish since the stroke.

"You sure you're ready for this?" Deirdre asked when we pulled up to the station.

"It's been two weeks," I replied. "I'm more than ready."

"If you ask me, you don't look ready."

"That's why I'm not asking." I smiled, getting out of the car.

Finally getting into Manhattan, I pulled myself up onto the sidewalk at 23rd and saw ol' Sonus banging away on his guitar. My impulse was to run away down 23rd, but I was no longer running anywhere. Spotting me, Sonus gave me a nod accompanied by a warm smile like he was greeting an old friend, and I felt compelled to return the smile while tossing a few bucks in his open guitar case. Attempting a hasty exit, I tried to mask that awkward hop and slapping left foot as I took off down 23rd.

"Where ya been, buddy?" the Puerto Rican vendor asked as I approached his cart. "You finally take a vacation?"

"Yeah," I said, catching my breath. "I took a vacation."

"That's nice," he replied. "The usual?"

An Orchestrated Mistake

"Sure."

"You want donut?"

"No, just the usual, thanks."

"Okay. I should take a vacation," he said while preparing my order. "Life too short. Can't work, work, work all the time. What life is that? You need vacation, no?" He continued preparing my order in silence and then added, "Yeah, have some fun. That is what life's about. It's good you had fun. It's good you took vacation." He continued sucking his front tooth. "Here you go, buddy. Maybe I take a vacation," he said with a wink.

Relieved that he hadn't any interest in the details of my vacation, I gave him a generous tip.

With Lulu and Zombie's breakfast tucked under my arm, I didn't dash across 6th Avenue like I usually did but waited instead at the intersection for the light.

Walking up to my office building, I spotted a few of my old smoking buddies standing outside enjoying their morning cigarette. They worked for a sound company on the same floor as Three Walls Productions, so I knew they would have heard what had happened. Phil was always in the midst of quitting smoking, so he never bought cigarettes of his own. In fairness, every few weeks he would buy a pack for those he mooched from, and he could often be heard asking, "Can I bum a smoke? Don't worry, I'm quitting right after this next film." Everyone in the industry who smokes is quitting 'right after this next film.' I hadn't smoked since that night I had dropped them in the trash. It's just too bad it took a stroke to get me to quit.

"Well, look what the cat dragged up," Frank, a Foley artist, said when I got close.

"That's the best you got, Frank?" I replied.

"I was going to say threw up, but I figured why kick a guy when he's down."

An Orchestrated Mistake

"We couldn't believe it when Laura told us you had a stroke," Dolly exclaimed.

"You're not still partaking in this nasty habit, are you?" Phil asked.

"Still leaving yours in the machine, Phil?" I said, quoting Rodney Dangerfield.

"Yep," he replied, taking a huge pull on his cigarette. "How are you feeling?"

"Worse than some, better than most," I replied. "I'll catch up with you guys later," I said, opening the front door. I wanted to hang out to reassure my friends I was okay, but before I was tempted to breathe in too deeply, I thought it best just to head upstairs.

No one at Three Walls had ever been the huggy-kissy showbiz type, and I was never more grateful for this than when I returned to work after the stroke. Of course, everyone was happy to see me, and there were general inquiries about my health, but it was business as usual. I needed to feel that normalcy.

I did, however, pick up a different vibe from Laura. Laura and I had worked closely over the years and knew each other well and trusted one another—not just as co-workers but also as friends. We weren't buddy-buddy type friends, let's go out for dinner once a week, but we genuinely cared about each other and took an interest in each other's lives. Over the years, Laura had inquired about my health from time to time, but not in an overbearing meddling sort of way, more of a concerned friend kind of way. I always gave Laura my standard answer: "I'm fine." She had no choice but to trust that my answer was truthful, but I had broken that trust when I had the stroke.

I had ignored diabetes for years, and the stroke proved I hadn't been truthful with anyone, least of all myself. My doctor back in Vancouver predicted I would face dire consequences in ten years if I didn't take diabetes seriously, and he was right. My reckless behavior had not only smacked me down but also inadvertently hurt those closest to me. Denial has a huge price tag, and the people who love you pay that price right along with you. Laura came over to me privately later in the morning to ask how I was truly feeling. My standard answer was out before I could think.

"I'm fine."

"Well, you seem fine," Laura replied. "But I'm not sure if that means anything."

She was right. It didn't mean anything. My words had proven to be hollow, and that left me feeling incredibly guilty. Later, I gave Mike a call to tell him I was back in the saddle.

"About fucking time," he replied. "I was beginning to think you joined one of those annoying subway mariachi bands and were off touring Canada."

"And pass on the experience to work with you? How could a producer pass on that? Although I'm sure you've been told *pass* for years."

"Fuck off."

I kept telling myself, *Mike's written the script you're going to produce, and he does love dogs. That must make him redeeming, right?*

"We don't have time to piss around," Mike said, getting serious.

"I know."

"No, you don't," he replied. "There's going to be a writer's strike, and if that happens, I can't work on *Thaddeus*. The rumor is this could be a long one."

"You're also a producer," I reminded him. "Take off your writer's hat, put on your producer's hat, and to hell with the Union."

An Orchestrated Mistake

"That's what you'd do because you're a prick," Mike replied. "I, on the other hand, am a word artist and will stand in solidarity with my artistic brethren."

"Oh, please! If you're going to get sanctimonious, you'll have to excuse me while I puke."

"I'll wait."

I didn't have time for a writer's strike, and if the writers did go on strike, I couldn't understand why Mike wouldn't want to switch hats and keep working. Mike told me he wouldn't change a word so long as the writers were out on strike. I respected his loyalty to the Union, but why did he have to pick now to get sanctimonious? It ticked me off. I understood it on one level. Mike needed to know he was still relevant as a writer. He'd been unemployed for so long he must have felt that by walking the picket line with his fellow scribes, he could say, 'Look! I'm still a writer!' I couldn't fault him for that. Everyone needs to feel they're still relevant, especially artists.

What had me so upset about Mike's unwillingness to keep working was since the stroke, I had been aware of a ticking clock in my head. It wasn't loud, just a very subtle realization that time is limited. The ticking was there when I searched the deserted canyons of my mind for words needed to express myself, but it was the loudest when I thought about my future. I didn't understand the ticking—or like it—it was just there. It made me a far less patient person, and the ticking along with the vocabulary challenges had me reaching for the easy access expletives to make a quick point.

"Oh, for fuck sakes, Mike, we don't have time for this bullshit. Let them walk. We keep working, and when the strike's over, we're already on the ground running."

"Nope," Mike said. "The only running I'll be doing is to a picket line."

"Christ!"

"He'll be joining us."

The writers did walk out, and Mike was true to his word. He wouldn't even discuss any possible changes to the script. The only thing he would discuss with me was the high-profile writers he was walking the picket line with.

"Mike, I don't give a shit who's on the picket line with you," I said to him one afternoon over the phone. "You're a producer on this fucking project, and the writer's strike should have no bearing on two producers discussing a script."

"Of course you wouldn't understand," Mike replied. "You're not a word artist. You're a dumb Canuck who really just wants to be out hunting moose."

While Mike walked the picket line with his fellow scribes, I worked on the budget and schedule for *Thaddeus* under Laura's tutelage, but my struggles in the aftermath of the stroke privately continued.

I taught myself to compensate for the challenges I now faced. I could no longer run, but I found if I just slowed the pace of my walk by a few beats, the effects of the stroke on my left leg could not be noticed. This, however, at times, would pose its own challenges. Walking with others, I was constantly bringing up the rear, and I needed a controlled intersection to make it across the street. Walking with Blake, Laura, and a few others from the office to lunch one day, they bolted across 9th Avenue against the light, but the signal from my brain to my left leg never quite made it, and I'd only just stepped off the curb before blaring car horns chased me back.

Making phone calls now required making notes ahead of time to help me articulate what I wanted to discuss. I didn't do this when I was calling Mike, of course. I didn't need a note to remind me to roll my eyes. When the call was over, I would slide my cheat sheet back under the phone. Sometimes it would only be a few words I would scribble on the paper; other times, it would be my completely fractured thoughts.

An Orchestrated Mistake

I also used these cheat sheets when I stepped into Laura and Andre's office. These notes were completely undetected, as it was common to see me carrying invoices or some paper around the office. I was using Word or Google to assist me in drafting correspondence, and what was extremely important to me was I try and mask any outward signs from the stroke and not show any moments of weakness.

There were times, though, this was not possible and uncharacteristic behavior would reveal itself. Explaining the plotline for a movie one afternoon to a director on the phone, I got so confused it was no longer clear whether I was describing a comedy or a drama. When the director questioned me on this, I shot back in frustration, "I don't fucking know! It's a fucking funny movie! Go see it!"

"Nicholas!" he replied. "Just breathe!"

I may have been describing a comedy to the director, but the phone call sure had turned into a horror show.

Communicating, like everything, now took longer to accomplish. My speech pattern hadn't noticeably changed, but the holes in my vocabulary had me searching for words I could no longer find. Instead, I would choose words with a similar meaning to what I was trying to say.

It wasn't just the physical and cognitive disabilities that were a challenge. Without health insurance, the cash I was paying for everything was flying out the door.

Dr. Kaye was happy I had given up smoking, but there wasn't a needle big enough to hold the insulin required to counteract the effects of my dietary habits. I wasn't eating fistfuls of M&M's anymore, but I was still abusing my body with take-out and eating out of a box in the freezer at my sister's.

I thought the insulin and other medications Kaye had me on were doing all the work and making the lifestyle changes for me. It was far easier to just shove in a pill or needle and forget about it than put any effort in to help my body heal itself. I didn't care what I ate anyway because the stroke had numbed the left side of my mouth and dulled my taste buds. The octane had to be pretty high for me to savor the taste.

Months after the stroke, the only thing that was gaining any real traction was my self-doubt. I was struggling in my ability to handle the day-to-day duties at Three Walls Productions and was also questioning if I had the energy to produce *Thaddeus*. The writer's strike was dragging on, so mercifully I didn't require the energy to deal with Mike on a daily basis, but I knew the strike wouldn't go on forever, so sooner or later, life was going to kick into overdrive. Even though I was only to be one of the producers on *Thaddeus*, I was going to have to wear many hats throughout the development, shooting, and post-production if there was any hope of this film making it to the screen. Working at an Independent film company, you have to be able to work in all departments, and sometimes you need to do that all at the same time. Everything is always due yesterday, and while I never used to have a problem with that, post-stroke I required a long time to prepare.

A few years before the stroke, I received a phone call from Andre late one Friday afternoon. At the time, Andre was out in Los Angeles filming a commercial, and Laura was on location in Arizona shooting a film. Everyone but my intern and I were out of town working on one of those two shoots. Fantasizing about a relaxing weekend, I had let my intern go home early, just moments before Andre's call.

"Nicholas," Andre said. "I just booked a commercial for Mercedes Benz, and we're shooting it in New York. I'll email you the details, but take a few notes now."

"Shoot," I said, picking up a pen.

"It's for the European market, so we need a PAL camera and a small lighting package. We need a sound man, preferably with his own equipment, and six ethnic college-age actors with strong improvisational skills. We'll shoot it around the boardroom table in our office. Make sense?"

"Sure. I'll start tracking down a camera first thing Monday morning."

"No!" Andre jumped in. "We're shooting this on Sunday, ya?"

"Andre, it's four o'clock Friday afternoon," I reminded him.

"Ya!"

I had heard Andre's 'Ya!' many times before and knew exactly what it meant: 'I don't care who you bludgeon, make this happen!'

"Okay," I replied, taking a deep breath. "You're flying out of LA tonight, though, right?"

"No. We're still shooting. You can handle this, ya?"

"Not a problem." I lied, feeling the production sweat already dripping. "I'll get on it right away."

I didn't have time to freak out or run around the office naked. I immediately called my intern's cell and hoped I could divert her to pick up the PAL camera. The call went straight to voicemail. I left her a message and immediately started calling camera rental houses. Finally finding a camera uptown, the fellow said he'd wait if I hurried.

By the time I returned with the camera and lighting package, two hours later, the intern had left a message claiming she needed to take care of a few things and that she and her boyfriend needed to get away to work on their relationship. If I didn't have a million other things to do, I would have called her in for pizza and lemonade. If she were serious about a career in show business, she didn't have time to consider her personal needs, never mind those of her relationship. I know, harsh, but there is no time for frivolities when there's a shoot to do.

An Orchestrated Mistake

I worked the phones that night, and by just after 10pm, I had hired a production assistant, but he wasn't available until the shoot on Sunday. I had also found a sound man with his own equipment.

"I do have one problem, though," the sound man told me. "My regular boom operator is going away this weekend, so I don't have anyone to work the boom."

Someone else with a personal life. How annoying. "Never mind, I've got a PA," I shot back. "We'll use him."

"Great," he replied. "Oh, and one more thing. I won't have time to pick up some DA 88s," he said, referring to sound tapes. "Think you can send the PA to pick some up."

The tapes were going to have to be picked up Saturday, which meant I was going to have to do it, and I had nothing but time. "Sure," I stammered. "Done."

The European production company was handling the rest of the crew, so by the time I got back to my Brooklyn apartment just after midnight that Friday I was tired, but everything seemed under control. I'd pick up the sound tapes between my phone calls, and even though it was just me, I didn't think it would take long to prepare the office for the shoot. Saturday was shaping up to be another long day, but I wasn't worried. How long could it take to find six ethnic actors? This is, after all, New York.

Saturday morning, I was back in the office by eight. I pulled out an old file box where I had been storing headshots and resumes. There were about three hundred of them in the box, and knowing the client only wanted ethnic types, I immediately tossed aside all the White folks. It's a non-union gig, so those containing a union affiliation were also tossed. The remaining resumes that contained too many school plays were tossed—inexperienced. Any headshots with the actor dressed in character, say looking like Attila the Hun, were also immediately tossed—if for no other reason than they look like a total amateur. Any actor who had listed under special skills 'watching television,' they're gone.

An Orchestrated Mistake

You'd be surprised how many people list the most mundane activities under special skills. One resume I saw, the actor had listed 'bird watching,' and in the composite photo on the front, there was a picture of him looking through a set of binoculars. Cornballs like this and those looking like Attila the Hun tend to look at the camera, so they're tossed.

By ten o'clock Saturday morning, 70% of the headshots and resumes I started with were in the garbage. I didn't have time to set up auditions, so I had to interview these people and hire them over the phone. I got my pitch down and began calling. After leaving a few voice messages, I interviewed a sleepy Asian fellow, and after telling him he had the gig, he came to life and screamed, "You mean I really got it?"

"Yes," I replied, taking the receiver away from my ear. "You got it."

"I don't even have to audition?"

"You just did," I told him. The young fellow screamed so loud with excitement you would have thought I had just turned the air back on for his grandmother. I only had to think back to my life as an actor to appreciate this fellow's genuine joy at a job offer. The life of a journeyman actor can be depressing as hell, and I believe it's listed on the depression scale just below that of a Bangladeshi garment worker. The professional life for a journeyman actor often goes something like this:

FADE IN:

A NONDESCRIPT CASTING OFFICE IN NEW YORK CITY. A CASTING DIRECTOR SITS IN A DIRECTOR'S CHAIR LOOKING INDIFFERENT. HE'S COMPLETELY BORED WHILE WATCHING AN ACTOR POUR HIS HEART OUT IN AN AUDITION. THE ACTOR FINISHES THE SCENE AND STARES OUT AT THE CASTING DIRECTOR, WAITING FOR ANY FEEDBACK.

SEVERAL BEATS OF SILENCE. FINALLY.

An Orchestrated Mistake

CASTING DIRECTOR: Wow! Thanks for coming back for the fifth time. You're a brilliant Richard the Third! You nailed it!

ACTOR: Thank you.

CASTING DIRECTOR: I was right there with you. Really, I was. I was back in the 1800s.

ACTOR: 1400s.

CASTING DIRECTOR: What?

ACTOR: Richard the Third lived in the 1400s. 1452 to 1485, actually.

CASTING DIRECTOR: Sure, 1400s. That's what I meant. Anyway, I was right there with you. The director will adore you. As a matter of fact, I'm going to go out on a limb and say you probably have the part.

ACTOR: Really?

CASTING DIRECTOR: Absolutely! There's a solid 50/50 chance the director will love you. I mean, you are Richard the Third!!

ACTOR: (EXCITED) Thank you!

CASTING DIRECTOR: No. Thank YOU! Wait a minute! Turn your head that way again. Just a little further. That's it. Now step a little closer into the light. Stop! Oh, man! NO!

ACTOR: What?!

CASTING DIRECTOR: You can't be Richard the Third.

ACTOR: I can't?

CASTING DIRECTOR: No! You have a green spot in your left eye.

ACTOR: What? No, I don't!!

An Orchestrated Mistake

CASTING DIRECTOR: Yeah, you do. I'm sorry. I can see it as clear as a bell. It's a green spot in your left iris about the size of a pinhead. Well, maybe not quite a full pinhead, but at least half a pinhead. No one is going to believe you're Richard the Third. It's too bad, really. I mean, you have the limp, the withered arm, the humped back, and everything. What a shame. Well, thanks for coming in.

ACTOR: Wait! I can wear contacts! What color do you want my eyes? Blue? Brown? Blue and brown?

CASTING DIRECTOR: I'm sorry. You just won't be believable. Would you mind closing the door on your way out?

FADE TO BLACK

I wish that were hyperbole, but I can assure you it's not. A director once said to me after an audition, "That was wonderful, but I'm looking for a Cadillac, and I think you're more of a Lincoln. Can you be more Cadillac?"

Minus the time it took me to get the sound tapes, I worked the phones all day Saturday, and by midnight had hired my cast. I think I was having difficulties hiring a cast because many of the actors I called didn't think I was legit. "Who the hell books a commercial over the phone?" Can't really say I blamed them.

My production assistant's call time was 7am Sunday; the crew's call was for eight. The cast's call was for nine, but by 7:20, I had left my third voice message for my PA as I ran down 14th Street in search of an open deli to pick up the crew's breakfast. Dashing back to the office with sandwiches and coffee, I tweaked my groin but managed to hobble into the office just as the first of my crew was arriving.

"You have those DA 88s?" the sound man asked right away.

"Here," I said, limping over to my desk to retrieve them.

"Hey, Nicholas," the director said, pouring himself a coffee, "I know I told you yesterday on the phone that we don't need tape stock for the camera, but I was wrong. We need some. You don't have any laying around the office, do you?"

"For a PAL camera?" I said. "Ah, no."

"Oh. I would have thought you'd have some."

"Normally we do." I lied. "But we just shot a Swedish feminine hygiene commercial."

"Oh. Well, can you get some?" the director asked.

"B&H opens at nine on Sundays," I said, referring to the New York industry landmark store. "I can run up there, but you're going to have to introduce yourself to the cast when they get here."

"Can't you just send a PA?" the director asked.

"I don't have a PA," I muttered.

"Oh," the director replied. "Well, that wasn't very good planning, was it?"

"No," I grumbled, limping for the elevator.

By the time I got back from B&H with the tapes, the director was rehearsing the cast. I had just poured myself a coffee when the sound man hollered, "Hey, Nicholas! Where's my boom man?"

"Um, well," I said, looking to see if the PA had shown up while I was gone. "I guess that's me."

"Great. I need you now."

"I'm all over it," I said, putting down my coffee.

The PA never did show up, but to the others, the shoot went off without a hitch. The director loved his cast, and if my arms hadn't felt like soggy spaghetti from holding the boom all day, I, too, probably would have enjoyed their performance. When everyone had left except the advertising executive from London, I sat down for the first time and realized I was too weak to hold a cigarette. The executive walked over and, taking a donut from the crafty table, said, "I really didn't think we could pull this off in the time we had, but we did. The cast, everything was great. This was a piece of cake, as my mother used to say."

I stared at him a moment. "Absolutely," I replied, nodding. "A piece of cake." I'm far too Canadian to tell him what I really thought of his mother.

Of course, not every production is as crazy as that weekend, but some are pretty close. It doesn't matter whether you're a producer, director, or production assistant. Every position has the ability to whisk you to the edge.

I kept asking myself in those months after the stroke, *Can I still do this?* The answer that always came back was, *I don't know.*

Heading into the Christmas season, Laura hired Gerald, a young filmmaker, to work in our media department and help me out with the day-to-day running of Three Walls Productions. Gerald was talented and a great help to me. As I came to rely on him more, I knew the writing was on the wall for me whether I wanted to admit it or not. At our Christmas karaoke party, I felt more depressed than I normally do during the Christmas season. I've never liked the hypocrisy of Christmas. I'm an all-or-nothing person. Either every kid around the globe receives a gift and celebrates, or let's scrap the whole Christmas thing. As a ten-year-old, I had my best Christmas morning when I took off on my bike and hung out with the kid behind the counter at the local Seven-Eleven. We drank Coke Slurpees and played pinball all morning. It was great. I didn't ride home until I figured the whole Christmas thing would be over. My mother wasn't sure whether to hug me or wring my neck.

At the Three Walls Production Christmas party, I sang my traditional Yuletide favorites that I did every year, Elvis Presley's "In the Ghetto" and R.E.M's "Losing My Religion," but even this didn't pick up my spirits.

An Orchestrated Mistake

Before we left for Christmas break, it was decided the office would be painted over the holiday, so all the furniture had to be moved away from the walls for the painters. I was no help in preparing the office for the painters, and anytime it even looked like I was going to move something, one of my colleagues would jump in, saying, "That's okay, Nicholas, I've got that!" I knew what they were all doing, and I loved them for it, but it hurt like hell to feel so useless.

To get away while all the moving was going on, I decided to take Lulu and Zombie for a walk—something I had always done before the stroke.

"Are you sure you're okay?" Laura asked after I took the leashes off her desk.

"I'll be fine, Laura. It's just a walk."

The dogs and I only got halfway up the block before Lulu started doing that doggie circle thing. You know, that circling and sniffing while the back is arched and the butt is poised like it's about to fire the opening salvo of the Armageddon. Then Zombie began jumping and encouraging Lulu on the other leash, and I knew I was in serious trouble. Without a stable sense of balance, I couldn't control the two dogs, and after Lulu had done her business both dogs began bouncing and running around in a victory celebration. In the excitement, Lulu jumped on me and knocked me to the ground. Both dogs were immediately all over me, and as I was trying to stand, Lulu knocked me back down again, and I was laid out on the sidewalk with my face inches away from a massive pile of dog shit. I didn't have the strength to get the dogs off me, and as I stared at that steaming pile, reality gutted me. I knew I couldn't do this anymore.

I finally admitted to myself what my body knew months ago. I had gambled with my health and lost, and now I needed medical treatment if there was going to be any hope of recovery. Without health insurance in New York, I couldn't afford that help, and that left me only one option. I needed to return to Canada. But where in Canada? Vancouver? Or Halifax, a city in the Maritimes that is close to New York and where my dad now lives with his new wife. Since the treatment I had envisioned had me returning to New York posthaste, I opted for Halifax, where I could temporarily stay with my dad.

I wrestled over the Christmas break with my decision, and once we were back at work, I struggled to find the words to tell Laura and Andre. Then after ricocheting my way into work one morning in mid-February, I stepped into the office and was immediately overwhelmed with a sense of loss. I knew that day was the day I had to tell them.

Lulu and Zombie gobbled down their breakfast that morning, but instead of charging back to Laura's office, Zombie stood guard while Lulu walked back to me with her tailing wagging and rested her head on my lap. She looked up at me and let out a sigh. It was like she knew what I was thinking and was giving me permission to leave. I reached down to pat Lulu and looked around the office and knew I was going to miss them all terribly.

Before I could go in and speak to Laura and Andre in their office, Laura came out to see me and we had a private conversation. "I know you're struggling," Laura said, "because your work is suffering. There were so many mistakes in that letter you gave me to sign yesterday that I rewrote it myself. I need to know the truth. How are you really feeling?"

"Not good," I said, almost succumbing to a rush of emotion. "It's been a struggle. I know I need help."

"Yes, you do," Laura said. "I think you need to return to Canada for that help." Laura voiced what I hadn't been able to, but instead of feeling sorrow at those words, I felt instant relief. I nodded in agreement, and Laura and I spoke about my situation, and although I didn't tell her exactly what a struggle the last five and half months had been, I was more truthful that morning than ever before. By the end of our conversation, it was decided April 30th would be my last day at Three Walls Productions. It wasn't a tearful decision. We both knew I had to step back to move forward. The two and half months gave me ample time to help

An Orchestrated Mistake

Gerald take over the day-to-day duties at Three Walls Productions and also gave me time to introduce him to Rachel so he could step in and take over as producer should they both choose. I would also use the time to get as much done on *Thaddeus* as possible and bring Heather up to speed so she could fill in as the producer on that project during my absence.

I met Mike for lunch a few days after my talk with Laura to inform him about my decision to return to Canada. "You okay with everything?" I asked, leaning on Mike as we exited the diner.

"Sure, I'm glad you're leaving," he finally said.

"You don't have to sound so happy," I replied. "I'll be back to produce *Thaddeus*. I just need to focus on my health for a while."

"I know," Mike said. "I once got a colonoscopy without any anesthetic, and the only thing more painful than that has been watching you these last few months."

"Did I just hear a tone of concern for another human being in your voice?" I asked.

"No, that wasn't a concern," Mike replied. "I was just pointing out the cause of my pain."

Every script needs a producer who will champion the material through the development maze. While Heather was a fine producer, I was concerned *Thaddeus* wouldn't get the attention it needed and end up buried amongst the other projects at Three Walls Productions. I did express these concerns to Mike, warning him about development hell, and he brushed me off in usual Mike fashion, telling me to go pop a pill with a moose.

The two and half months flew by, and after my last day at work, Laura and Andre threw a party for me at a midtown Mexican restaurant. Mike was there, along with industry people I'd worked with over my eight-plus years at Three Walls Productions. My ten years in New York and Independent film

An Orchestrated Mistake

were coming to a temporary close. "I'm a word artist," I heard Mike say over drinks at the party. "I wrote *Thaddeus*." I looked at whom Mike was talking to, and I didn't have the heart to tell him he was talking up the girlfriend of a lighting technician. Mike was going to be Mike no matter what I said, and I just hoped he and *Thaddeus* would navigate their way through the development maze without me.

I came to New York to write and be a producer of Independent films. I spent my ten years in New York working on other people's material and never wrote a word, and my goal of becoming a producer was achieved on a Thursday, but by Monday, my future as a producer was derailed by a stroke. Five days. I believe we are all the writers of our own life script, and I sure hope I'll write a better ending to the next act. Ultimately, I now understood that how my movie ends will be entirely up to me.

The next day, I headed into the office to say my final goodbyes. When I got off the subway at 23rd & 7th, I could hear Sonus banging away up on the sidewalk. *Man, what a noise*, I thought as I pulled myself up the stairs.

When I reached the sidewalk, I looked over at Sonus and was taken aback by the pure joy etched on his face. He was watching a small Black boy of about five dancing with a magical energy while he pounded away on his guitar. I was spellbound by the perfect bliss these two souls were sharing. The boy danced over to his father, who had been standing there watching with other New Yorkers. "Daddy, can I have a quarter?" the boy asked, taking his father's hand. His father reached into his pocket and gave him some change, and the boy danced back to the open guitar case and tossed the money in. Sonus and the boy shared a luminous smile that lit up everyone's universe on that sidewalk, and waving goodbye, the boy danced and skipped his way across 7th Avenue with his father.

That morning I heard Sonus' music for the first time, and it was beautiful. I listened long after the little boy had danced away, and reaching into my pocket, pulled out my wallet and tossed a twenty-dollar bill into Sonus's case. Sonus gave me a warm smile. I just nodded, turned, and walked away. Crossing the street, I thought of how that little boy showed me that, sometimes, if we only reframe the picture, we too can hear the beautiful music. I wondered that if maybe one day soon I'll also be able to skip and dance my way down 7th Avenue.

The next day it was strange not to be heading into the office on a working day, and at the end of the day I got an email from Laura that simply read:

Hey Nicholas - How was your first day of freedom? – LK

I wrote back:

Not sure yet. I'll let you know. – NA

CHAPTER EIGHT

Forty-eight hours after leaving Three Walls Productions, my sabbatical commenced at JFK with a search for Al-Qaeda in my shoes. I had been watching another TSA agent grilling some fellow about carrying a jar of mustard onto the plane, so why, I thought, was my agent interested in my shoes? Al-Qaeda was obviously in that guy's mustard. It had been over seven years since I watched the Twin Towers fall from the rooftop during a film shoot on the Lower East Side, and it had been ten years since I had flown. So much had changed. Police no longer sauntered through airports giving directions to the Duty Free or boarding gates. Now they strutted around carrying automatic weapons looking like Robocop. How inspiring it is to witness the progressive evolution of the human spirit.

"Sir, put your shoes on the belt, please," the female TSA agent ordered.

"You already asked me," I said. "I told you, I need to sit to take them off. I can't stand and balance…"

"On the belt, please, sir."

Leaning on the X-ray machine, I snapped. "You want my feet still in them?"

"Please don't lean on the machine, sir. Your shoes on the belt."

"Jesus!"

I dropped cross-legged to the floor, and getting my shoes off, struggled to my feet before tossing my shoes on the belt. As they passed through the machine, the bored, expressionless agent didn't even glance up at her screen. "You could have at least looked," I snarled as my shoes reappeared.

"Sir, please remove your shoes from the belt. Next!"

An Orchestrated Mistake

I can't stand someone in a costume and a badge with a false sense of authority. I've always had an overwhelming urge to tell them to go pound sand, which is the Canadian version of *go fuck yourself!* The theatrics of national security could be the comic relief in any scripted drama.

I found a seat to put my shoes back on and was surprised when I looked past security and saw Deirdre still standing there waving madly. I had discreetly left my sister five thousand dollars in the hope she would pack up my nieces and leave her emotionally abusive marriage. It wasn't a lot of money to start over with two children, but it was most of what I was able to save after months of medical expenses. I figured I was going to be gone about two or three months and would be staying with my father and his wife, and with socialized healthcare, what did I need money for? I was happy to leave my sister a little nest egg. I just hoped it would be enough for a down payment on her freedom.

Boarding the plane at JFK, I got that feeling I used to get as a kid on Sunday nights. That lonely, empty feeling that only Sunday nights can bring. That feeling you'd get while you were lying on your bed just before a cold nose nudged your arm. You broke away from counting the glowing stars you'd stuck to your bedroom ceiling from back in the day when glowing stars were cool and realized the owner of that nose is probably the most trusted pal you have in the entire world. You scratch your pal under his chin, and then it hits you. You played all weekend and forgot to read the book, and the report is due tomorrow morning. There is nothing you can do about it now, so you just lay there playing with your pal's ears while staring up at those glowing stars. It was those lonely Sunday night feelings. Well, anyway, that's the feeling I got when I boarded the plane at JFK.

Minutes later, Lupe Fiasco's "Day Dreamin" was blaring from my iPod as the borough of Queens faded and we slipped out over the Atlantic Ocean. That New York chapter had officially ended, and I was embarking on a new adventure. An adventure I wasn't particularly enthusiastic to take.

An Orchestrated Mistake

Less than two hours later, the announcement was made we were descending into Halifax. I looked out the window, and there wasn't a manmade object in sight. All I could see were trees. We were landing in Sherwood Forest, and I was flooded with that feeling again that my life seemed guided by a series of orchestrated mistakes. Staring out the window, I wondered if I had made the right decision to come to Halifax. How did I go from an employed producer in New York City to an unemployed dreamer in Halifax? I don't recall writing that show business exit scene in my life's script.

I almost walked away from show business years ago before a chance meeting erased my self-doubts and infused me with the flicker of hope I needed to continue. I was a struggling actor making $136 a week appearing in a show at the Arts Club Theatre in Vancouver. It was at a time when many of my friends were graduating from University and beginning their careers, and I was getting tired of making tomato soup out of ketchup. A friend of mine offered me a job with a large salary, company car, and great company benefits. The offer was tempting, and I was mulling this over when, needing money, I took work as an extra on the film *Mrs. Delafield Wants to Marry Again*.

Extra work can be boring, so I took Clifford Odet's play *The Big Knife* with me to read. I was sitting just off set reading the play when I heard that distinct voice ask, "Are you reading that play for the theater?"

I looked up and was gazing into the eyes of the star of the movie we were shooting. "No, no," I stammered. "Just, I'm just, you know, reading it."

"Ah."

"But, but I am doing a play at a theatre here in town," I said, not wanting to disappoint.

"I love the theater," she said. "It's the artist's sanctuary, you know."

125

An Orchestrated Mistake

"Yesss."

"The actor has the opportunity to really find himself in the theater," she continued.

"Yesss."

"It's magic."

"Ready for Ms. Hepburn, please!" the first AD called out.

"Be patient," Katherine Hepburn said.

"Yesss."

"Good luck," she said as she smiled, turned, and walked onto the set.

I was stunned. The only time I've ever been starstruck. How did she know I was questioning my creative passion? Or maybe the more poignant question is, how did she know what I needed to hear? Maybe it wasn't the message but the messenger who had influenced me. Whatever it was, the doubts I was having at that time in my life were replaced by a burning desire to reside in the 'artist's sanctuary.' I called my friend and passed on his job offer.

Several years after that encounter, I wrote a play I co-produced in Vancouver, and one of the passages in it is based on that brief encounter:

"...in the theater words ring home like truths. It's magic. You go places that the soul dare not go, and when you're there, the soul cries out for more, never to let the truth subside. The theater is the artist's sanctuary. A place where men like O'Neill and Odets wept like babies as their words ripped into the heart of humanity. The theater, my dear, is a place where the artist finds himself..."

Anyway, that's what I was thinking about when the plane touched down in Halifax. How my life has just seemed like a series of chance encounters, orchestrated mistakes, and just dumb luck. I wondered if that trend would continue in Halifax.

An Orchestrated Mistake

"Hi, welcome to Halifax," the immigration officer said. My eyes were drawn to her hip. Where was her automatic weapon? And she was actually smiling. "Door number two, please," she said, stamping my papers. I noticed all the other passengers were going through door number one and then straight out into the terminal. I wanted to go through door number one.

Two Canadian immigration officers were sitting behind booths in room number two, one female and one male. I was the only one in the room with them, so right away I felt uncomfortable. I never liked being alone with authority figures. I've had this aversion ever since junior high school when I was busted throwing an egg and then sent to the vice principal's office. There, I endured a lecture on egg throwing and was sentenced to a week's detention. Quite extreme, I thought, for just one yolk.

The young male officer waved me over. As I handed him my papers, my eyes were scanning the officer's hips for weapons. Again, there were none. Not a six-shooter in sight. How tough can these Canadians be?

"Welcome," the officer said, going over my papers.

"Hi."

"What's your postal code?" he asked.

"Excuse me?" I replied.

"Your postal code. You didn't fill in your postal code on your customs form."

"Zip code, right. I'm staying at my father's. I don't know his zip code," I said.

The female officer chimed in. "Give me the address. I'll go look it up for you."

I stared at her as she got out of her booth, took my papers, and disappeared in the back. I almost had a second stroke. This doesn't happen in the US. If they had asked me for my zip code

An Orchestrated Mistake

in New York and I didn't know it, I would have been interrogated under bright lights, perhaps waterboarded and pepper-sprayed for good measure. People in uniforms in the US don't like it when you can't answer their questions.

"How long do you think you're going to be back in Canada?" the officer asked while we waited for the female officer to return.

"Hard to tell, maybe a couple of months. I had a stroke."

"Oh, I'm sorry."

"Nothing to be sorry about. I brought it on myself."

He pulled out a paper, filled it out, and handed it to me. "In case you stay longer, this will make your items tax-exempt if you decide to send for them within a year."

"I have everything with me," I said, looking down at my two tired old suitcases.

"You do?" he asked, staring down at the suitcase held together with duct tape.

Looking down at the suitcases, I thought, *My life boils down to this?*

"You're right. I have more stuff coming later," I said, lying to the officer.

He took the form back from me. "What kind of stuff?" he questioned, poised to write. "You'll need to be specific so you don't get taxed on them."

I bit the inside of my lip. I didn't have anything coming. Not even my picture of the three wolves, but I must be the proud owner of something. Maybe I should tell him I have some exotic art from the Far East or rare artifacts from an Egyptian dig. Something... I couldn't admit my life had boiled down to hand-me-downs from the wardrobe department.

"I'm just expecting some stuff," I finally offered.

"Yes, but what kind of stuff," he asked with pen still poised.

"Books," I finally said. "I'm expecting some books."

"Do you know the approximate value or any of the titles?"

"That matters?" I asked, regretting that I had said anything at all.

"It matters if you don't want to pay any taxes on them."

I couldn't think of any books, so I just said the last book I had read. "*Behold a Pale Horse* and I think *Catcher in the Rye*."

"That it?" he asked.

I could only think of a book my sister had purchased for me years ago at a garage sale, *Writing for Dummies*. "*Writing for Dummies*," I blurted out. "It's a writing book. It was a gift. I think it was like ten bucks."

"I see," he said, trying not to sound judgmental. "Anything else?"

"No. Well, yeah! A few plays. Shakespeare, Ibsen, Pinter," I added with a shrug. "You know, the classics. You can just put down 'classic plays.'" He shook his head and wrote on the form. "I won't be expecting anything else," I added.

"Right," he said, stamping the form. I hoped he didn't open my suitcases to see them stuffed with used clothes and a tired copy of my play that I never worked on while I was in New York.

The door burst open with such force I almost executed a duck and cover before realizing it was the female officer returning with my father's postal code. "Here you go," she said, handing her partner the form. The male officer quickly rechecked the information and stamped it. "Welcome home," he said, handing me the paper.

An Orchestrated Mistake

"That's it?" I questioned.

"Yep."

I shot through the doors into the terminal, and spotting an Australian Akubra hat seated in the waiting area, walked over to greet my seventy-eight-year-old father. He stood up and gave me a hug, and looking down at my tired suitcases, he asked, "Is that it?"

I looked down also. "Books," I said, looking back up. "I'm expecting books." And as easily as that, I was repatriated back in the land of Anne Murray, Michael J. Fox, and Celine Dion.

"Ah! Christ," my dad groaned as we both reached zero gravity after he hit the curb while entering the mall parking lot.

"Where we going?" I asked with my hand pressed up against the windshield.

"I need to pick up some cigarettes."

"For who?" My dad hadn't smoked since Deirdre was born.

"June."

"June smokes?" I questioned.

"Sort of."

"Sort of?"

"She doesn't inhale. You want to come in?" he asked.

"I'll wait."

I didn't have much of an opinion of June. My sisters had gone orangutan when they found out Dad was marrying her about six months after our own mother's death from leukemia. I couldn't have cared less. I've never had any interest in other people's relationships. Hell, I'd barely shown any interest in my own. I'm just not wired that way. Nothing can make my eyes glass over more quickly than listening to someone drone on about their relationship. Well, that's not quite true. An addict with a violin has the same effect on me. You know, those people who at every break in the conversation feel compelled to remind you that they're an addict? Well, my eyes glass over with them too.

I think the only time I really took notice of June was driving her to the airport with my dad after their brief visit to New York. On that drive, June wouldn't shut up about how good the Indigenous Peoples of Canada have it, and I was waiting for my dad to say something to set her straight, but when he didn't, it was all I could do not to hit the brakes to take her out with an airbag. Up until then we lived in different cities, so I didn't care. The most contact I would have with her would be discussing the weather for two minutes on the phone. At the time, Deirdre had asked Dad why he felt the need to marry her so soon after Mom's passing. "Well, she does make a good waffle," was my father's response.

"Maybe that's the problem with your marriage," I said to Deirdre after she told me. "You just can't make a good waffle."

Waiting for Dad to get June's cigarettes, I rolled down the window and was taken aback by how quiet Canada was. I didn't remember things being so quiet. I reached over to turn on the radio, which was tuned into some talk show, and instead of screaming and yelling about some political point of view, I heard a female caller going on about a black bear up a tree in her backyard. "I'm here in Sackville," the woman said. "And we have a problem with bears too. I was doing my dishes, and I looked out the window, and I'll be! There's a bear right in our backyard!" I shut off the radio and locked my car door.

"Where's Sackville?" I asked Dad when he got back in the car.

"Just over the hill," he said, pointing. "Why?"

"They have a bear problem," I said.

"That's Sackville. We're in Clayton Park. Maybe you'll see a deer or a raccoon."

"Raccoons have rabies," I replied as I rolled up the window.

On the drive to my dad's condo, he regaled me with stories about life in Halifax. The reverse culture shock pushed me into a funk, which had me looking out the window for a tree with a branch strong enough to hold the rope.

"You live in the middle of the forest?" I asked as we pulled into the condo parking lot. "I thought you said you lived in Halifax."

"We do. Just not downtown."

"I haven't seen anything that even resembles a downtown."

Dad opened the front doors to his building, where an elderly Asian gentleman sat in a wingback chair in the lobby. In front of him, in a stroller sound asleep, was what I assumed was his granddaughter with a teddy bear on her lap and a thumb falling out of her mouth. I smiled at the old fellow, and he nodded and smiled, mercifully never lowering his gaze to my left thumping leg or my shabby suitcases.

Dad called out to June when we entered the condo, and the silence had me thinking that perhaps she had jumped out the third-floor window at the thought of my impending arrival. June came around the corner, and like two city bus drivers passing each other on a city street, we give each other a two-finger wave, both mumbling hello. June asked for her cigarettes and escaped out onto the balcony while Dad showed me to the guest room.

"I'm taking you to see my doctor tomorrow morning," Dad said after I emerged from the guest room.

"I'd rather you just take me back to the airport."

"We'll go first thing after you get your health card."

An Orchestrated Mistake

"Can't wait," I said, walking into the kitchen.

"Where you going?" June questioned, charging in from the balcony.

"To get a glass of water," I said, stunned.

"I'll get it," she said, getting a glass.

"Ah, okay. What the hell's that?" I said as I pulled a refrigerator magnetic off the freezer door.

"It's a Tar Baby," June replied, taking it from me to place it back on the fridge.

"I know what it is," I said, staring at it.

"Then why did you ask?"

"I've never seen one live before."

"Here," she said, pouring me a glass from the tap.

Moments later, standing there looking out the window, I drank in the silence as my whole body exhaled. It had been seven months since the stroke, and I was completely physically and emotionally spent. My legs weakened, and I steadied myself on the back of the couch. I had never allowed myself the luxury of a healing sleep after the stroke. At my sister's place in New York, there were always three televisions blaring with some reality show or a children's cartoon cranked at full volume. It was a loud house. Jay was constantly bellowing at my sister or nieces. Their home could only be described as the darkest form of chaos. It was toxic, definitely not a place to heal. It was only after arriving in Canada I realized how much I had deprived my body of sleep. I had fought sleep for seven months in New York, and now back in Canada, I waved the white flag in surrender. "I need to lie down," I announced to no one in particular. I barely shuffled into the guest room before my body shut down and I fell into unconsciousness.

An Orchestrated Mistake

In what seemed like seconds but comprised the whole afternoon, my dad was at the bedroom door and woke me. "Nicholas! Supper!" I didn't have an interest in rising or eating, but I knew I had to make an appearance at the dining room table.

"Your friend was down in the lobby," my dad said to June as I let gravity drop me into a chair.

"Who? The Chinaman?" June asked. Dad nodded, shoveling in another forkful of mashed potatoes.

"You mean Asian," I said, staring at my plate.

"You know, he shouldn't sit there staring at everyone coming and going," June continued, ignoring my comment. "I don't like it. I don't want him watching me while he's stinking up the lobby like an egg roll." June giggled at her little joke. I dropped my fork.

My father grunted and continued shoveling in potatoes. June pushed her front teeth out over her bottom lip like a demented rabbit, and speaking through her nose in what I can only speculate was her attempt at an Asian accent, squealed, "Ouu yang ya gong hey hee haa!" Amused by her own wit, she let out another giggle. I was knocked speechless. I looked over at my dad, but he wasn't even coming up for air from those damn mashed potatoes. I considered asking her whether she was mocking the Asian fellow in Cantonese or Mandarin. I chose to bite my tongue and reminded myself I'm just a temporary guest. Please, sky gods, let it be temporary.

Splashing water on my face in the bathroom, I now felt trapped and claustrophobic on top of everything else. After giving the money to my sister, I barely had enough to cover incidental expenses, never mind paying for a place of my own. And even if I could afford a place, I had no idea where I was. I was out in the forest somewhere in Nova Scotia with a body that seemed to be breaking down further by the minute.

"You okay?" Dad asked when I returned to the table.

An Orchestrated Mistake

"Yeah. I'm just tired."

"How can you be tired?" June jumped in. "You slept all day!"

"I did, didn't I?" I said.

"What's for dessert?" Dad interjected.

"Rhubarb pie," June announced.

Feigning excitement, Dad grabbed her arm. "Oh, I don't know! Supper sure takes away a guy's appetite!"

June let out another giggle, and I fought the impulse to assume the fetal position in the corner.

I didn't recognize my dad. He looked familiar, I even recognized his corny jokes, but he wasn't the father I grew up with. Nor was he the husband that helped my mother with her thirteen-year battle with leukemia. I couldn't see the man who sat across from me building a massage table and learning Shiatsu massage to take away my mother's pain. I couldn't envision this man married to my mom, who, along with her sister, my aunt Vivian, had been pelted by stones in the Berlin peace marches of the 1950s. My mother was in no way a saint, but she spoke up loudly in her circles for social justice. I couldn't see this man married to that woman. He wasn't the same open-minded man who, because he had been an air-traffic controller for 35 years, chose his words carefully. What did he see in June? It was obvious she spent far too much time in the bingo halls of the Catholic Church instead of comprehending her scripture. I really needed to try those waffles.

"Just ring the buzzer," June said when I asked for a key. I had been in their home less than twelve hours, and I already needed to get out. I had noticed a Starbucks at the bottom of the hill when we drove up earlier, so I thought that was as good a place as any to seek refuge.

An Orchestrated Mistake

"Here," Dad, said tossing me his keys. "Take mine." I wasn't coordinated enough to catch them, and they hit the floor. "Sorry," Dad said, stepping towards the keys.

"I got 'em," I said, steadying myself on a chair to pick them up.

"He can just use the buzzer, William," June snapped, her natural venom appearing to catch even her by surprise.

"You don't have to wait up," I said, jingling the keys.

The hill down to Starbucks was steep, and without a strong sense of balance, gravity propelled me faster as my left leg thumped as a heinous reminder as to why I had come to Halifax. Halfway down the hill, I was able to slow and stop myself before I had completely lost control. I stood staring across the street at the trees, wondering where the hell I was and why I had let this happen to myself.

Toot! Toot! The sound of the car horn snapped me back to reality.

I looked over, and a car had stopped, the male driver waving me across the street. I wasn't even at an intersection. Puzzled, I looked the other way and a woman coming in the opposite direction had also stopped and was waving me across. I didn't even want to cross. I looked back and forth between the two cars. The male driver raised both palms to the heavens, and not wanting to disappoint, I crossed. Once there, I was left standing where I didn't want to be. I stared back across the street when two more cars stopped to wave me back. This is crazy. No intersection, no crosswalk. Canadians really are too polite. It was at that point I realized the phrase *playing in traffic* must have been coined in Canada.

I ordered a cappuccino at the Starbucks, and while waiting, counted the money in my wallet. I had one hundred and five dollars. Not even enough to buy a one-way ticket back to New York.

An Orchestrated Mistake

"Your cappuccino," the girl said, putting the drink down in front of me.

"Are you guys hiring?" I asked. So, one day I'm producing movies in New York, the next I'm producing café mochas in Halifax. At that point, I didn't care. I'd have produced anything. I needed to work to get my life back.

"Ah, no, we're not," the girl said. "But you're free to fill out an application form." My handwriting hadn't improved much beyond the red crayon in New York, so I decided to pass.

I found a table with an old newspaper, and flipping to the sports section, saw the Mets had dropped their last two games to Los Angeles. Back in New York, I would have glanced at the article, mumbled a few expletives, and moved on. Now I was clinging to everything that was New York. I visualized every swing of the bat. What I wouldn't have given at that moment to be there in that stadium sipping a cold beer and booing at the top of my lungs as the Dodgers rounded the bases. Walking out of the stadium, I would have commiserated with total strangers about the loss before jumping the 7 Train to Times Square so I could catch the subway to Brooklyn. In Brooklyn, I'd jump off at Avenue J, grabbing a slice of Di Fara's Pizza for the five-block walk home. Getting home, I'd hit the fridge to finish off the orange juice, right out of the carton, before tossing it across the kitchen into the garbage to claim the two points. Flopping on the couch, I'd turn on my old television just in time to catch the sports highlights where I'd relive the loss all over again.

I snapped out of my New York moment, finished my cappuccino, and slowly began to make my way back up the hill. I had to stop many times to catch my breath, but this time I made sure to face away anytime a car came. I wasn't playing that game again.

Dad and June had gone to bed. The country music had mercifully been turned off, so all I could hear was the dull hum of the refrigerator. I flopped on my bed, and even though I was physically and emotionally exhausted, I lay there desperately missing the speed of life in New York. I needed to get my old life back. I had no idea how long that was going to take or what it was going to entail, but like show business, I needed to achieve it yesterday.

I pulled out my laptop and signed onto their wifi to check my emails. I opened an email from Andre, and in it, he told me about a director they liked for *Thaddeus* who had shot comedy videos for Jimmy Kimmel had decided to pass. Andre went on to say the director decided to entertain studio offers. I forwarded Andre's email to Mike. Almost immediately, Mike wrote back, *Fuck him!*

I skipped down to another email from a friend in New York. It simply read: *How's the newest repatriated Canuck?*

I stared out the window at the trees for a moment before turning back to write: *To quote an old Canadian proverb, 'I'm as Canadian as possible under the circumstances.'*

I closed my computer and was unconscious before the glow had even faded from the screen.

CHAPTER NINE

"Nicholas, breakfast!" my dad yelled, poking his head in the guest room.

"Huh?" I groaned, sitting up. "What?" In that instant, I was back in my Brooklyn apartment and had no clue what my dad was doing there.

"Come on. Get up," he ordered again. Reality flooded in, forcing another groan. I really did have a stroke. I felt like I had been run over by a tank, and I really was back in Canada. I sure did do a crackerjack job at loading the silver bullet, aiming it at my career, and pulling the trigger. Hopefully, I hadn't killed it, but I sure put it on life support.

"What time is it?" I asked, dropping back onto the pillow.

"Seven-thirty. Come on. Get up. June has breakfast on the table."

"Waffles?" I asked, opening one eye.

"Just get up."

The energy of life in New York had kept me going for eight months since the stroke, but after returning to Canada, my body was taking what it so desperately needed—deep, healing sleep. The cognitive and physical challenges I faced in New York could no longer be masked. They were now magnified and screamed for me to pay attention.

I once again let gravity drop me onto a dining room chair. June had set out a bowl, a box of Raisin Bran, Special K, and an empty coffee cup. Not a Coco Puff, Pop-Tart, nor even a waffle in sight.

"We had breakfast. We couldn't wait. You want coffee?" June asked, putting a carton of milk on the table.

"Please," I said, staring at the boxes of cereal. I looked up, and June was in the kitchen putting instant coffee into a cup of hot water.

"You can add whatever you want," she said, moving a bowl of sugar closer to me. I stared at the coffee and the carton of one-percent milk.

"You don't have any cream or artificial sweeteners, do you?" I asked, looking up.

"You think this is a restaurant?" June giggled.

I looked over at my dad, who was changing the batteries in his hearing aids. He can't hear much of anything without his hearing aids, so he just grunted his agreement.

All my Canadian identification was expired and issued from the Province of British Columbia, except my health card, which for some reason was from the Province of Nova Scotia. I have no idea how I ended up with Nova Scotia healthcare, as you must live in a province for six months to get it, and other than the short sojourns out from Vancouver during my mother's illness, I had never stayed there.

"Where is everyone?" I said to my dad as we entered the Provincial Healthcare office. "Where's the overcrowded waiting area with crying babies? The bulletproof glass? Are we in a government office or a mausoleum?"

My dad grunted and pointed to the young man who was waving me over to his counter. I handed him my expired health card, and he disappeared for three minutes before returning and handing me a freshly minted one.

"That's it?" I said, stunned.

"Yeah," he said, stunned that I was stunned. "Did you need something else?"

"No, I just thought…forget it." I turned to my dad. "Let's go."

"That was amazing," I said to Dad as we walked out. We were in the office barely five minutes, and I was walking out with full universal health coverage. I looked back at the government building as I was getting in the car. I was expecting to get tackled at any moment.

Unlike receiving my health card, we had to wait to see Dad's doctor, but we didn't mind because it gave us a chance to chat and catch up. Our conversation roamed from my sisters to my deceased mother to analyzing the latest in Canadian sports.

"I forgot about the CFL," I said, referring to the Canadian Football League. "I used to love the B.C. Lions."

"They won it all a few years ago," Dad replied. "Not like the Canucks," he added, referring to the Vancouver hockey team.

"Figures the Lions win when I leave. I'm used to supporting perennial losers," I lamented. "I wonder what it feels like to see your team hoist a trophy?" I added, looking down at the Mets logo on my t-shirt.

Dad picked up a magazine and began flipping through it.

"Why didn't you say anything last night?" I finally asked.

"About what?"

"At dinner when June was mocking the Asian fellow down in the lobby."

"Why?" Dad questioned.

"Why? Because it was incredibly bigoted!"

"Nicholas, she doesn't mean it."

"*Doesn't mean it?* Then why say it? You heard her!"

"I tune it out. She'd never say anything in front of anyone."

"Of course not!" I exploded in a controlled whisper. "She'd be afraid someone may haul off and belt her in the mouth!"

"Nicholas Alexander!" a voice called out.

Dad nodded towards the hallway, and steadying myself on the chair, I pushed myself up. "Where are you going?" I asked, noticing my dad rising.

"I'm going in with you."

"Why?"

"Just get going."

"Deirdre called you, didn't she?" I complained.

"Never mind," Dad said, waving down the hall. "Just get moving."

Family trust.

I was finally able to get myself up on the examining table and noticed my dad sitting relaxed with his legs crossed in the corner. "You don't need to say anything when the doctor comes in," I said.

"You're the one seeing him. What am I going to say?"

"I don't know, but you look like you're going to say something."

"Never mind me," Dad chided.

The door opened, and a cheerful Doctor Roberts came in. "Hello," he said, his face registering surprise at seeing my father in the corner. "Hi, William. I didn't expect to see you here."

"Neither did I," I mumbled.

An Orchestrated Mistake

"Well, thought I best come in with Magee here," Dad said, pointing at me. I was instantly back to the burbs of Vancouver, the area where I grew up, back in Dr. Wilbee's office as a nine-year-old getting busted for faking an earache. During that visit, Dr. Wilbee spent less time looking at my ear and more time listening to my father explain how "Magee" shot a hockey puck through his basement wall. Looking at my dad speaking to Dr. Roberts, I suppressed the urge to blurt out, 'Dad, tell him about the puck and the wall.'

"You must be Nicholas," Roberts said, turning to me and extending a hand.

"Sometimes I go by Magee," I said. Roberts looked confused. "Nicholas," I added, taking his hand.

"I've looked over your records from New York, and you've had quite a time of it," Roberts said, stepping into his doctor's role.

I wondered if now might be the time to warn Roberts that he'd have an easier time climbing K2 without arms than dealing with me as a patient. I knew if this sabbatical to Canada were going to be successful, I would need to be honest and follow his medical advice. I was secretly harboring thoughts of him giving me some kind of magic pill that would cure my diabetes, eliminate the effects of the stroke, and have me back on a plane to New York by two o'clock that afternoon.

Roberts gave me a brief examination, and picking up my file from New York, went over what it said. "Your blood pressure was high in New York, and it's high here, 172 over 90. In diabetics, we like to see it about 130 over 75. Your A1C, or average sugars, for the last three months are almost five times what's considered normal." Roberts went all doom and gloom, telling me what rough shape I was in, and finished his monologue by mentioning diabetes causes not only amputations but also blindness.

"I've heard," I replied. When Roberts asked me if I had any questions, I couldn't think of any other than, 'Can I just get the pill? I have a flight to catch.' But instead, I just mumbled, "No."

Roberts asked me how the stroke affected me, and I kept it simple by explaining my obvious physical challenges, like the numbness on my left side, my thumping left leg, and my limited balance. I thought about mentioning my cognitive challenges, but I just didn't feel like getting into it. I definitely wasn't bringing up my emotional issues and the crying or anything that would lead him to question my sanity.

"I don't see anywhere in here," Roberts said, flipping through my file, "where you were seen by a neurologist."

"I wasn't."

"Your doctor in New York didn't send you to one?"

"He suggested it," I said. "Might have insisted."

"And...?"

"And I didn't want to go. It was too expensive."

"So, you received no therapy or rehabilitation of any kind while you were in New York?"

"No," I said. It crossed my mind to tell Roberts about Miss Healing Hands and the acupuncture, but I didn't think he'd count them as professional therapy or rehab.

Reading from the New York report, Roberts referred to a lesion on my brain. "This lesion has a nonspecific appearance but could represent a demyelinating plaque from multiple sclerosis or other white matter..."

"Wait! What are you saying?" I said, cutting him off. "I may have multiple sclerosis?"

"Your doctor in New York didn't go over this report with you?"

I vaguely remembered Kaye saying something, but then again, he said a lot of things, most of them negative. He usually had my file in hand when he said things, though I didn't remember that little tidbit. My mind was probably in some casting session for *Thaddeus*, so I might have missed hearing about lesions on my brain and possible MS.

"Look, we can't rule anything out at this point," Roberts said. "I need a detailed MRI, so we need to get you seen by a neurologist. I'm ordering more blood work, and I also want you seen by a cardiologist for your heart and an endocrinologist." I stared at Roberts, nodding in agreement like I knew what the hell an endocrinologist was.

Roberts handed me a fist full of prescriptions, including one for a new Canadian glucometer. "Have you ever attended a diabetes clinic?" Roberts asked.

"Yes."

"You have?" he said, raising an eyebrow.

"Back in Vancouver," I said. Roberts stared at me. "Really, I have."

"Maybe you should do a refresher. Will you go if I send you?"

"Do I have to? I mean, I've already been through a diabetes clinic."

"And we see how well that worked for you. I think you should do a refresher."

"Okay," I said, surrendering. There was no way I was making that two o'clock flight now.

An Orchestrated Mistake

"Good, I'll arrange it," Roberts said. "I'll get your other appointments set up as well, and in the meantime, I'd like to see you back here every two days."

"Every two days?" I protested.

"Yes. You're going to see me every two days until we get those sugars under control. I don't think you understand this, but you're in pretty rough shape. You're lucky to still be alive."

Whoa! I thought that last statement was a little bit melodramatic. Sorry that my dad had to hear that, I immediately looked over at my father. Fortunately, I don't think he did hear it because he had that 'I'm enjoying my mashed potatoes' look on his face.

"You've got a long road back, Nicholas," Roberts said as I was leaving. "You need to get started."

"What the hell is an endocrinologist anyway?" I asked Dad as we drove away from Roberts' office.

"A doctor." My dad smirked.

"I know that, but a doctor of what?"

"Medicine."

I shook my head, looked over at the car next to us stopped at the traffic light, and if there was any doubt I was back in Canada, the image and music next to me completely eliminated that. Rumbling beside us, while Bachman Turner Overdrive's "You Ain't Seen Nothing Yet" blared over the stereo, was a hopped-up late 60s red Chevy Chevelle, complete with a middle-aged driver wearing a denim jacket and sporting an 80s mullet. A hairstyle, incidentally, I briefly tried to import to New York, but it never quite caught on.

"I want to go home," I groaned.

"We will after we pick up your prescriptions."

An Orchestrated Mistake

"No, not your home. My home. I want to go back to New York. And not back to Deirdre and Jay's. I want to be back in my apartment in Brooklyn."

"Maybe if you took better care of yourself, you might still be living in New York."

I turned to glare at my father, who was just staring out the front windshield. Parental truths are so annoying.

****

"Nicholas, supper!" Dad yelled. I'd slept the whole afternoon. Like I did most afternoons at my father's. I wouldn't often dream, but occasionally I would, and they always seemed to revolve around some kind of abandonment: of a friend, a lover, a job, or just life. I would often wake up emotionally distressed. It got me questioning, was there really any difference between love and sorrow? If there wasn't, then I can safely say I've been in love my whole life.

I'd never eaten with such regularity as those meals with Dad and June. I guess that's what happens when you retire. You eat with regularity. It wasn't just the constant state of fatigue that seemed to reduce my appetite, but also June enjoyed having the network TV news on while we ate. I've never cared for network news. Eighty-five percent of it is establishment propaganda, thirteen percent of it is utter bullshit supporting the propaganda, and two percent is some feel-good story about a kitten playing with a string. June's take on the news was much more black and white. Any news story with anyone protesting the government or standing up to authority needed to get a job, and anyone with brown skin who had an unfortunate incident occur in their lives probably brought it on themselves. If you had brown skin and you were protesting, forget it. '*Those* people have no right!' would be the opening statement of her rant. 'Everyone is entitled to their own thoughts and opinions. That's why they make red shirts and blue shirts,' my dad would often say. But when those comments go against the grain of your soul and you say nothing, well, then that silence will manifest itself in other ways.

An Orchestrated Mistake

*****

"That's not good." Roberts grimaced. Both my lower legs had been scratched completely raw, and the wounds were scabbing over. "How long have your legs been like this?"

"Two weeks."

Roberts gave me a cream and said the scratching was probably caused by nerve damage as a result of diabetes. I had to agree. It probably was caused by nerve damage, but not because of diabetes. I'd scratched my legs raw once before, long before I was diagnosed with diabetes, and the only thing that stopped the mad scratching was removing myself from the stressful situation.

While I was experiencing a lot of separation anxiety from New York and my career, I also knew the stress of my silence to what I deemed June's bigotry contributed to my uncontrollable self-mutilation.

In fairness to June, there is probably nothing more maddening than having a liberal invading your space when your values are obviously much more conservative. If I were a conservative and a sickly liberal came to live with me, I'm sure I'd look for ways to spike their medication.

I did my best to keep my head down and mouth shut on contentious issues, but it wasn't much safer to engage her even through a casual comment.

"This is nuts," I said one morning, sighing. "Almost a month and the only doctor I've seen is Roberts."

"Why don't you go back to the States if you don't like it here," June suggested from the kitchen.

"I'm just saying, I thought I would have seen other doctors by now."

"And I'm saying, you don't like it, leave," June shot back with a giggle in an attempt to alleviate the tension.

An Orchestrated Mistake

Subsequently, I braved the hill and spent a lot of time down at Starbucks.

A few days later, June lost it one morning. Her slippers slapped her feet as she stormed around the condo, cleaning up an already impeccably spotless home.

"Good morning," I said from the dining room table, trying to sound as perky as possible. My greeting was returned with the sound of more slapping from her slippers as she stormed around. "Happy Birthday," I said, taking my breakfast bowl to the kitchen. I'd barely got it in the sink when those slapping slippers were right behind me.

"Leave it!" June said curtly. Just when I wondered whether or not I should attempt a birthday hug, June snapped up my bowl, threw it in the dishwasher, and stormed off. Well, that eliminated that potentially awkward moment. I retreated to my bedroom and chuckled when I saw the birthday card I had bought for her the night before sitting on the nightstand. My signature was still illegible, so there was a chance she would think the card was actually from someone else.

"I don't need this! This is my house too!" I heard June yell as she slammed the kitchen cupboards. "I'm sick of it! I'm just sick of it!"

I was contemplating in my mind what she could possibly be sick of when I heard my dad's voice. "What is it, hon?"

"I'm just sick of it! I do everything, and I'm tired of it!" June wailed. "I'm not doing it anymore!" she howled. "I'm leaving!"

"Hon! Hon!" my dad protested between slapping slippers and slamming cupboard doors. "What's the matter? What's going on?"

"I don't need this! *He's* ungrateful!! This is my house!!" June shrieked like a wounded animal. "I won't stand for it! I'm leaving!"

An Orchestrated Mistake

It didn't surprise me that I was the cause of June's unhinging, but I did believe I had done my best to keep a low profile since I arrived. I'd spent most of the time in my room, either sleeping or working on the budget and schedule for *Thaddeus*.

The slapping slippers got louder as she passed my open bedroom door, and immediately my father, whose arms are outstretched as he tried to corral her into a hug, followed. "Hon, calm down," he said as June twisted free, turning back to the kitchen. Her protests became louder and shriller.

I had no idea what had set her off. I thought I had been on my best behavior. I was even consistently raising and lowering the toilet seat. I needed to get out of there and down to Starbucks. I was sitting on my bed putting on my shoes when June appeared at the door. "I won't have it in my house!" she snapped. I looked up, confused. "And don't go running to Daddy either!!" she wailed.

"Hon! Hon! No! Calm down!" my dad shouted, putting his arm across the open doorway to block her from entering. June twisted and turned in an attempt to break past my dad's outstretched arm, and I wondered what she'd do if she got past him. I still had a lot of things on my bucket list, but brawling on the floor with a 75-year-old woman wasn't one of them.

"Watch him run to Daddy!!" she shrieked in a final burst to get by. "Run to Daddy!" she screamed as she stormed off into her bedroom. My dad looked back at me in the room and just raised his palms to the heavens.

Getting down to the lobby, I realized I hadn't tied up my shoes in my haste to leave their condo. I felt a pang of guilt having left my dad, and I could still hear her ranting while I waited down the hall for the elevator.

Sitting in the lobby was the Asian fellow, and I took a seat beside him and his granddaughter so I could tie up my shoes. He smiled at me while his granddaughter took her thumb out of her mouth long enough to shoot me a near toothless grin. I could only force a smirk in return. My thoughts and emotions were preoccupied with breaking the hell out of Halifax.

"I'm telling you, she just snapped," I said to Deirdre on a payphone in the hotel lobby across from Starbucks.

"Well, you must have said something to set her off."

"I didn't. I've tried to be good all month. I have no idea what set her off."

"Well, something obviously did," Deirdre said.

"Probably that the stroke didn't kill me," I said. "Look, I need to move out. I knew coming to Halifax was a dumb idea."

"What are you going to do? Go to Vancouver?"

"I would if I had the money. I hate to ask this," I said, taking a deep breath. "But you know that money I left you in New York? Can I borrow some of it back? Just like two grand so I can get a room until I figure out what I'm going to do." My request was greeted with silence. "Hello? Did you hear me? You can keep the other three grand. I just need to get away from here and think." I could hear my sister breathing. "I'll pay it back. I'll get a job delivering pizza or something. Hello?"

"The money's gone," my sister finally said through a sigh.

"It can't be. I left you five grand less than a month ago. What did you spend it on?"

"What does it matter? Stuff."

I couldn't imagine how my sister had gone through five grand in less than a month, but then I remembered my nieces saying goodbye to me with pink and blue hair. She'd also just bought a home stereo unit out of the back of a van in a New York parking lot and was stunned when I told her it was stolen. Yeah, of course the money was gone. Blown on 'stuff.'

An Orchestrated Mistake

After hanging up with my sister, I was completely demoralized, flat. I went to Starbucks to look through the classifieds, but I didn't know if I was looking for a room, a job, or both. But since I had no clue about Halifax anyway, I might as well have been reading the obituaries for all the good it would do me.

I spent the day at Starbucks going through old and new newspapers. Returning late in the afternoon, my dad came into my room to see me. "You coming with us to June's birthday dinner tonight?"

"You're kidding, right?" I said, looking up from my computer.

"No," Dad replied. "Her whole family's going to be there, and I think you should come."

"Dad, you saw what happened this morning. The last thing I want to do is go out and celebrate."

Dad looked away and saw the envelope with June's name on it. "What's that?" he asked.

"Her birthday card."

"You going to give it to her?"

"No."

"Why not?"

"Dad, do you even remember this morning?"

"It would be a nice thing to do," Dad said.

I was about to say no, but I could see he felt embarrassed and wounded. I felt sorry for him. "Okay, I'll give her the card."

"And come with us for dinner. June went out and got her hair done."

An Orchestrated Mistake

The sign of a true psychopath. Ranting and raving one minute, then getting your hair done the next.

"Well, since she got her hair done," I finally said, "I'll go."

I gave June her card, and she managed to mumble a thank you, and I managed to mumble that her hair looked nice. At the restaurant, though, June had never been nicer to me. I knew it was a show for the others. However, I also was more than aware that my presence in her home was a struggle for both of us.

After dinner, everyone walked down to the lake, but I didn't feel secure enough on my feet to tackle the grassy incline, so I took a seat on the observation platform. After a few minutes, June's son, David, walked up the hill and joined me.

"How you feeling?" he asked, leaning against the railing.

"Fine. I just didn't feel like going down to the water." I lied.

"What are the doctors saying?"

"Canadian healthcare is like making movies," I said. "Hurry up and wait. But I'm fine."

David nodded and looked back down at the lake.

"Where do you think is a good place to live in Halifax?" I asked David after a moment. I figured with David being a Halifax cop, he would be as good as any to ask.

"Why? You thinking of moving out of Mum and Dad's?"

"I have no idea how long this health thing is going to take, and I can't stay at their place forever," I said. "Problem is I haven't a clue where downtown even is. I know their place and the doctor's office. That's about it."

"What do you want to spend?" David asked.

"Know anyone who wants to rent their couch?"

An Orchestrated Mistake

"You worked in film, you must have lots of money."

"Independent film. Our budgets are twenty bucks and a six-pack."

"No money, huh? Well, the cheapest area is the North End, but you don't want to live there. It's pretty rough."

"David, I lived in Brooklyn for years," I replied, omitting the fact I lived in the Jewish area of Brooklyn, so my biggest fear was getting taken out by a stray matzah ball. "I'm not worried about living in the North End of Halifax."

"I have some court cases this month," David explained. "Let me get those out of the way, and I'll take you around. Couple of weeks sound good?"

"I'd appreciate it." I still had one huge problem, though. How was I going to pay for a place once I found it?

A few days later, I was speaking with Deirdre from the hotel lobby when she told me Mom's sister, our Aunt Vivian in Vancouver, wanted me to call her. I got off the phone with Deirdre and called Vivian, collect, as instructed.

"Oh, hi," Vivian said in her familiar Australian accent. "How are you?" She laughed like it was some grand conspiracy we were speaking on the phone.

"Fine, how are you?" I replied.

"Oh, fine. Now that we have the lies out of the way, how are you?"

I told Vivian a little bit about how I was feeling, and when I asked her about the state of her leukemia, she just laughed and said, "Deirdre called me the other day. You have to get out of there, Nicholas. That woman is completely off her rocker. I can't believe your father married the fool."

"Well, Vivian, it's probably me too. I mean, I'm not exactly the easiest person to live with."

"I remember," Vivian said with a laugh. "You were ten, but I still could have smacked you for pushing my buttons, you little twerp."

"I enjoy pushing buttons."

"Let me send you some money," Vivian said, getting serious. "You can pay me back if you want when you start working again."

"No, Vivian! Thanks, but I don't want your money. I'll find a job."

"Rubbish!!" Vivian said, her Australian accent dripping. "How are you going to get a job? You're damn lucky you're still walking."

"I don't know. I'll find one. I'll deliver pizzas if I have to."

"You bloody fool! If you won't let me help you, then call up Nova Scotia Social Services and claim disability."

"Vivian, I'm not disabled."

"You damn fool, you've had a stroke! Put your damn ego aside and listen for once. You've had a stroke, and the only way you're going to get better is if you allow people to help. Now stop being a fool and call them up!"

"Okay, okay, I'll call."

I had no intentions of calling Nova Scotia Health and claiming disability, but I knew it would only be a matter of time before I sent June onto the edge of insanity.

I actually like that June takes care of my dad, but she and I are just not meant to live under one roof. When there was another dust-up a few weeks later, I immediately retreated to my room. Seconds later, my shoes were on and I was walking down the hill, but instead of going to Starbucks, I walked to the hotel lobby to use the phone. I looked up Nova Scotia Social Services in the phone book and dialed.

The next day someone from the agency came out to meet me at the condo. Dad and June waited in the other room while I answered the fellow's questions, and two days after he had received the forms from my doctor, he called to say I had been approved and placed on disability. It wasn't a lot of money, but it was enough for me to get a small place and to live on my own. When he dropped off my first check, I got a copy of the medical form that Doctor Roberts had filled out, and I was shocked and horrified by his assessment. I was suspected of having heart disease, and beside the question *'How far can this person walk?'* Roberts checked *'1 to 2 blocks.'* *'How much can this person lift?'* He had checked *'5-10 pounds.'* *'How many stairs?'* He had checked *'5-10.'* But what struck me the hardest was he had checked the box *'Permanent.'*

David drove me around to look for a place when I got my disability assistance. Miraculously, my scratching stopped.

"You don't want to live there," David said as we drove by a building in the North End of Halifax.

"Why not?" I asked.

"It's a crack house. We busted it last night."

"So rent is cheap," I said, crossing it off my list.

June could barely conceal her excitement when I announced I had found a place on the second day. It was in the North End, much to David's displeasure.

"This ain't the North End," Ken, the rotund superintendent, a shoo-in for Captain High Liner, admonished David as he slid me the lease. "This is a respectable place. Used to be a Catholic monastery. The white trash is north of here."

"I see," I said, looking at the lease.

"So, why did you leave New York to come to this whistle-stop?" Ken asked.

"I had a stroke."

"Stroke? Awfully young to be having a stroke, aren't you?"

"Long story. I have diabetes."

"I have diabetes!" Ken said.

"Well, I ignored it and just ate what I wanted," I said.

"I ignore it and eat what I want!" Ken replied.

"I smoked."

"I smoke!" the exasperated superintendent announced. "Jesus! I'm going to have a stroke!" Ken was staring at me with genuine fear in his eyes. I looked over at David, who raised an eyebrow and shrugged. We both looked back to Ken, who was staring up, waiting for one of us to say something.

"I'm sure you'll be fine," David finally said.

"Christ, I hope so," Ken fretted. "I retire at the end of this month. As a matter of fact, I'm taking the apartment just down the hall from you. You and I are going to be neighbors."

"See, things are looking up already," David chimed.

"Sign here, and we'll make it official," Ken said.

I looked over at David, and he nodded, so I took the pen and signed. As I handed the pen back to Ken, a huge grin broke out across his face, and for the first time, I noticed he was missing all his teeth.

"Welcome to the asylum."

CHAPTER TEN

Medications can cause nausea, vomiting, headaches, dizziness, fainting, and loss of coordination. It may also put you at risk for heart attack, internal bleeding, and difficulties in breathing. It may cause drowsiness while lying down. Not to be taken while listening to a political pundit, as it may cause eye-rolling and induced vomiting.

I was experiencing every side effect listed on my medications and some that weren't just to ensure I was, in fact, a sentient being. It wasn't just the side effects of the prescription drugs that had me feeling lousy. I was also sleeping on the floor of my Halifax studio apartment. My flat was about the size of a large walk-in closet. This meant I didn't have far to roll before crashing into a wall as I writhed around at 3am, caused by cramps that felt like a spike being repetitively driven through my calf muscles. On the bright side, I didn't have to worry about falling out of bed as I contorted around because I was already on the floor. Unlike the incident I had while house-sitting for Laura. There, I got up in the middle of the night, forgot where I was, stepped off the loft, and fell seven feet to the hardwood floor below. Dogs and cats executed a duck and roll as they scrambled for cover when my knees hit with such a loud thud that Laura's Upper Westside apartment groaned and shuddered. I was lying on the floor, moaning in so much agony as my left knee swelled up like a grapefruit. Lulu came over to lick my face, making any emergency room visit completely unnecessary. Much easier to suffer and walk with a limp for a month than tolerate an emergency room visit. So, yes, I am a sentient being, but one without wisdom.

Just before I took possession of my Halifax apartment, my dad offered to buy me a bed and some basic furniture, but I wasn't open to receiving charity from friends or family. Charity is more palatable when it comes from total strangers. I know that's dumb and irritating to those that want to help you, but there have been times when my stubbornness served me well, although other times it volleys against my self-interest.

After a visit with Doctor Roberts, I asked my dad for a ride to the Furniture Bank. "What for?" he asked.

"What do you mean 'what for?'" I replied. "They're raffling off designer furniture and I want to get my name in."

"I mean, why do you need to go to the Furniture Bank?"

"Because a furniture store will want actual money, and you probably noticed, I haven't got any."

"I told you I'd get you a few things," Dad said.

"No."

"Why not? I can at least get you a bed."

"You could, but I wouldn't sleep in it."

"Christ. Why?" Dad asked, genuinely confused.

"Because I don't need you to buy me a bed," I told him. "They said on the phone they'd have a bed for me in a few weeks, a month at most."

"A month? Where are you going to sleep for a month?"

"My apartment comes with a floor."

"Christ, Nicholas, stay with us, at least until you get a bed."

It had only been a couple of days since I moved out, and I couldn't imagine returning to their place while waiting for a bed. June had been doing a celebratory jig from the moment she heard I'd found an apartment, and if I returned, that would have her guzzling from her proverbial religious goblet and me executing a swan dive off their third-floor balcony. No, I wasn't accepting any handouts from Dad, and I definitely was not moving back into their condo.

Leaving the Furniture Bank after putting in my request, I did wonder what my dad was thinking when I noticed him glancing down at my thumping left foot as we crossed the parking lot. I knew all of this wasn't easy on him, and I wondered if he mourned my lack of independence as much as I did, especially in those moments when I was forced to use his then seventy-nine-year-old shoulder for support. The most tragic consequence of any illness is the loss of independence and freedom, and sadly they're always the first casualty.

I did get another charitable offer from my middle sister, Sonya, who called from California after June's second meltdown. This first call from Sonya was nine months after the stroke, six weeks after I returned to Canada, two weeks after my birthday, and only happened apparently after much goading from Deirdre. I'm sure when Deirdre told Sonya the day after I had the stroke in New York, Sonya's response was probably something like, "Well, is he still breathing?"

"Yes," Deirdre would have said. "But…"

"On his own?"

"Well, yes, but…"

"Oh, well, nothing to worry about then!" Sonya would have announced before claiming she needed to get back to work and attend to the horses.

When Sonya finally called me in Halifax, I could hear by her voice she was already on the defensive. "I called your cell in New York on your birthday, but you didn't pick up," she claimed.

"Sonya, my birthday was over two weeks ago," I said, glancing up at the heavens. "I gave up my cell when I left New

An Orchestrated Mistake

York six weeks ago. In case you're confused where you just called, I'm here at Dad's in Halifax."

"I know," she replied, ignoring my sarcasm. "I'm just saying I called your cell on your birthday. So, what are you doing?" she asked.

"Sonya, what the hell do you think I'm doing? I know Deirdre told you I had to come back to Canada because I had a stroke."

"I know. I mean, what are you doing for fun?"

"For fun? Sonya, are you serious?" I asked, stunned. "Sonya, I had a stroke! I came to Canada to watch a damn hockey game! What the hell do you think I'm doing?"

"I know," Sonya said, realizing her conversation was charging down a dead-end street. "I thought that maybe you would want to come to California and live here with Mark and me instead of in Canada."

"No!"

"Why not?"

"Well, for starters," I said, "my medical bills would have you guys bankrupt in a week, and secondly, no offense, I'm done living with family."

"Oh."

"Yeah, 'oh.'" I could almost hear the relief in her voice.

"Well, up to you. Think about it. I have to get back to work. Love you!"

Sonya always said 'love you' before hanging up. It's like 'love you' made her indifference palatable. There is one nice thing about Sonya's annual calls—they're always brief. It did cross my mind, however, to tell her, 'Yes, Sonya, I'll be on the next plane to LA,' just so I could listen to her gag and stutter.

I knew I would have to eat humble pie and accept some charity from somewhere if I wanted any semblance of my independence and freedom back. However, it was hard enough to put my hand out to the Furniture Bank, so I was nowhere near ready to accept handouts from family.

Unless you've got an emergency, the Canadian healthcare system can be much like show business, and like many other medical systems throughout the world, it can be very much about the hurry up and wait. After moving into my apartment six weeks after my return to Canada, I finally started meeting with the specialists. If my meeting with the cardiologist was going to foreshadow my recovery and path back to New York, I was in for a long journey. While the cardiologist seemed like a nice fellow, my visit didn't shed any light on anything about my current state of health. In fact, once he found out I had worked in film, the bulk of my visit was taken up with a discussion about movies. Meeting my father as I came out of the examining room, my father asked me, "Well, what did he tell you about your heart?"

"Nothing really," I replied. "But he did think that *Capote* should have won for Best Picture."

He did schedule me for a stress test a few days later back at the hospital, and it was during this test I realized there is no room at all for your ego in the recovery room. A beautiful young technician led me to a small cubical, and drawing the curtains, asked me to remove my shirt.

"What?" I stammered, gazing into the most amazing eyes ever.

"You need to take off your shirt so I can see if I need to shave your chest before hooking you up." After unbuttoning and removing my shirt, Miss Universe quipped, "Oh, this won't take long."

After my shave, Miss Universe walked me to the treadmill, and while she was hooking me up to a blood pressure cuff and the EKG machine, a doctor walked in, and reading from a file, asked, "Which side of your body did the stroke effect?"

"Neither," I said, in what has to be one of the more delusional statements I've ever uttered. Standing there shirtless with my few remaining wispy chest hairs, I'd long since given up trying to flex my bicep for Miss Universe. I resigned myself to the fact I was indeed the poster boy for a pasty, undefined, middle-aged white guy. The doctor asked if I'd mind if a few medical interns sat in on my stress test. As I nodded my consent, six young *GQ* model interns entered, and my shoulders immediately sagged as I mumbled, "Why not?"

My left foot began slapping the moment the treadmill was turned on. "The left side," the doctor announced to the room. "The stroke affected his left side."

My performance on the treadmill never reached the level of a brisk walk. The doctor gave a running commentary on my sad performance to his models, and after six minutes and six seconds, he announced I was weakening and needed to call it. The interns got up and immediately filed out, grateful, I'm sure, they didn't have to pay for such a disappointing performance.

The cardiologist's final report said my stress test was inconclusive, as my target heart rate was never reached. He stated my issues were more neurological than cardiovascular, and further investigation was required by neurology. I, on the other hand, gleaned from the test that I'd become a frumpy middle-aged white guy in pathetic shape, which, without a keen sense of balance, had become terrified of treadmills. Oh, I also learned Nova Scotia has one hell of a good-looking cardiovascular department. But don't tell anyone, because if word ever got out, the single population of the province will be clutching at their chests and dropping like flies.

If I thought the stress test smacked down my ego, it was shattered like frozen glass during my visit to the Halifax Diabetes Clinic.

I had picked up a lot of information over the years during my struggles with diabetes, but I never folded that information into my own life. Again, for whatever reason, there was a disconnect to that information and applying it to myself.

During the shooting of one of our films, a background actor became listless in his chair, and, speaking to him, I recognized right away he was probably hypoglycemic or experiencing low blood sugars. "Here, drink this," I said to him, holding the straw of the juice box. Within moments he was coming back around and regaining his strength. I asked him, "What's your name, buddy?"

"Greg," the fifty-something man replied.

"You're a diabetic, Greg?"

"Yes." He nodded.

"Why do you think your sugars dropped, Greg?"

"I took my medications this morning," Greg admitted sheepishly.

"And then I skipped breakfast."

"Greg, Greg. You know you should never do that," I said. "Diabetics constantly have to be aware of when they took their medication and when and what they are eating. It's the cardinal rule of living with diabetes."

"I know," Greg said to the floor.

I told Greg to call it a day and call someone to come pick him up. Greg agreed, and on my way back to producer's holding, I walked past the crafty table, reached down, scooped up, and inhaled a fistful of M&M's. I'm sure that's the cardinal rule for the definition of delusional: believing you're exempt from the rules.

"I have your latest blood work, and I've gone over the results," the nurse at the Halifax Diabetes Clinic told me. "All the numbers from your blood tests are quite high. Your A1C, triglycerides, your bad cholesterol, blood pressure, all of it is high. Well, except for your good cholesterol, that was quite low. Why don't you tell me in your own words how well you control your blood sugars?" she asked.

"I don't think I'd use the words 'well' and 'control' in describing my diabetes," I said.

"I can see that," she exclaimed, pointing to my test results. "Why don't I just ask you some questions, and then I'll get a better idea about why your numbers are where they are."

"Shoot."

"How many times a week do you exercise? Zero to two times a week? Three to four? Or more than four?"

"Three to four." I lied. She looked up and furrowed her brow.

"How long do you exercise? Zero to twenty minutes. Twenty to forty-five, or more than an hour?"

"Twenty to forty-five minutes, I'd say." She looked up and glared at me again. "Okay, probably zero to twenty," I said, changing my answer, but judging by the look on her face, she wasn't buying that either. "Okay, closer to zero. Fine, okay, it is zero. I don't exercise at all. Happy?"

"This isn't a test, Nicholas. There are no right or wrong answers, but it is helpful if you can be truthful."

"Fine," I said, shifting in my chair. "I'll be truthful."

"Good," she said, picking up the questionnaire. "Erectile dysfunction?"

"What!!??" I gasped in a falsetto.

"Do you have difficulty…"

"I know what it is!" I stammered. "I just don't know why it's relevant."

"It's relevant if I'm going to get a clear picture of your current state of health."

"I'm not in a relationship right now," I stammered to the floor. I looked up, her unblinking eyes demanding a more complete response. Now even the soles of my feet were perspiring. "Okay, okay. I haven't been in a relationship in quite a while. Okay, I don't even remember my last relationship!"

Truth was, I hadn't been in a relationship for a long time, and ED, or erectile dysfunction, brought on by diabetes, played a role in that. As my diabetes had become worse, I had pulled further away and refused to open myself up to the possibility of a relationship that might lead to intimacy. The reasons behind impotence in diabetics are complicated, but it involves diabetes causing impairment in the blood vessels, nerves, and muscle function. About 95% of men, should they live long enough, will experience some form of erectile dysfunction, but for uncontrolled diabetics, this emotionally crippling malady can hit ten to fifteen years earlier than those without the disease. Those like myself who chose to continue to ignore the disease will find themselves sooner rather than later shooting pool with a cord, which had me terrified of intimacy. It's not just the physical carnage that diabetes causes, but the emotional day-to-day struggle of living with the disease can bring a whole host of emotional baggage, and that in of itself can be debilitating. Dealing with ED is just one aspect of the psychological damage diabetes brings, but I guess being single does allow you to watch *Sports Page* in peace.

"So that's a yes?" the nurse asked.

"Yes!"

"I just want to be clear," she said, writing in my file. "Yes to erectile dysfunction."

"Yes! Yes! Jesus! Who would have thought your health would be so damn personal!"

"I'm sorry. I'm just trying to get the big picture. So, you've been diabetic since…"

"I was thirty-one."

"Type two?"

"I guess," I mumbled, still stinging from the last statement.

"Does diabetes run in your family?"

"No."

"No?" the nurse questioned, looking up. "No one else in your family, maybe your grandmother or grandfather, was diabetic?"

"No. I'm the only lottery winner."

"You're sure?"

"Yes. I asked my mother when I was diagnosed. She told me 'no.'"

"Did you have weight issues when you were diagnosed?"

"No."

"Has a doctor ever explained to you how you may have developed diabetes?"

"Nope. And I never asked." I had figured with about 422 million confirmed diabetics worldwide and another possible 352 million with prediabetes or impaired glucose tolerance, it was probably just the luck of the draw, so I had never given it much thought.

"It is a little strange there is no history in your family," she said, writing in my file. "How long were you hospitalized because of your stroke?"

"I wasn't."

"What??"

"I was living in New York. I couldn't afford a hospital."

"Oh my God. You weren't hospitalized? What about rehabilitation therapy?"

"I haven't even seen a neurologist yet."

"Your stroke was like ten months ago."

"Yes."

"And you've never been seen by a neurologist or had any therapy?"

"No."

An Orchestrated Mistake

"Not in the US or Canada?"

"I've only been back in Canada about three months. I'm on a waiting list."

"That's incredible. What kind of work did you do in New York?" she asked, looking through my file.

"I was a production manager in Independent film. Well, I was actually a film producer for two days, five days if you count the weekend." I could tell by her low-hanging jaw she wasn't sure whether she should laugh or be concerned, so I helped her and let out a chuckle.

After the nurse and I finished shocking each other, her with her questions, me with my answers, she passed me off to the dietician at the clinic, but not before telling me she may have to increase my insulin injections beyond the current 34 units per day.

The meeting with the dietician was full of more good news. "Well, your weight has gone up considerably," she told me as I stepped off the scale. "One hundred and seventy-five pounds." At only 5'8" I thought that explained the man-boobs. I had put on about fifty pounds in roughly ten months.

Since the stroke, my life had become even more inactive, if that were possible, and my eating habits had gone from bad to worse. There was a brief improvement while I was staying with Dad and June, but now that I was on my own, my diet mainly consisted of things that came out of a cardboard box. Having given up cigarettes also had me stuffing my face with anything that wasn't tied down, especially if it came with sprinkles and frosting. It wasn't just my sedentary lifestyle and diet that had me packing on the pounds—insulin turns on the fat storage switch in the body, and I had been on significant amounts of insulin since seeing Dr. Kaye back in New York after the stroke.

An Orchestrated Mistake

High, out-of-control sugars can cause the body to lose weight as the body literally devours fat and muscle in an effort to fuel the body. Insufficient insulin prevents the glucose from the blood from entering and nourishing the cells. When this happens, the body starts eating at fat and muscle for energy. It's why I only weighed 136 pounds at the time of my stroke. I've read where young girls who are diabetic will run high blood sugars to stay thin. This, of course, is a highly dangerous practice, as the complications from diabetes are far more severe than a few extra pounds. For me, I always felt best when my weight hovered where it had been for most of my adult life, around 150 pounds.

Overall, the report by the Diabetes Clinic to my doctor wasn't much better than the one sent by my cardiologist.

The clinic's report stated I had poor diabetes control, which led to a whole host of medical issues. A major factor contributing to this lack of control was poor meal spacing, poor meal balance, and nutritionally inadequate meals. Both the nurse and the dietician voiced concerns over further complications from diabetes, and the nurse stated I needed to see an ophthalmologist regarding small blood vessel damage in my eyes, known as retinopathy, the leading cause of blindness in diabetics. I thought their report focused a little bit too much on the negative. I mean, who would have thought my sloth-like lifestyle and eating out of a package would cause so much damage? They could have at least said something positive, like, 'hasn't touched a cigarette in ten months.'

A few weeks after my uplifting visit to the Diabetes Centre, I found myself at the endocrinology clinic. "So, what is it that you do?" I asked the endocrinologist after taking a seat in his office.

"I specialize in internal medicine."

"Ah."

An Orchestrated Mistake

"Basically, I study the different hormones and the glands that produce them and how imbalances in the endocrinological system may contribute to disorders in the body. In your case, diabetes."

"Of course," I said, hoping my vacant stare didn't reveal the fog bank rolling through my head.

"And it looks like you've got a few things out of balance," he said, looking back down at the results of yet another blood test.

While the science to what this doctor was explaining may have been over my head, breaking down his tone and body language screamed volumes. 'You're up shit creek and in for a whole other world of hurt if you don't get things under control.' He also recommended I see an ophthalmologist for my retinopathy in my eyes and pointed out that the numbness I had in my feet was brought on by nerve damage by a condition called neuropathy, a direct result of my high blood sugars. His parting shot as I left his office was that my weight had gone up by four pounds since my last weigh-in at the Diabetes Clinic, and perhaps I should try and get some exercise, "even if it is only walking," he added before I left the room.

"Even if it is only walking," I grumbled as I left the clinic at the hospital. I had only walked about two blocks before my thumping left foot had me feeling like a captain listening to the horrid sound of twisting metal and popping rivets as his ship sunk to the bottom of the ocean.

I stopped to quell the thumping and catch my breath when the sound of sobbing distracted me from my anguish. I looked over, and there was a woman kneeling by a gravestone with her shoulders heaving toward the heavens with each sob. I felt trapped. I wasn't in the mood to listen to this open wound, but I also didn't have the strength to continue. Where was I going anyway? Back to my tiny apartment? I now had a table, chairs, and bed, so I could stare at the wall in comfort, but I was tired of staring at the wall. I looked around and saw an old couple sitting at a bus stop across the street, and never having experienced downtown Halifax thought I was in need of a bit of sightseeing.

I tried to dash across the four lanes of Robie Street when there was a break in the traffic, but unlike the days when I used to run across 6th Avenue in New York, there was no dashing to be done. My left leg wouldn't move at the speed I needed it to, and I barely managed to hop to the center median before a stream of traffic prevented me from going any further. Doubled over, catching my breath, I straightened up and noticed the old man at the bus stop had put down his paper, and he and his wife were watching me like a painful reality show.

When I finally made it to the bus stop, I was greeted by disapproving glares from my senior traveling companions, and the old man snapped his paper, and lifting it, said to his wife, "Did you read this in the paper today?"

"Read what?" she asked.

"Five leading causes of death," he said from behind the paper.

"No, I must have missed that."

"Says here, heart disease, stroke, diabetes," and lowering his paper, he stared at me, "and accidents."

"In that order?" his wife asked.

"What the hell does it matter about the order?" he groused. "You're dead!"

I wanted to point out to the old-timer he'd only named four out of the five leading causes of death, but since I already had three out of the four, I decided I didn't need to hear the fifth. I looked across the street at the woman still kneeling by the grave and wondered if I wouldn't have been more at ease just remaining over there.

I was only on the bus very briefly before it pulled up to the intersection of Spring Garden and South Park Street. I asked the man next to me, who, like me, had been forced to stand on the crowded bus, if this was downtown.

"Spring Garden is one of the main drags downtown, sure," he replied.

"Thanks. Hold the door, please," I shouted as I crashed and bumped my way to the front door.

Stepping off the bus, I was greeted by a poster in the window of a Dairy Queen storefront that serenaded me with the slogan, 'Cool Treats!' I used to love Dairy Queen and hadn't seen one in years, never mind being in one. Rather than being an adult and acknowledging I was more than a little fragile at that moment, so I should walk the other way, I waited for the light to change and made a beeline for the front door.

Moments later, I was standing before the counter perusing the menu with all the brightly lit photos of banana splits, chocolate sundaes, and ice cream cones when the young girl behind the counter asked, "Can I get you anything?"

I wanted to say, 'Yes, I'll have that half of the menu,' but without taking my eyes off the menu, I said, "No thanks, I'm just looking."

"Oh," I heard the now nervous girl reply.

"Oh, wait!" I shrieked, pointing. "You guys actually have chocolate soft ice cream! Oh, forget it, I can't."

I decided I'd just start to walk down Spring Garden after getting my soft chocolate ice cream peanut buster parfait with chocolate sauce. The girl had to ask me twice before making it to make sure I really wanted it made with chocolate ice cream because it came covered with chocolate sauce. "It's impossible to have too much chocolate," I had assured her. I figured if I was going to continue to commit suicide, I should at least go out happy. It only took a couple of spoonfuls of this decadent treat to start my feet tingling, a symptom I was now used to when I indulged my ravenous sweet tooth. I just told myself I'd take an extra shot of insulin when I got home. Sometimes I'm an idiot. Other times I act like one.

Strolling down Spring Garden, taking in the atmosphere of my recently adopted city, I was amazed at how many street buskers there were. Kids playing banjos, an old guy whistling while keeping time with what I thought were spoons but turned out to be a butter knife and a salad fork. That had to be worth at least a quarter in his bucket. Further along, a young girl was holding up a sign that read, "Good Karma! Only 25 cents!" I stopped, took a spoonful of chocolate ice cream, and, reaching into my pocket, pulled out a loonie, the term for a Canadian dollar, and tossed it into her upside-down hat on the sidewalk. "There's a buck," I said. "See what you can do."

Strolling along the sidewalk, I'd forgotten how quiet Canada was compared to the US. When I thought I heard a car horn, it turned out to be just an old Chevy belching. Everything seemed so much more relaxed than I remembered. I spotted a cop on foot patrol walking towards a car stopped in a bus zone and thought, *Now it's time for a good old-fashioned Canadian smackdown.* I'll see a little pent-up institutional aggression now. A car stopped in a bus zone. This has to be good for a huge fine. Perhaps a verbal beat down because the driver is some young guy, a punk that you have to know is oozing an attitude that only a narcissistic punk who stops in a bus zone can have. The cop will get him to step out of the car, check his ID, perhaps a pat-down, and give him a stern lecture. I'm sure he'll get in the kid's face like I've seen a thousand times on the streets of New York. "Hi!" the cop said cheerfully after tapping on the driver's window. "You know you can't stop here. This is a bus zone."

"Yes, I know, Officer," the kid replied. "My girlfriend just ran in to use the bank machine."

"No worries," the cop replied. "But if a bus comes, you know you have to move."

"I know, sir," the polite kid replied. "She'll be out any second."

"Enjoy your day," the cop said, tapping the fender as he walked away.

What the hell just happened? Where was the ticket? The lecture? He didn't even yank the kid out of his car through the window to check his ID! And what about the trunk? For all we know, Al-Qaeda was hiding in this kid's trunk. Well, it's possible! After all, the Americans thought Al-Qaeda was hiding in my shoes. In New York, this kid would have had to mortgage his firstborn to pay that ticket! He would've had to show his ID. He probably would've been pulled out for a little frisk and a couple of shots with a Taser to make sure he never stopped in a bus zone again—maybe even a little waterboarding for good measure! But here, 'no worries, enjoy your day?' I agree with Americans. Canadians are too damn friendly and obviously soft on crime. When a bus pulled up moments later and gave a couple of friendly toots on the horn to the kid, I turned and walked away in utter disgust.

Ten years away from Canada, and I honestly don't remember Canadians being this damn congenial. It wasn't just the blaring car horns and the aggressive Robocops that were absent. Where were all the TV pundits screaming about social issues? It's so socially quiet in Canada I can once again only hear the hum of the refrigerator. Where is all the shouting about abortion? Gun control? Gay marriage?

How will I know what to think if religious and political leaders and the screaming heads don't tell me? Oh my God! How will the human race excel if these myopic visionaries don't guide us? I'll be forced to rely on my own thoughts and ideas, and I've already demonstrated how inept I am at that. Well then, if being back in Canada means I'm expected to think for myself, I say getting upset with gay marriage is like being a diabetic while furious with your neighbor for enjoying a chocolate cake. It's got to be the highest form of lunacy. Although, I will admit I have found myself jealously scowling at a person happily savoring a decadent pastry on more than one occasion.

Walking further down Spring Garden that day, it became clear it wasn't just living on my own I had missed. I also missed living in Canada. It seemed Canadians had found a new confidence for what Canada stood for, what it meant to be Canadian. Or maybe I just hadn't noticed it before, but even now, French Canadians no longer howled to separate. They appeared content to just smoke cigarettes and sip their wine. Maybe it's true that you do have to move away to appreciate your own country. I don't know, but one thing was for sure, it sure was nice to see human acceptance dominate the Canadian social psyche that day.

Later on, I found myself at the downtown library reading and taking out a few books on health and diabetes. I was surprised by how much I enjoyed learning about and understanding the nature of the disease. For example, I was interested in reading about hyperglycemia, meaning high blood sugar, not to be confused with hypoglycemia, which is low blood sugar, and the damage that these two conditions can cause the body.

In my case, as a type II diabetic, my body is not responding properly to the insulin my pancreas is producing. Therefore, the glucose from the food I eat can't get into the cells effectively to nourish my body. Think of that excess glucose that can't get into the cells as minuscule balls with spikes bouncing through and damaging the blood vessels that supply blood to my vital organs. The tearing and damaging of these arteries lead to diabetic complications such as blindness and a whole host of other problems—in my case, a stroke. That tingling I was feeling in my feet from eating the peanut buster parfait was caused by overloading my system with more sugar than my body could handle and was the excess glucose damaging the arteries and nerve endings where I could feel them in my feet. In a non-diabetic, the body utilizes insulin efficiently so the glucose can enter the cells. For me, the tingling feet was a sign the permanent damage was happening. Sure, I'll just take another shot of insulin when I get home. But that will be too late. The damage will have been done.

One of the most frustrating things about a chronically underfunded and overworked public healthcare system is the waiting. It was six months since my return to Canada before I was finally able to see the neurologist. It seemed every medical appointment up to that point I was told or asked the same question, "What does neurology have to say?" Or, "We'll be able to move forward after you see the neurologist." It appeared to me that this doctor held my future. This neurologist must be some sort of a sky god. Perhaps it will be him that gives me the little colored pill that will have me back to New York. I couldn't wait to see this man.

****

I knew I didn't like this neurologist the moment I met him in his examining room. I no longer thought he was God, and it was obvious nobody ever told him he wasn't either. He reeked of attitude. He came across as condescending and arrogant, and no way was that going to work for me, especially since my patience and fuse had been drastically cut since the stroke. It didn't take much to set me off.

An Orchestrated Mistake

Only weeks earlier, I had been standing five or six people deep in a lineup at a sandwich shop when the server stopped making a sandwich to ask a customer how his weekend was. "It's fucking Wednesday!" I roared from the back of the line. My outburst even surprised me. When everyone turned to stare at me with their mouths agape, I just shrugged, mumbling, "Well, it's Wednesday. Who the hell remembers Tuesday?" I did apologize to the young man when I got up to the counter. He said no, he was sorry for chatting instead of just making the sandwiches. We both tripped over each other apologizing. It was the quintessential Canadian moment.

"What were you doing in New York?" the neurologist asked without looking up from my file.

"Working."

"What kind of work?"

"Film."

He looked up briefly, seeing me for the first time. "Tell me what happened in New York?" he asked, tossing the file on his desk. I had barely started telling him before he reached for his cellphone and started scrolling through it. My blood began to boil as I recounted that afternoon in New York. I could have been telling him a recipe for meat pies for all the interest he was paying. "Tap your left foot," he said, looking up from his phone. I awkwardly tried to tap my left foot. As usual, it was devoid of any rhythm. "The right?" he asked. My right foot moved with a little more fluidity, but not much. "Yes, you've probably had a stroke," he announced, looking back at his phone.

"My nine-year-old niece could have told me that," I said, struggling to keep my voice even. My assessment of his prognosis didn't even register on his face. "My doctor told me you'd be giving me an MRI," I continued, trying to get his attention away from his phone. "He said there's a slim chance this could be MS."

"Oh, I don't think so." He chuckled, looking up. "But, yes, we'll do an MRI."

"Can we do it now?" I asked.

"Now?" he questioned as his chuckle moved to outright laughter.

"No, no. It will be at least another few months."

"Months?"

"Yes," he said. "I don't see this as a priority."

'Don't see this as a priority?' I screamed inside. It's not he whose reality shifted in the seconds it took for the elevator doors to open. It's not he who is numb on one side of his body with a thumping left foot. Or can barely walk two blocks. Or developed a fear of stairs. It's not his thoughts that now have a stutter. It's not he tearing up over a happy image one moment and in a blind rage the next. It's not he who now feels so incomplete that he wonders if he would just be better off to leap off some bridge. He's not the one in midlife watching the sun set on his future. *'I don't see this as a priority.'* Maybe it's not to him, but I sure think about it once or twice a day! If doctors don't have anything positive to say, shouldn't they at least offer hope?

"Months?" I said again.

"Yes," he replied. "You people can't expect everything right away."

"You people?"

"Yes. You know, you show business types."

"What the hell does show business have to do with anything?" I spat.

"Well, you know…"

"No, I don't know."

"People in your business. They're always fucking getting something. You know what I mean? Look at Michael J. Fox."

I searched for any kind of smile—something to show me that he was joking. There wasn't one. "Michael J. Fox has Parkinson's. I had a stroke," I said, incredulous. "What we do, or did, has nothing to do with what happened." I searched again for a smile on his face. Nothing. My mind began stuttering in overdrive. "That's just… That's just… I don't…" Just then, his cell rang, and he, seeing who it was, raised a finger to silence me.

"I really have to take this," he said unapologetically. "It's my mechanic. I'm having my brakes done." I flopped against the back of my chair, stunned while he discussed disc brakes. I couldn't believe he was blaming show business for Michael J. Fox's and my ailments, never mind the differences between Parkinson's and a stroke.

"Okay?" he said, finally hanging up his phone.

"Yes, I guess that's it," I said, standing. In the old days, I would have had a smart-aleck comment to let this doctor know precisely how I felt, but at that moment my mind was all over the place. I just needed to get out of there, because without the words I didn't trust I wouldn't take a swing at him just to wipe away the smugness.

"My office will give you a call about the MRI," he said, opening the door for me.

An Orchestrated Mistake

No, they won't, I thought as I exited. Two doctors had dumped me, but now it was my turn to do the dumping.

There was going to be no storming out of the office or files subtly left on the receptionist's desk. There wasn't even going to be any pizza and lemonade. No, I was going to dump him the old fashion way. I was walking out and simply not coming back.

In his report to my doctor, he stated I had probably suffered a brainstem stroke and needed a change in my therapy. His comment "change in therapy" made me laugh. What therapy? Unless, of course, you want to count 'Miss Healing Hands' and practicing my signature with my niece's red crayon as therapy. As soon as I got home, I made an appointment with Roberts about seeing a new neurologist. I didn't explain or give any details. I just told him I didn't think the neurologist and I saw eye to eye.

Sometimes the greatest gift for healing a doctor can give their patient is hope. Hope that the doctor and patient will work together to make them complete again. Hope sometimes is all a patient has, and if hope is taken away, the chances of them being whole once again and moving forward are diminished. I needed to get my freedom back. I needed my life back, and I wasn't willing to give up hope that I couldn't make that happen.

Shortly after that visit to the neurologist, I got an email from Mike in New York. *Hey, Prick! It's been six months, when are you coming back? We need to make this fucking movie. Why don't you go fuck a moose or do whatever it is you Canadians call healthcare?*

I have no idea anymore when I'm returning, I wrote back. *I would try anything, but because of cuts in Canadian healthcare, fucking a moose is no longer an option. It's a shame, really, because we were going to export it as a therapy for angry screenwriters.*

Mike shot back, *Fuck you!*

An Orchestrated Mistake

CHAPTER ELEVEN

I am a *social* introvert. What I mean by that is on the surface I may sound like I've revealed a lot about myself, but in truth, I've divulged few details and instead gotten others to talk about their own life. If the conversation does come around to me, I'll only discuss events, not my personal relationship to those events. Life for me has always been about my emotional deflection.

I mentioned earlier my mother's mantra was, *Never bare your soul.* One of the side effects of this belief is I had to learn to be my own best friend. This lesson also came to me innocently enough growing up in the suburbs of Vancouver. Back then, the area was more forest and single-lane dirt roads than it was urban sprawl. There just weren't a lot of other kids to play with in those early days. But that didn't matter. I was more than content to hang out on my own with a bucket full of trucks and a pile of good dirt. Countless hours were spent pushing those trucks through the dirt while building a town called Truckton. It wasn't until I was eight years old that my first real boyhood friend, Bill, moved into the neighborhood, and Truckton got its second resident. Bill was a great pal, and we grew up together. However, by eight years old the imprint was already on my psyche—you have to enjoy your company and be your own best friend.

I've fallen back and relied on this lesson many times during the rough patches in my life, like relationship turmoil, auditions or jobs that flew south, or just anytime I felt the grey clouds of life closing in on me. I would not reach out to others for the answers or my happiness, but instead, search inward for my old friend. In my early twenties, I had a pal drop by after a long absence and ask, "Well, did you miss me?" I thought about it for a millisecond, just to give the impression that I had given it some thought before answering, "No, should I have?"

It didn't matter whether it was a friendship or an intimate affair. I have always been able to turn relationships on and off like a light switch. Relationships of any kind are simple for me. They are like any other classroom in the school of life. When the lesson is over, you shut off the lights, close the door, and move on. I think that's why so many of us struggle with family relationships. It's more difficult to close that door. Family relationships aren't of our own choosing. They're forced upon us by fate, not by a common interest in a path we mutually choose, and so there is often limited space for them to grow and develop. That crazy uncle, or the nutty sister-in-law, or just that family member who is always out on a limb—we're stuck with them forever as a part of our lives. We can shut them out if we choose, but that often creates an additional crack in an already fragile family dynamic. I believe you can revisit relationships after years or even decades, but for me, if there isn't anything to be learned I'm quickly bored, and without malice or judgment, I'm just turning off the switch, closing the door, and moving on to the next classroom.

What I found after my health crisis was that when more than ever I needed to be my own best friend, I no longer desired nor enjoyed my own company for the first time in my life. The loss of my freedom and independence left me feeling lost and isolated, and not even my daydreams about the future could bring me peace because I no longer knew what the future held. That first meeting with the neurologist had stung my ability to hope, and sometimes hope is all a patient has to cling to.

I did my best after the stroke to give the outward appearance that nothing had changed, but inside I knew things were different. I did not want to be alone with what I perceived myself to be—a broken man. A man who was not only broken, but after the visit to that neurologist, devoid of hope. I needed social interaction to distract me—not only from the torment I felt for a career I had let slip away but from a silent mind that only seemed to speak when reminding me I was damaged and empty. I could no longer live in the thoughts of my head.

An Orchestrated Mistake

I had always turned inward for answers or peace of mind, but now I needed to reach out to others. I needed others to distract me from the empty echo chamber that was banging in my head. I didn't want to talk about what had happened or the lack of substance now in my own life. I've always hated small talk, but now more than ever, I wanted and needed to hear about other's hopes and dreams. I didn't want to hear about their opinion of the weather or what they had for dinner. I wanted to hear about their travels to far-off lands and the dreams they held for tomorrow. I'm not interested in the mundane.

I only wanted the movie trailer to their life story. I wanted to see, hear, and feel the highlights of their story. Unfortunately, the effects of the stroke had me withdrawing instead of reaching out, which left me far more isolated. Far beyond the normal isolation of a social introvert.

Subconsciously, days after landing in Halifax, I knew I should be reaching out instead of withdrawing. Without the distraction of Three Walls Productions, the reality of the miracle needed for recovery began to come clear, and I began to get less comfortable within the solitude of my mind.

Soon after arriving at my dad's house in Halifax, I emailed Jan, following an email introduction from Andre. Jan had visited our office in New York to work with Andre on a project, but I had never met her, which was surprising considering I had met most of the people who came through the doors at Three Walls Productions. I wasn't eager to meet new people given my condition, but I was desperate for real social interaction, and after only days with Dad and June, I figured I needed a reprieve just as much as June probably needed one from me.

Within minutes of my email to Jan, she invited me out to her home on St. Margarette's Bay, about forty minutes outside of Halifax, to have dinner with her and her husband, Geoff.

An Orchestrated Mistake

Jan immediately greeted me with a hug when she picked me up at the rendezvous point, and on the drive to her home, she cheerfully spoke about her and Geoff's life in Nova Scotia with their six dogs and two cats. I knew Jan and Geoff were also in the entertainment industry, so I immediately thought, *This woman is far too nice to be in show business. Where's the cynical edge?* She energetically filled me in on the status of the Nova Scotia film industry, and I have to say I never felt so immediately at ease with someone—especially someone in show business. As I listened to Jan and gazed out the window at the beautiful coastline, I thought, *This woman is much too genuine to be in the film industry. It must be her husband who's the prick.*

I've never been so wrong. Geoff was just as genuine and kind as Jan, and I was instantly at ease with them both. Even though I've tried to see the glass of life as half full, I'll be the first to tell you that glass has a great big crack in it, so while outwardly I may appear warm and accepting, inside I'm very solitary and guarded, even skeptical. Given my state of mind at the time, I would have thought I'd feel that way with total strangers, but with Jan and Geoff, not so. I was totally relaxed and at ease.

It would be easy to say that I felt a kinship with them because we all worked in the same industry or because they're both wonderful storytellers, but it wasn't that. It was about the type of people they are. As they told me over dinner of the many places around the world they'd visited, the cultures and experiences came to life and I could feel the imprint that those trips had made upon them. It was their oneness with humanity that they so generously shared that drew me to them.

Geoff hails from the States, and over after-dinner coffees mused about his dad, who designed sets for the great American playwright Eugene O'Neill while he was a student at Harvard.

"Wait a minute!" I interrupted. "*The* Eugene O'Neill?"

"You know another one?" Geoff laughed.

"O'Neill, Odets, they're my heroes!"

Geoff would later tell of his father working at Paramount Studios, where he had befriended Buster Keaton, and my mind went right back to those old black and white silent movies. "Just before he passed away," Geoff said about his father, "I guess he must have been about ninety. He was up late one night watching an old black and white Claudette Colbert picture. I walked up behind him, leaned on the doorframe, and looked in on him. He looked so peaceful sitting there in his chair, covered in his blanket. As I stood there admiring him for the full life he had lived, I heard him mumble, 'That bitch still owes me twenty bucks.'"

The personal stories were shared freely that night, and the laughter flowed easily. I was a little sad when the time came for them to drive me back to my stark reality in Halifax.

"We'll have to have you out another time," Jan had said as I got out of the car.

"Sure, I'd like that," I said before turning to walk into my dad's building. Truth was, I wanted them to ask me out again. I knew the role friendships can play in the recovery of someone stricken by an illness. However, the stroke hadn't just shattered my brain. It had devastated my confidence. So, when I should have been reaching out and embracing old and new friendships, I was withdrawing.

Without others putting in an effort to reach out, I was more than content to pull back onto my private island. Like so many others, I just kept in touch with Jan and Geoff through emails— not even phone calls, just emails. It felt safer that way. Other than the calls from doctors' offices and my dad, my phone would only ring when Deirdre would call to inform me about the latest spat she had had with Jay. My old self would have cut her off if she went on some rant about her marriage, but in Halifax, I had nothing but time, so I'd let her vent until she either got bored with the topic or the battery in my cordless phone died. It was more often than not the latter. Even with today's technology, emails, Skype, etc., I was amazed how my illness had shrunk my social circle so quickly and the negative impact this was having on my already fragile psyche. Pre-stroke, I craved solitude. Now I craved social interaction as a distraction to that endless solitude. Complete withdrawal after such a health crisis was not healthy for me. Mainly because my natural default position is to pull back and observe rather than engage.

Long waits in any healthcare system can only feed into a patient's uneasiness and anxiety brought on by their malady, and I was no exception to this rule as I waited to see a new neurologist. To help me pass the time, I would take books out of the library to read on nutrition and diabetes and search online for answers to the questions the books raised. I was surprised at how engaged I was to find out how diabetes had affected me and why the stroke happened. It was also around this time I decided I needed to rehabilitate my communication and writing skills.

I began by doing something I wanted to do before I got distracted by filmmaking when I first moved to New York. I rewrote my play. It was difficult because my thought process had changed so much. The squiggly red lines *Word* uses to highlight misspelled words left my manuscript looking more bloodshot than the town drunk's eyes on a Sunday morning. It was incredibly maddening and frustrating.

It wasn't just to overcome my spelling and vocabulary deficits. As a desperate need for some kind of social interaction, most importantly as a way to scratch my creative itch, I began a blog that most of this book is based on. I would try and write in it every day and post the chapters online every few weeks. It was terribly written, filled with typos and grammatical mistakes, but I didn't care. I needed to fall before I could stand up. I'm sure my

An Orchestrated Mistake

neighbors heard me on more than one occasion scream out in frustration as I struggled with spelling a word or searched for the right word to illustrate a thought. To relearn how to write, I would have to sit in front of my computer for countless hours and bleed. I don't know which writer it was that said something like, *I write so I know who I am*—and there was never more truth to a statement than when it applied to me after the stroke. Not only were there numerous times I wanted to quit, but the truths I was finding out about myself and my life were, at times, leaving me shocked, stunned, and even hurt.

In Halifax, I decided to rewrite my play about a father and son. During press interviews years ago when it was staged, I was adamant it wasn't about my relationship with my father. Turns out I was right. It wasn't about my relationship with my father, but it was about the relationship I had with my mother. I didn't see that rogue wave coming. It became obvious to me why I didn't rewrite the play when I was in New York. If one writes to know oneself, I simply didn't know myself and wasn't ready—or probably closer to the truth, didn't want to visit the shadows that roam inside me. If we don't seek to cast a light on our shadows, life has a way of eventually doing it for us, and life's way is usually harsher than if we do it ourselves.

It took a stroke to get me to sit down and begin writing and looking at my own life. Sometimes our greatest opportunity for growth comes to us disguised as personal misfortune.

For the most part, Halifax is a university town, so there were many students in the building where I lived. There was also a happy little group of maritime curmudgeons who would sit around the table in the back parking lot drinking beer while imparting six-pack wisdom and hyperboles. This was the extent of my social circle. Pre-stroke, I would have never given this group the time of day. Outside of a few high school pals, my social circle tended to be with people in my same industry. That's where my interest was, so that was the type of people I hung out

An Orchestrated Mistake

with. How shallow and, quite frankly, boring. The stroke gave me permission to slow down and really listen to all who make up the spectrum of life.

This little group that met out back had obviously been doing this for decades. If I felt I needed a break from my books or writing or just craved a social distraction, I'd go out and sit with these characters. They were safe. There were no demands or expectations, and often I'd just sit there without saying a word. To them, I was just a CFA (Come From Away). I was 'Buddy' who had a stroke.

"I wonder what it feels like to die?" Denise, a middle-aged woman who had never mastered the art of rolling her own cigarettes, questioned. Silence ensued, and looks were exchanged all around the table. When all eyes finally settled on Bobby, the seventy-something retired postal worker shot back, "How the fuck should I know!?"

Everyone at the table got along. Well, everyone except Ken, the old superintendent, and Bill, the new super. If Ken was a toothless version of Captain Highliner, complete with his long-winded stories from his two years in the Navy, Bill was an older, fatter version of the Michelin Man. In Ken's eyes, Bill could do nothing right, and it wasn't long before Ken had dubbed Bill 'Dufus.'

"Hey, Dufus," Ken would bark across the table. "When are you going to cut the lawn? And you should cut some of those branches back on the trees while you're at it."

Ken would badger Bill relentlessly. Nothing Bill did would meet with Ken's approval. For the most part, Bill took Ken's jabs in stride, but that was because Bill was usually stoned. He had somehow convinced his doctor he needed medicinal marijuana, and so long as Bill got his pleasant puff, Ken had nothing to worry about. But if the government was ever late sending Bill his herb, look out, Ken.

Sure enough, one morning the door to the outside burst open in front of me as I was about to walk through it. Ken stumbled in, clutching his chest. "I've just been assaulted!"

"What?" I said, stepping back.

"Dufus! He attacked me! I think he's on crack or something! He assaulted me! I need the police!" Ken hollered as he staggered down the hall towards his apartment.

I stuck my head out the door and saw Bobby sitting alone at the table sipping a beer. My left leg thumped as I crossed the parking lot to Bobby. "I hear I missed the main event," I said when I got close.

"Na! Ya missed nothin'," Bobby said, taking a swig. "Couple of fat old ladies slapping each other. Kenny tripped over the bench there and ran inside."

"Where's Bill?" I asked.

"Ran in the other door squealing like a little girl."

Grudges didn't last long at the table in the back parking lot. The next day, Ken, a newly stoned Bill, and Bobby were back drinking beers, sitting around the table. Standing up after telling a particularly long-winded story of an Atlantic crossing, Ken announced he needed to go inside and get another beer.

"Am I the only one who notices that the seas get rougher with each of Kenny's crossings on that damn frigate?" Bobby said after Ken disappeared inside.

I shrugged my shoulders.

An Orchestrated Mistake

"He was a fucking purser for Christ's sakes," Bobby said, looking over at Dave, a long-since retired cop who had fallen asleep on his electric scooter. "You'd think he'd sunk the fucking Bismarck!" Bobby added as he reached into the basket on Dave's scooter to steal a beer.

I'd never spent time with such a, well, uniquely interesting group of characters before. They each had an epoch in their life that they enjoyed reliving over and over again. I wondered as I listened to Ken retelling the same Navy stories or Bobby's retelling of the time he almost threw a no-hitter as a teenager in the minor leagues if the epoch I would be reciting would be my years at Three Walls Productions. Had I, too, already lived my life's highlight reel?

Despite Ken's badgering of Bill, I quite liked Ken. He was a bit gruff and had a financially challenging life, and although you wouldn't know it if you watched him with Bill, he had a great sense of humor about himself and life. I'd often go down to Ken's apartment at night to take in a Blue Jays baseball game or some hockey game, and I enjoyed asking him questions and listening to him prattle on. The only time Ken wasn't sucking on a cigarette was when he was sleeping, and even then, I'd lay odds he was probably hooked up to some nicotine drip. It could get pretty smoky in his apartment, which could be a little hard to take at times, but it was the price I had to pay for a little social interaction.

"Do you ever think about quitting?" I asked him one night as he extinguished one cigarette and lit another.

"Yep."

"And?"

"Then I never think about it again until some clown like you brings it up." Ken got up from his chair. "I'm getting a bowl of ice cream. You want some? It's chocolate."

"You're diabetic," I said, stunned.

"So."

"So, you shouldn't be eating ice cream. Besides, you just lit a cigarette."

"I did, didn't I?" Ken said, looking at the cigarette between his fingers. "Ice cream is better this way. Think of the cigarette as the whipping cream," Ken said, flashing a toothless grin. "Sure you don't want a bowl?"

"You know I'm diabetic too," I said, watching Ken open the freezer.

"I know," he replied. "Matter of fact, you know Fern? The big woman in the apartment next to me? She's diabetic. I guess that makes our side of the building diabetic row!" Ken chuckled.

"Wait. Fern is diabetic?"

"Yup."

"But I've seen her come in many times with an open bag of chips or cookies."

"Yeah, so. Who are you, the diabetic police?"

"But I thought you said Fern was a church minister?"

"Semi-retired. But what's that got to do with it? Religious people aren't delusional like the rest of us?"

"What about Gus?" I inquired about the man living next door to me.

"Oh no. Gus is not a diabetic," Ken replied. "Gus is an alcoholic."

An Orchestrated Mistake

Interesting that Ken chose the word delusional when describing an uncontrolled diabetic. I don't know why so many of us are delusional. Perhaps it's because the consequences of our destructive behavior aren't initially felt right away. It takes time for the effects of high sugars to be felt, and high glucose levels only further exacerbate the cravings for more sugar. This can be seen clearly in the consumption of Chinese food. That old joke about being hungry a few hours after eating Chinese food is not an old wives' tale. The high rice content of Chinese food spikes your glucose levels and leaves you hungry hours later, and your pancreas works overtime to release enough insulin to bring those sugars down. High insulin levels induce hunger. We all have an Uncle Bert who retires to the couch to saw logs after gorging himself to the breaking point at the dinner table. Diabetic or not, imagine how hard Bert's pancreas is working to release enough insulin to bring his body back into balance. It's no wonder he's having a good snooze.

Our world is not the most diabetic-friendly place either. Many social occasions have food as the centerpiece, and many of our traditions require the giving and sharing of sweets. You can't say 'I love you' on Valentine's Day without a box of chocolates, and that Easter Bunny isn't laying celery sticks. Of course, let's not forget every diabetic's favorite occasion, Halloween. This one is diabetic hell. Don't think I don't fight the urge every year to throw a sheet over my head to get that pillowcase full of neighborhood candy. Christmas is another one where coffee tables around the world are laid out in chocolates, candies, and pastries. Yes, navigating through the social calendar for a diabetic is pure torture. It's akin to social waterboarding. If you manage to stay strong over a holiday, don't gloat too much because those holiday treats will be offered at half price the day after. Who amongst us isn't tempted to throw a few half-price chocolate Easter treats into our grocery basket?

An Orchestrated Mistake

Perpetual high sugars for a diabetic only lead to cravings for more sugar, and before you know it, you're popping in more snacks to satisfy those cravings, which in turn only drives the sugars up further. High sugars can cause anything from headaches to problems thinking and reasoning to memory issues and just leave you struggling to stay focused. High sugar levels will also have you feeling fatigued and exhausted, so what do you do? Eat more sugar. It's a conveyor belt of dysfunction. Looking back, I'm surprised I was able to function at Three Walls at all.

****

Fall turned into winter, and it became obvious I wasn't returning to New York anytime soon, but I was going to experience my first Canadian winter in ten years.

"What's that?" I asked Dad when he handed me a bag after dropping by my apartment.

"Crampons."

"They're spikes," I said, pulling them out of the bag.

"That's right. Clamp them onto the bottom of your boots so you don't slip and fall."

"Dad, I don't need crampons." I laughed. "It's not like I'll be hiking across the tundra."

"Nicholas, it's supposed to snow this weekend. Don't forget you're back in Canada now, and with your balance issues…"

"Dad, I used to live in Canada, remember?"

"Vancouver, not Halifax. Just use them."

I had no intentions of clamping spikes to the bottom of my boots, but to put Dad's mind at ease, I told him I would. Besides, winters in New York can be no cakewalk either, so I wasn't worried about experiencing a Canadian winter. Perhaps a little winter experience might help to get my mind off things.

As luck would have it, that weekend I saw grapefruits on sale in the little community of Spryfield, which is about a twenty-minute bus ride from Halifax. I love grapefruit, and living on a limited income, snow or no snow, I was taking the bus to Spryfield to get some grapefruits.

It was colder than I thought, and the mild snowfall on the ride out turned into a full-blown blizzard for my return as I waited at the bus stop for over an hour with my shopping bags full of grapefruit.

"I didn't think you were coming," I said to the driver as I struggled to get on when he finally arrived.

"I didn't think anyone would be dumb enough to be out here," the driver shot back.

"Well, surprise," I said, paying my fare. I was cold and in no mood to sit next to a sarcastic driver, so I made my way back towards the middle doors of the empty bus. The bus crept along through the weather, and as the only passenger, I somehow felt responsible for causing the driver to make the arduous journey. "Well, at least the storm keeps the crazies off the road," I hollered towards the front of the bus.

"What?" the driver snapped, glaring at me in his rearview mirror as if I'd just taken the last chicken wing.

"I said the storm keeps the crazies off the road."

"No." He scowled. "It's only the crazies that would be out here."

"Guess you're right," I mumbled out the window at the blowing snow.

An Orchestrated Mistake

Riding the rest of the way in silence, I pulled the bell as we neared my stop. I dragged my four bags of grapefruits towards the middle doors and waited for the bus to stop and the doors to open. I looked down at the accumulation of snow on the sidewalk and realized right away it would be risky to step off the bus with four heavy bags. "I've got four bags," I hollered up to the driver. "I'll just take two at a time. It'll take me a sec!" I grabbed two bags and had no sooner stepped off the bus than the driver began to close the doors. "Wait a minute!" I cried out, slipping on the snow but managing to stick my arm in the doors to block them from closing completely. "I have two more bags!" I yelled through the crack. After a brief moment, the doors opened and I stumbled back onto the bus. "Thanks!" I hollered sarcastically as I stepped off. But as my right foot hit the sidewalk, I lost my balance in the snow and crashed to the ground, sending grapefruits flying everywhere. One grapefruit landed just under the bus. "Wait a sec!" I hollered, scrambling to my feet. "One sec!" I yelled again, losing my footing and falling to my belly. I reached for the grapefruit under the bus at the moment the bus left the curb. "Hey!" I yelled, yanking my arm clear of the rear wheels and banging my fist on the side of the bus. The driver ignored me and drove on, revealing a flattened grapefruit on the road. I scrambled to my feet and tried to kick the grapefruit at the departing bus. "Prick!" I screamed as my right foot completely missed the flattened fruit, and I landed on my butt. "Asshole!"

I retrieved all the grapefruits, and once home, managed to stuff them all into the fridge before standing back, exhausted, but admiring the citrus treats. I took one, sat down, and began to peel it as I opened a book to a chapter I was reading on nutrition and the side effects of pharmaceutical drugs.

Grapefruits are known to interact with blood pressure medication and may cause dizziness or fainting. Eating grapefruits while on statin drugs may also cause severe leg cramps and liver or kidney damage. "Perfect," I grumbled, glaring at my fridge now full of grapefruits. Turning

An Orchestrated Mistake

my attention out the window at the blowing snow, I added, "I hate Canadian winters."

By mid-December, I was finally seated in the new neurologist's examining room. I thought if this new guy was anything like the first, I was declaring a full recovery and heading straight for the airport and back to New York.

A young intern entered, and after introducing herself, said she'd be asking me a few questions before putting me through a few physical tests. Her first question was one that I had been asked many times before: "Tell me about the event." To me, an 'event' is heading out to a concert or a Mets game—that would be an event. But, certainly not a stroke. I briefly told her what had happened, omitting the fact I smoked during the blessed event, or that, to date, my only rehabilitation consisted of practicing my signature with my nieces' red crayon and navigating the three steps on Deirdre's back porch.

During the physical test, my chest swelled with confidence when I proved my eyes could follow the tip of her pen, but that confidence disappeared when she asked me to walk heel to toe across the room. I had walked straighter lines after wrap parties. Following a battery of more tests, the intern stated she was leaving to brief the doctor and both would return in a few minutes. Even though it had been fifteen months since the stroke, I still couldn't recognize the man who had just struggled to complete a few simple physical tasks. I wanted to run after the intern and tell her that wasn't me who she just tested. I can do those tasks easily. But who was I kidding? I could not do them, and probably closer to the truth, I wasn't running after her or anyone. I couldn't run at all.

A few minutes later, the intern and neurologist returned, and he greeted me with a handshake and a warm smile. Already this new fellow was head and shoulders above the last. His demeanor of friendly confidence put me at ease, instantly filling me with a sense of optimism. He went over my test results with me, but I did bite my bottom lip when he asked me to repeat the heel-to-toe exercise.

"You really want that one, huh?" I asked, pushing myself up out of the chair.

"I'd just like to see for myself." He smiled.

No amount of concentration was going to change my drunken sailor routine, and after he told me to relax and try again for the third time, he mercifully told me, "That's okay, just have a seat." Taking a seat, my state of morosity was replaced with indignation when he asked me if I'd ever thought about using a cane. "No," was my curt reply, and he immediately dropped the subject.

He said he was going to order an MRI to determine "Exactly what has happened up there," but this time I was under no illusion that the MRI would take place that afternoon. He was troubled I had never received professional rehabilitation since the stroke and was concerned about a few near misses I had had with respect to falls. He looked me right in the eye at one point and said, "People with disabilities…" Instantly, his voice changed to that of the teacher in the *Peanuts* cartoon, and I glanced back over my left shoulder to see whom he was talking to. I looked back, realizing it was me, but I was still struggling to get my mind wrapped around those words and how they related to me when he asked, "So would you be agreeable to that?" I realized I hadn't heard a word he said since, 'disabilities.'

"Sure, of course," I absently replied, demonstrating Canadians truly will agree to just about anything just to get along.

"Good," the doctor said, writing in his notepad. "So, the occupational therapist is going to come to assess the safety of your apartment. They may want to put some grab bars in your bathtub."

"Some what?"

"Grab bars. Bars for you to hang on to while you get in and out of your bathtub."

Doctor Roberts had suggested grab bars after I developed an extremely sore right shoulder from using the shower curtain to support myself while in the tub.

"It's still really sore," I had told Roberts during one visit.

"Can you lift your arm over your head?" he asked.

"No. I don't think those drugs you gave me for the pain are working."

"I didn't give you any drugs for pain."

"No?" I questioned.

"No."

"Oh. Well, you should have."

"I suggested you get some grab bars," Roberts said.

"I don't want grab bars. Today it's grab bars, tomorrow it's orthopedic shoes. No, I'll just use my left arm to hang on." Roberts didn't think that was much of a solution, so he made an appointment for me to see an orthopedic surgeon. When I received my notice to see him and saw my appointment wasn't for a little over two years, I called right away.

"There's no mistake, sir," the secretary said. "That's the correct date."

"Two years?" I asked.

"Yes, sir."

"You do realize while I'm waiting to see the surgeon if I apply myself, I mean really apply myself, I could attend medical school, graduate, and perform the surgery on my shoulder myself." I waited for her to answer, thinking she might offer up a better solution.

"Sir, does that mean you want to be taken off the waiting list?"

Shortly after the call, I found there are two lists: a waiting list and a cancelation list. I called up again and got on the cancelation list, and two days later I was in seeing the surgeon. It didn't really matter because the surgeon told me after a cat scan there was a small tear, and what my shoulder needed was rest. I still wasn't big on getting those grab bars. I did trust this new neurologist, and if the occupational therapist said I needed grab bars, I'd get them. But I was going to draw the line at orthopedic shoes.

"You'll also be hearing from the physiotherapy department at the rehab center," the neurologist said. "They'll be able to fully assess you and offer special treatment. They may suggest the use of a cane," he added, looking up from his pad.

"They can suggest all they want," I replied.

"You'll be hearing from the Cardiovascular Hearts in Motion Program. I'm glad you agreed to that. It's a twelve-week program focusing on diet and exercise. It will help you build some positive habits."

"Oh," I said. Not realizing when I had said I agree, I had agreed to so much.

"We'll get you in a driver's program to get your license reinstated."

"I never lost my license."

"You could end up with some insurance issues because of the stroke, so it's a good idea that you do this."

"Fine."

"Hey, I know this sounds like a lot," the neurologist said, picking up on my tone. "But this is all going to help you get back to contributing to society. I assume you want to get back to being a contributing member of society?"

"Sometimes I wonder how much I ever contributed," I lamented.

"We'll just stick to the post-stroke issues." The neurologist smiled. "We don't know yet to what extent the brain can rewire itself after an injury. There's a chance that you will make a full recovery. We just won't know until you get the professional help that you need."

In the months after the stroke, I had dreamt many times about being able to run again, about being whole and returning to New York and my entertainment career. What this neurologist restored in me was that this was, in fact, possible. It wasn't just a dream to be interrupted by the morning sun. He couldn't guarantee I would be whole again, but he gave me the one thing a doctor can always give. Hope. That's what he gave me. No promises, just hope. Perhaps if I worked hard and believed in myself and remained faithful to that hope, one day I would once again run against the light across 6th Avenue.

CHAPTER TWELVE

Not only had I completely transposed the digits of the phone number, I had also written down the wrong name before I erased the message from the ophthalmologist on my answering service. After several hours on the Internet tracking down the correct doctor and explaining to the receptionist, she quipped, "Perhaps it's not your eyes that need testing, but you're ears."

"Perhaps you should stick to the details about my appointment," I bit back.

"Perhaps that would be wasting time for the both of us. Perhaps I'll just mail them to you."

The sarcastic receptionist had a point. I'd be less likely to screw up an appointment with a confirmation letter in my hand, but it was annoying to have that pointed out.

I had never had a problem remembering numbers, names, or even useless information—I remembered it all. I had, and enjoyed, a photographic memory I employed not only in my acting days when studying scripts, but often used it to memorize routes and drop-off locations back in my undercover agent days. I have never been an attention to detail kind of guy, always instead focusing on the big picture, but the photographic memory served me well with the small details. I never forgot a line on stage, but if for some reason my concentration waned and I did trip up, my mind would instantly locate the words on the page in the script before I had missed a beat.

In my early years at Three Walls my memory was solid, but after years of high sugars and perhaps a year or so before the stroke, I definitely noticed memory and concentration issues. Looking back, at least several years before the stroke I was feeling the accumulated effects of diabetes, but I had become so adept at living and compensating for them I simply pushed them aside.

An Orchestrated Mistake

Taking a phone message for Laura one time, I didn't write the number down, and being called away before I was able to email her the message, I incorrectly typed out the last number when I finally sent her the message from memory a few minutes later. I didn't know then my struggles were due to high sugars, but there was no doubt my visual-spatial processing was severely impaired after the stroke.

"When was the last time you had your eyes thoroughly examined?" the ophthalmologist in Halifax asked when I finally got in to see him. "And I don't mean just by a regular optometrist, but an ophthalmologist," he added.

"I don't know. Must have been back in New York, I guess." I lied. In truth, I had never seen an ophthalmologist. For that matter, I wasn't even sure what an ophthalmologist was until I spoke to his cheeky receptionist.

"You guess?" he questioned with a raised eyebrow.

"Yeah."

"Did they tell you that the diabetes is damaging your eyes? That there are some significant signs of retinopathy?"

"I don't remember." I shrugged.

"You are diabetic?" he asked with the tone of his sarcastic receptionist.

"Yes, of course."

"That wasn't a question," he said, glaring over his reading glasses.

"Oh."

"How are your sugars?" he asked.

An Orchestrated Mistake

My sugars were still at least two to three times as high as what they should have been. As long as the foundation of my diet continued, eating like a child whose parents aren't home by eating food out of a box, controlling them would remain a huge struggle. "Better." I lied again. He waited for me to elaborate, but when I didn't, he twirled his hand in the air, encouraging me to continue. "Better than in New York," I added.

He dropped his pen, holding his head with both hands. "Look," he said, finally looking up. "The eyes reveal what diabetes is doing to the arteries of your internal organs, and in your case, it doesn't look good. There are significant signs of retinopathy in your eyes. In other words, there is significant damage done to the small blood vessels in your eyes, and you're going to need laser surgery to correct it."

"Okay." I shrugged.

"No, it's not okay. There's only so much we can do with laser surgery, and only so many times we can do it."

"Okay." I nodded again.

"I'm saying if you don't get a handle on your diabetes, there is no question you're going to lose your eyesight. Understand?"

"Yes." I nodded, suppressing the urge to call him an alarmist. He continued his lecture on the perils of diabetes, and I could tell from his tone he was exhausted to have to deal with patients like me. I can't blame him. It must be depressing and frustrating for doctors to see patient after patient who will not lift a finger to help themselves. How defeating it would be to go to work every day and have ninety percent of your sage advice completely ignored. It's a shame that for so many of us, short of a disastrous event, fear has to be the primary motivator for healthy change.

When he finished his rant, he told me I needed to see his receptionist to make an appointment for a further eye evaluation at the hospital. "Maybe you should just mail me those details," I said to her after setting up the appointment.

"Oh, I intend to," Miss Sarcasm replied. "In triplicate."

I wasn't experiencing any dramatic changes to my vision from the retinopathy, but from my own readings and research, there was little doubt I was feeling the effects of peripheral neuropathy. One of the results of this condition is the damage to the peripheral nerves, often in your feet or your hands. This condition can result from traumatic injuries or infections—and a host of other problems—but in my case, it was caused by uncontrolled diabetes.

I was experiencing nerve damage in the form of numbness in my feet, and after the ophthalmologist's report, Dr. Roberts felt I should go for a nerve function test to determine the level of damage. The test is performed by shooting an electric current through the affected area to determine the level of nerve damage. In my case, the feet.

"Hmmm," the technician conducting the test mumbled, taking the electric cattle-prod device away from my lower leg.

"What does 'hmmm' mean?" I asked.

"I just shot enough volts through you that should've had you clinging to the ceiling."

"Hmmm," I agreed.

"You really didn't feel that?" he asked.

"Not really," I said, adjusting my hospital robe.

"Let's try the other leg," he said, putting the prod against my other lower ankle. "You feel that?" he asked, turning up the device.

"Maybe a faint tingle."

"This is not good," he lamented. "You want me to touch your arm with this so you can feel the volts I just shot through you?"

"Not really," I replied, shaking my head. "JESUS FUCK!" I yelled, bolting upright when he touched the prod to my arm.

"Yes, exactly," he exclaimed.

"I said, 'No,'" I snapped, rubbing my arm.

"I'm sorry, but I just wanted to give you an idea of the level of damage we're looking at here."

"I don't need an idea. I get it. I'm the perfect spy. I'll never give up information as long as they only torture below the knees."

"That's one way of looking at it."

"Well, this mission is over," I said, getting up off the table.

I'd had numbness in my feet for several years, even before the stroke, but if the stroke hadn't shown me the writing on the wall, this little experiment put an exclamation point on the damage caused by diabetes.

The more I read about diabetes and the more I wrote in my blog, the more confounded I was about how I had developed this disease. There is a genetic component to the disease, but carrying the gene does not mean you're destined to develop type II diabetes. What it does mean is you may have a predisposition to developing the disease if you play into it with your lifestyle of poor eating habits. At the time of my diagnosis, I have to admit I was leading a pretty sedentary lifestyle. The most exercise I was getting was opening and walking through the door at a fast-food joint. Long gone were the teenage years of ice and grass hockey. I wasn't overweight or any more sedentary than the next guy, and my mother had clearly stated diabetes wasn't in the family, so why did I develop this disease seemingly out of thin air? There had to be a reason, and the answer came from a rare phone call I received from my cousin Michael in Australia.

Michael's father and stepmother raised him and his twin brother, Anthony, following his father's divorce from my mother's sister, Aunt Vivian. Michael's reunification with his mother after a thirty-five-year global search is a sad tale and a book unto itself, but until that phone call in Halifax, I had only spoken with him once, shortly after he located his mother.

The call wasn't completely unexpected. Deirdre had told me Michael had called her recently in New York, and when she told him I'd had a stroke, he asked for my number. While I may have expected his call, what was unexpected was the amount of maternal family knowledge Michael had gleaned during his thirty-five-year search for his mother. We joked about how secretive our mothers were, and eventually the conversation came around to me, diabetes, and the stroke.

"Well, Nicholas," Michael said in his Australian drawl, "diabetes is not something you can ignore. You can't just put your head in the sand and it goes away."

"I know, Michael. But I just don't get how I developed it. I mean, I wasn't fat when I was diagnosed. Alright, so I wasn't the most active person, and most of my food was coming out of a factory, but there are people who treat themselves far worse than I ever did."

"Nicholas, Nicholas. Listen, mate, you know diabetes runs in our family."

"That's what I don't get. It doesn't."

"Nicholas, Nicholas," Michael said, laughing, "you know our grandmother had diabetes?"

"What?"

"Yes, mate. She had it in the worst way. She got terribly sick because of diabetes. So sick she had to come live with us when Anthony and I were very young. My father and stepmother nursed her back to health. Nanny, as you called her, almost died!"

"You're kidding," I said, stunned.

"No."

"From diabetes?"

"Yes! Her kidneys were failing. My father took her in, and they nursed her back to health. You didn't know that?"

"No."

"Diabetes got her in the end."

"I know she died of a heart attack," I said, still reeling from the shock of Michael's information.

"Diabetes, mate! Cardiovascular disease. She had it for years."

"Jesus."

"Killed our grandmother, mate. So, it does run in our family in a big way. My mother and your mother both knew it, so I don't know why they didn't tell you. You've been a diabetic bomb waiting for the right environmental conditions to detonate. You carry the gene, mate. I'm sure I probably do too."

"You have it too?"

"Luckily, no. But I've been aware it runs in the family and have done my best to stay active. At one time, I was also a male nurse, so I've seen firsthand what kind of damage it can do. I don't know why you weren't aware of this."

An Orchestrated Mistake

"I don't either."

I was gutted when I got off the phone with Michael. Not just because I'd found out my grandmother had died from complications brought on by diabetes, but also because it asked the bigger question: Why hadn't my mother told me? I thought I might know the answer to that, but my mother had died over a decade before from leukemia, so there was no way to ask her. I thought about calling Aunt Vivian out in Vancouver, but she was having her own battles with leukemia at the time, and I knew my conversation with Michael about the family would upset her. It really didn't matter anymore anyway. If I knew I had a predisposition to developing diabetes, would I have made the lifestyle changes to prevent the disease from taking hold? Probably not. I think I knew why my mother neglected to tell me, but it was what Michael revealed to me in his second phone call months later that prompted me to pick up the phone and call Vivian.

****

Temperatures plummeted, the snow flew, and my first Canadian winter in ten years had the country in its usual chokehold. Despite the weather, the occupational therapist came over to assess my apartment. Once again, I had no idea what an occupational therapist actually did, but I told myself for once I needed to agree and cooperate if I was going to stand a Canadian snowball's chance in hell at a return to my old life.

"There's really nothing to assess," I told Carol, the occupational therapist, when she arrived at my apartment door. "I'm not kidding," I continued, standing back to let her enter. "I mean, I can vacuum my whole place without changing plugs. I just turn it on and off and I'm done."

"I'd still like to assess your living environment if you don't mind," Carol replied.

An Orchestrated Mistake

Besides my dad, the only visitor I had in my apartment was ol' Ken from down the hall, and even then, he only stood at the door while I rummaged through my junk drawer searching for stolen ketchup packets to give him.

Reading from a file in her hand, Carol asked, "So you're having problems picking things up off the floor?"

"Sometimes." I shrugged. I decided not to tell her about the orange that had rolled and been living under my bed for the last two days. "It's a balance thing," I said. "Bending over to pick things up can be a little tricky."

"There was some mention you are having problems standing in the shower," Carol said, poking her head in my bathroom. "I'd like to see you get in and out of the bathtub if I may?"

"You're joking?"

"Please."

I walked into the bathroom, pulled the shower curtain back, and stepped into the tub. "Do you hold on to anything while you're lathering up?" she asked. I reached up with my left hand and held on to the curtain rod. "That's it?" Carol questioned with an incredulous tone.

"Yeah. Well, I used to hold on with my right hand, but I tore my right shoulder."

"That's not going to hold your weight if you slip. You're going to need grab bars."

Carol helped me out of the tub, and we took a seat at my kitchen table while she continued her questioning. "So, what you're telling me is you have problems with your buttons?" she asked.

"Yes. No. I mean sometimes. Well, I mean, who doesn't have problems with their buttons?"

Carol suppressed a frown, pulled out a catalogue, and flipping the pages, stopped and turned the catalogue around for me to see.

"I can order you a buttoner if you like. It's easy to use and will help you button your shirts."

"No."

"Well, if you're having problems…"

"I'm not." Carol raised an eyebrow. "Well, just sometimes, and it's only because I don't have much feeling in my left hand," I said. "I only have problems when I'm in a hurry."

"Let me order one for you."

"No! I mean, no, thank you." Carol almost looked hurt. I knew she was just trying to be helpful. "Look, there's no need for me to be in a hurry in my life anymore," I said. "And besides, I'm more of a t-shirt and jeans kind of guy anyway."

"Okay, fine," Carol relented. "I noticed you don't wear a diabetic identifier, like a bracelet or necklace."

"More of a fashion choice, really," I said.

"Oh."

"But I did wear an earring when I was younger." Carol looked at me, confused. "Just one," I added. "I was never cool enough to wear two."

"I'm going to leave you this medic-alert brochure. You should really consider an identifier."

"Fine. I'll consider it."

"I also noticed your gait when you walked back from the bathroom. Have you thought about a walking stick?"

"What?" I asked, snapping up my head from the brochure.

"A walking stick. A cane."

"I don't need a cane!" I said with more venom than I intended.

"Okay. It's just a suggestion, that's all. It could make it easier for you to get around."

"Look, you're right about the grab bars. You're probably even right about the bracelet, but I definitely don't need a cane."

Carol mercifully dropped the subject of the cane, but when she returned the next day with the grab bars, she dropped a duffle bag on my floor with half a dozen colored aluminum canes inside. "I know you don't want one, but I brought a few for you to try just in case. I'll fix the grab bars on your tub. Why don't you try a few canes while I do?"

Carol disappeared into the bathroom while I just sat there staring down at the open duffle bag full of canes. When she came out, she saw that I hadn't touched them. "I really think you could benefit by using a cane," Carol suggested. "Look," she continued, taking a cane out of the bag, "this one comes with an extendable ice pick for those icy sidewalks."

"I'm sure you'll find another Canadian who will find that very useful," I said. Carol looked a little flustered. "Look, Carol, I appreciate and get what you're trying to do, and I thank you. I'm sure I'll even learn to appreciate the grab bars, but I don't need a cane. I start rehab at the Hearts in Motion Program in a few days, and let's just see how I make out there."

An Orchestrated Mistake

"I understand." Carol nodded. "There is one more thing I think you should check out. There's a screening of the movie *The Diving Bell and the Butterfly* at the Queen-E-II Hospital tomorrow night, followed by a discussion. I think you should go. You know the movie?"

"Actually, I do," I said. Laura and the rest of the gang at Three Walls had driven up to the Woodstock Film Festival in Upstate New York and had come back raving about the film just before I had my stroke. "It's about a guy who had a stroke and can only communicate through blinking," I said.

"That's right," Carol agreed. "I think you could get a lot out of the evening. I think you should go."

"Sounds like a perky evening." Carol looked almost hurt by my remark. "I'll go."

"You will?" Carol almost squealed.

"Who wouldn't want to see a movie about a stroke? Especially when you've had one."

I did go the next night, not so much because I was interested in seeing a film about a guy who had a stroke, but because the old gang at Three Walls had raved so highly about it. Of course, little did I know back then that the film's subject matter would end up directly relating to my life.

After watching the movie, I wasn't surprised I enjoyed the film but was surprised there was so much humor in a film that dealt with such a dark subject. Who knew a film about a stroke could almost seem like a comedy?

My neurologist headed the panel discussion afterward, and when he began recounting a stroke patient who would always cry at happy things, I sat up. "You know that TV commercial?" he said into the microphone. "The one where the fluffy white kittens are coming down the stairs beside a roll of toilet paper? Well, every time this patient saw this commercial, he burst into tears and the nurses would have to run into his room and change the channel."

"My God! I do that," I mumbled. The elderly lady sitting next to me looked over. "Well, not with kittens," I shot back after I caught her glare out of the corner of my eye. "But I cry at happy." The lady looked at me uneasily. "Well, I don't mean I bawl," I said. "I just tear," I mumbled, turning back to the stage.

"It's called emotional labile," my neurologist went on to explain. "It can be brought on by a significant brain injury, such as a stroke."

"That's it then! That's what I have!" I said, turning to the elderly lady again. "I'm not losing my mind!"

Weeks later, when I had an appointment with my neurologist, I told him about the revelation his discussion had provided. He told me about another stroke patient of his who laughed uncontrollably at sad things. "She was actually attending a friend's funeral and had to be escorted from the church because she was laughing so hard."

It's not just uncontrollable laughing or crying that happens with this condition, but also incredible mood swings can take place in the patient. I definitely had mood swings. That little incident in the sandwich shop was proof of that, but on the bright side, the neurologist told me the effects of the labile should begin to lessen over time. Of course, if they don't, some form of therapy or treatment may be necessary. I already felt my mood swings had dissipated dramatically in the last few months, although my sporadic ability to articulate my thoughts did seem to keep my temperament on a constant simmer.

An Orchestrated Mistake

Carol's final report to Doctor Roberts stated: *Nicholas has difficulty with bathtub transfers and functional mobility, especially outside. I'm hopeful that this will improve with his enrollment in rehabilitation. He also has decreased engagement in meaningful activities, but I'm also hopeful rehab will correct this. We discussed the benefits of using a cane, but given his feelings about the stigma of a cane, this is not an option at this time.*

Rightly or wrongly, the acceptance of a cane at that point in time, before I had even begun any form of rehab, would be an admission of failure. Fear and doubt already permeated my psyche. Not only because I was fearful that the programs would not help put me back together, but because I didn't trust myself to give the one-hundred-ten-percent that would be needed in order to succeed. I'd let myself down one too many times.

****

"What did you say your wife's name was?" the elder woman seated directly in front of me turned around and yelled.

"Excuse me?" I said, looking up from the handout I was given when I entered the Hearts in Motion room at the Dartmouth Sports Center.

"Your wife's name!" she said, exasperated. "What did you say her name was?"

I looked around, thinking she must be talking to someone else, but then I wondered why she was staring straight at me. Or maybe more to the point, why was she yelling? "Are you asking me?" I asked, mesmerized by her hair that was such a bright burgundy and coiffed so tightly it looked more like a hockey helmet.

"Yes! What did you say her name was?"

"I didn't."

An Orchestrated Mistake

"I thought you told me her name."

"No. I just sat down. I never said anything."

"Oh, I wasn't talking to you?"

"No."

"Oh! I must have mistaken you for someone else."

I looked around the room at all the Hearts in Motion Program members and wondered who she mistook me for. They all looked like they had first-hand knowledge of the Great Depression. Also, everyone in that large classroom looked to me like aging movie stars. There was Mickey Rooney sitting in the corner talking to Phyllis Diller. Ernest Borgnine, whose eyebrows joined his hairline, was talking to Estelle Getty while the other Golden Girls talked among themselves. It literally was a who's who of the golden years of Hollywood.

"Yes. I thought you looked like someone else," the elderly woman said, who looked like a badly aging Audrey Meadows. Taking in the room, I wanted to ask her who she thought I looked like, but she had already turned around and was explaining her morning gas to Minnie Pearl.

There were three components to the program, each with its own practitioner. There was the nurse who monitored our overall health, a physiotherapist who was in charge of the exercise portion, and a dietician who monitored our dietary habits. That first day was just a meeting with each practitioner to determine which areas we needed to work on for improvement. Safe to say, I needed to work on all three.

"Do you always have cookies for a snack?" the dietician asked without looking up from my food chart.

"Sometimes," I said. "I mean, I used to love grapefruit, but yeah, I've always loved cookies."

"I see that. Your meals aren't really balanced, so we'll need to improve that. But I see that one day you did have chicken, potatoes, and peas for dinner, not bad."

"Yeah, not bad," I said smugly, thankful I'd had the brainstorm to list everything separately that was in that TV dinner.

She weighed and measured me, and at close to one hundred and eighty pounds and a thirty-nine waist, she asked me if I thought I could lose a few pounds. "I suppose," I reluctantly agreed, and she began developing a weekly meal plan that was sadly devoid of cookies.

I didn't fare much better with the physiotherapist when she asked me what physical activities I participated in. "I wouldn't use the word 'participate' when describing my activities," I told her.

"But I do amble a few blocks to the grocery store a couple of times a week."

"Amble," Janet, the physiotherapist, wrote down in my chart. "Low intensity." I wanted to tell her my intensity increases if I'm going for cookies but figured why raise expectations. Janet asked me if I'd have any problems exercising for about an hour per session on treadmills, bikes, and lifting weights.

"Not a problem," I said. "I don't think I'll have any issues."

Janet raised an eyebrow.

"I think we're going to need to increase your insulin," the nurse said when I sat down in front of her. This was disappointing but not surprising, given my weight had shot up and I didn't have a handle of any kind on my diet. "I'd like you to check back in with the diabetes clinic," the nurse said. "And how long have you had that cough?"

"Not sure. Since New York anyhow."

"Before the stroke?" she asked.

"Yes. I'm on a waiting list to see a pulmonary specialist."

"I'd like you to bring it up again with your doctor. Let me ask you," she said, tapping her pen on the desk. "Do you think you'll be able to handle this program?" I looked at the desk, and when I didn't answer right away, she continued, "I'm just asking, but has anybody spoken to you about the use of a cane?"

"Yes! And I don't need one!"

Pam, the nurse, raised her hands in self-defense. "Okay. I was just asking."

I could tell she didn't believe me, but I immediately started tripping over my words, trying to explain I had been through this with the occupational therapist, so she just dropped it. "Do you have shortness of breath?" she asked after a moment.

I nodded. "Sometimes."

"When?" she asked.

"Walking to the store. Sometimes just making my bed or a sandwich," I said, looking down at the floor. "But only sometimes," I added, looking up.

"Next time you see your doctor, I want you to bring up again your shortness of breath and this cough. Also, talk to them at the diabetes clinic about increasing your medication. This is just a reminder. You can pass it to them," she said, handing me a slip of paper. *Get SOB making a sandwich* was written at the bottom of the page.

An Orchestrated Mistake

"Get SOB?" I said, looking up.

"Shortness of breath," she replied.

"Right. Don't know what I was thinking."

We were all sent to change into our workout clothes to get ready for our first physio session. Days earlier, my dad had given me a pair of white plastic sneakers when I told him I needed to buy a pair. "Have these," he said, retrieving them from his hall closet. "You can have them. I've never worn them."

"I can see why," I mumbled, picking them up. It's not like I had the money to go out and buy new sneakers, so I took the shoes, but my dad seemed a little too eager to get rid of them.

When I came out of the changing room at the sports center, I looked at all the old Hollywood stars in their latest fashionable workout attire. Borgnine wore high-end trainers like he was expecting to run a marathon, and Phyllis Diller wore a jogging suit with color-coordinated shoes and matching headband. Even Mickey Rooney's sweatshirt matched his track pants. I looked down at my sad outfit, which consisted of a Mets t-shirt that now groaned as it stretched to cover my girth, a pair of old grey track pants that were cut off below the knee and often doubled as my pajamas, and then, of course, those damn white shoes.

Janet had us all stand in a circle while she put the Sister Sledge song "We Are Family" on the stereo. "All right, march on the spot!" Janet yelled over the music. "All right, use your arms! Punch the air in front of you!" As I was marching and punching, I realized I was now in one of those groups that I saw at the local community center as a kid and thought, *Please, God, don't ever let my life come to that!*

As I punched and marched, I looked across the circle at Estelle Getty, who was thoroughly enjoying herself doing a little two-step number to the music. I looked closer and did a double-take at what I saw. Estelle Getty was wearing my shoes! Now I knew why my dad was so eager to give them away! I was wearing old lady shoes! I looked beside me, and the sight of Borgnine marching and punching the air made me smirk, but I chuckled when Ernest looked over to me, raised those eyebrows into his hairline, and said, "I really feel like an asshole!"

I shook my head. "You have no idea!"

There are a bunch of old magazines on a table in the waiting area at the rehabilitation center, and as I waited for the physiotherapist to come out, I picked up the one that had a picture of the lead actress of one of Three Walls' films on the cover. I flipped through the magazine to the article about the actress's nomination for an Academy Award. Reading the article transported me back to the pre-production of the film in our busy New York office. But that was life then. Now the grey walls of the rehabilitation center in Halifax surrounded me. I tossed the magazine back on the table but couldn't stand the sight of the actress staring back up at me, reminding me about the life that could have been. I picked up some other old magazines and tossed them on top of her.

"Nicholas Alexander?"

"Yeah," I said, turning in the chair to face the voice.

"Busy?" the young woman said, nodding towards the magazines.

"Yeah. No. No," I said as I tossed the last magazine on the pile.

"Good. I'm Lori, your physiotherapist," she said, smiling.

Lori told me she had read my file and suggested we walk and talk as we made our way to the rehabilitation gymnasium. I was there for physical rehabilitation, and Lori was my physiotherapist, so why was I walking so slowly to control the slapping of my left foot? Lori's powers of observation penetrated my smokescreen of small talk.

"You're from Halifax?" I asked her, increasing the volume of my voice to cover the thumping on the tile floor.

"Cape Breton, actually. I went to university here in Halifax, but my family is from Cape Breton."

"So, you graduated…yesterday?"

"Who said I graduated?" Lori smirked.

Lori opened the doors to the gymnasium. "So, this is the gym and much of the equipment we'll be using," she said, ushering me inside.

The gym had about a dozen patients in various stages of repair. A wheelchair sat empty, its older occupant laying on a table as a therapist gently rolled her legs from side to side. A young man dragged his legs slowly between two parallel bars as an attendant walked beside him. A grey light lit the gym that was obviously haunted by exhausted dreams and smelled of burnt hope. I couldn't imagine spending two minutes in there, never mind twelve weeks. I wanted to run from the room, telling Lori there had been some terrible mistake, that I didn't belong, but I could neither run nor utter the words of such a gross lie. I swallowed hard at the realization that I needed this room. I needed Lori if I wanted my freedom again.

Lori sat on a bench and told me to take a seat beside her. "So why are you here today?" she asked after I sat down.

"Halifax? It's close to New York."

"Not Halifax. Here, in rehab. Why are you here?"

"Not sure. My doctors told me I need help and thought I should come here."

"And you don't think you need help?"

I looked over and saw the strain on an elderly woman's face as she fought to turn over on a therapy table. Her face contorted with the agony of the struggle, and when she was about to give up, a therapist reached out to help her.

"I don't know," I uttered almost inaudibly, looking back at Lori. "I really don't know how I've ended up here."

"You've had a stroke," Lori said, checking off points on her fingers. "You've never been hospitalized or had any kind of therapy. From what I've read and what I can see, you've never done anything to help yourself with recovery, and you're still not sure if you belong here?"

"Well, when you put it like that, you make it sound like I need a psychiatrist more than a physiotherapist."

"You think?" Lori asked rhetorically. I shrugged. "I can help you," Lori said. "I can't guarantee that you're going to be as good as new, but you'll be back together. However, you're going to have to do something for me first." I looked at her. "I need you to check your ego at the front door. Look around," Lori added, "there's no room in here for an ego."

I looked around the room as a young boy of about nineteen inched his way into the room with the help of an attendant and two canes. I watched his painfully slow progress, and looking back at Lori, I nodded.

Lori put me through a battery of assessment tests in the next hour, most of which measured my balance and coordination and the level of assistance I required to complete each task.

An Orchestrated Mistake

"Wait! Wait!" I told her before she dropped a chalk brush on the floor in front of me for the third time. "I can do this without using the wall for support," I said. Lori dropped the brush, and I bent over to pick it up but lost my balance and fell against the wall. "I wasn't ready," I said. "Drop it again."

"You weren't ready to bend over?" Lori asked sarcastically.

"Yeah," I replied. "I mean, I was ready, but I'm not used to picking things up. Now, if you had asked me to drop the brush, I would have aced it!"

Next, Lori had me walk as quickly as I could to pick up the chalk brush that she had placed twenty feet away and return to the starting line.

"It's hard," I said after an attempt that seemed to take forever. "And I can hear you clicking the stopwatch. Maybe I'd be faster if you didn't click that thing."

Lori stared at me with her head cocked to one side before dropping the stopwatch in her pocket. "Okay. Happy? Now do it again. Ready? Go."

Waddling like a duck, I moved as fast as I could to the brush and back the twenty paces to the starting line. "See!" I said proudly.

"I'm much faster without you timing me."

"You forgot to pick up the brush," Lori said, looking like my first-grade teacher.

"Try just standing on one leg," Lori told me after we had moved on. I tried several times, but I couldn't do it without leaning on the wall. "Who stands on one leg anyway?" I snapped in frustration.

An Orchestrated Mistake

Standing at the top of a flight of stairs, Lori asked me if I could go down without using the railing. Looking down the stairs threw my balance off, and I could only make it down to the landing by holding on to the railing with two hands. "Can you come back up without using the railing?" Lori yelled down to me.

"No," I said without even trying.

Lori took a seat beside me on the bench with her clipboard when all the tests were over. "The first balance test wasn't bad," she said after several minutes. "You scored forty-seven out of fifty-six. That's acceptable. The next CBM test didn't go quite as well. Thirty-six out of ninety-six. In the last test, you traveled 450 meters around the third floor in the time I gave you."

"What does that mean?" I asked. Lori smiled. "Well?" I asked again.

"Six-hundred meters is considered marginal in order to function independently in society." Sensing my slipping mood, Lori added, "It's going to improve. That's why we're here, to make things better."

"Sure."

"Nicholas, have you ever given any thought to using a cane?" My glare switched from the floor to Lori. "All right! All right!" Lori surrendered. "I needed to ask."

I had promised Lori I wouldn't bring my ego into the rehabilitation gymnasium, but my ego would not permit me to bring a cane into my life. The more it was suggested, the more I used it as motivation to win back my freedom. I told Lori about my right shoulder and the problems it was giving me.

"Have you tried acupuncture?" she asked.

"Not for my shoulder. You can do acupuncture?"

An Orchestrated Mistake

"I poke around a little, but I eventually hit a nerve," Lori said, smiling. "Look, you're on my team now," Lori added. "And my team doesn't lose. You commit to me in this program, and I'll do everything I can to get you to use those stairs without the railing…or a cane."

I wasn't sure I believed Lori, but I had to. I had learned to compensate for my limitations, but there was no way I was just going to phone-in the next twelve weeks. Especially when I had such a committed and passionate person like Lori helping me.

Before I left, Lori had me fill out a questionnaire asking about my physical challenges and what I felt I needed to work on. All the questions were pretty standard, but at the end I came across a question that made me pause before I answered. 'What are your expectations from physiotherapy?' it asked. I was afraid I wouldn't be able to live up to my or anyone else's expectations, and that scared the hell out of me. Failure terrified me. I chewed on the end of the pen for a moment and then wrote down, 'Miracles.'

An Orchestrated Mistake

CHAPTER THIRTEEN

I've always loved big cities. It's not that I don't enjoy the country, I do, for about half the weekend—unless I'm asked to help out in the garden, then I just want to get the hell out. Growing up south of Vancouver is about as rural as I ever wanted life to get, but as soon as I could, even back then, I ran to reside in the city. I love the anonymity a big city provides along with an abundance of character studies. For me, the city is an enlightening classroom.

I guess Halifax technically is considered a city, but in contrast to New York, or even Vancouver, I've always considered Halifax a big village—a nice village, but nevertheless, a village.

Waiting one day five cars deep at a traffic light, my dad announced with disgust, "Aww Christ! Bloody rush hour!" I glanced over at him, stunned, and his only retort was to point to the cars in front and exclaim, "Well!" I was used to busy traffic, jammed subways and buses, but I never really gave it much thought. It was just the price to pay to live in a large city.

"Dad, we're five cars deep at a traffic light. The delay to our lives will be maybe five or six seconds at most."

"I'm damn near eighty." Dad smirked. "I don't have six seconds."

The craziest commute I ever had was probably driving home to Brooklyn from Manhattan during the blackout of 2003. What would typically take about an hour, whether by subway or car, took me a little over nine hours after I commandeered a production vehicle from our Manhattan office. I even managed to tag on to the back of a VIP motorcade heading down 7th Avenue for several blocks before being sternly waved out by a trailing motorcycle cop. The blackout was one of the more amazing times I ever experienced in New York.

An Orchestrated Mistake

Arriving home well past midnight on that warm August evening, my Brooklyn neighborhood was alive in a festive atmosphere. Kerosene lanterns dotted the streets, and the children ran around with flashlights. Neighbors sat out in chairs swapping stories as the smell of spices from Middle Eastern cuisines cooked only hours before on barbeques saturated the air. I had never seen my Brooklyn neighborhood so alive. I sat on my front stoop smoking a cigarette listening to the sounds and laughter that seemed to rise up so effortlessly between my predominantly Jewish, Arab, and Russian neighbors.

The next day, with the power still out, the carnival atmosphere continued. Mrs. Chen, my landlord's wife, knocked on my door mid-morning to bring me some homemade Asian soup she had made out back on their barbeque. I thanked her, ate the soup, and decided to go out. I hadn't walked outside ten feet before a Lebanese neighbor who I only knew by sight waved me over to share in his wife's tabouli.

"Have kabob too! I make," the smiling neighbor said in his thick Lebanese accent. "You like falafel? He make," he said, pointing to his next-door neighbor. He spoke to his neighbor in Arabic and said what I can only assume was, "Bring this skinny white boy some food!" because moments later, a falafel dripping in tahini sauce was in my hand. I sat with them for a while, mostly nodding and smiling, as their stories vacillated between Arabic and broken English. When I had barely managed to force down my third kabob, I knew I had to make a polite retreat.

After thanking my hosts, I had progressed not more than two houses down the street before a young man called out to me, "Hey! We have cold drinks! Come! Come!"

"I'm fine, thanks!" I waved, but my answer didn't satisfy the young man, who came running towards me, opening up a cold beer.

An Orchestrated Mistake

"Join us!" he said, thrusting the beer in my hand.

"No, really, I'm just walking to the store to get some cigarettes," I said, trying to hand the beer back to him.

"We have cigarettes! Come!"

Minutes later, I was sitting in his front yard around three coolers full of cold beer, vodka, and melting ice. Who I assumed was his mother appeared shortly and doled out borscht soup for everyone. Their English was much better than my Lebanese neighbors, but again, I said little as I sat listening to the group of about a dozen people. They were all super friendly, but coming from the prissy world of show business, I didn't have much in common with this hardcore group of construction workers, plumbers, and electricians. I did try and make an effort by asking a fellow what the difference was between AC and DC current, but just like in electricity class in high school, I was dazed and confused by his first words, "Za plug..."

After sampling more Russian cuisine and a couple of beers, I thanked them and excused myself to pick up that pack of cigarettes. Rounding the corner onto Coney Island Avenue, I immediately stopped and stared at my usual corner store that two twenty-something Iranian twins owned. In front of the store were about 25-30 kids excitedly chatting, assembled en-masse near the entrance. One of the twins was attempting to keep the kids in an orderly line when he spotted me at the back. "Hey!" he yelled, waving me to the front, past the horde. "We are giving away our freezer treats before they melt! Come! Have some ice cream?!"

"No," I said, weaving my way through the kids. "I just came for cigarettes."

"I know you like ice cream! My brother hook you up inside," he said, making room for me to enter the store. Inside the store, his twin brother and their sister were making ice cream cones and handing out the treats to the kids, who excitedly shouted out their requests.

"Hey! Ice cream?" the brother asked when he spotted me.

"No! No, just a pack of Winston's," I shouted over the kids.

"I know you like chocolate! It's free!" He smiled, obviously enjoying himself.

"I've had enough to eat already today, thanks. Just the cigarettes."

He turned and spoke to his sister, who began making a chocolate ice cream cone. He grabbed a pack of cigarettes off the shelf, and handing him the money, he gave me the Winston's and the cone his sister had made.

"Enjoy!" He smiled.

"Thanks," I said, taking the cone. I turned around and saw a set of dark five-year-old eyes staring up at me. "You like chocolate?" I asked the boy.

"Yes!" he beamed.

"Merry Christmas!" I said, handing him the cone.

That afternoon I got talked into joining a group of men and boys in a game of street soccer. Naturally, I played goal. My future as a soccer goalie was about as bright as my future in hockey, and when a boy of about nine or ten scored on me, a man winked at me as if saying, 'Nice of you to let the kid score.' Of course, I winked back, but truth be told, I did try to stop the kid's shot. It's just that he had more soccer prowess than the forty-year-old man standing between the two pylons.

That evening generators were brought out to power floodlights that joined the lanterns illuminating the streets and the stereos pumping out music from foreign lands. Chairs around me were filled and emptied while salutations and introductions were made, and by the conversations, I could tell some long-standing neighbors were meeting each other for the first time. Others I could tell were visiting friends or relatives, like the Jewish fellow up from Philadelphia who lost a brother on 9/11 and shared his story with a Muslim man who was a complete stranger only hours ago. I listened intently with a lump in my throat and thought about my own time on the Lower East Side during 9/11, but I just listened and didn't offer any remembrances of my own.

Mothers from different ethnic and religious backgrounds shared a laugh about their children's discoveries and adventures while they sampled and savored one another's cuisines. Food and drinks were in abundance, and there wasn't just a sense of neighborliness amongst the people but a real sense of social kindness and understanding. You could feel and taste the sense of peace and belonging.

A young man came out with an oud, a short-neck Middle Eastern guitar, and began to play. He was about three-quarters of the way through his first song before a young teenager joined him with his komuz, a long-neck guitar-like instrument. I gathered around with the others who hadn't opted to join another impromptu soccer game, and moments later a girl joined with an acoustic guitar, and I strained my neck to see who had joined with the bongo drums. Stereos began to soften as music from the quartet resonated throughout the neighborhood, and rather than standing there, I decided to cross the street and enjoy the concert and soccer game from the steps of my home.

I wasn't listening and watching for more than ten minutes before Mr. Chen came out the front door and joined me on the stoop.

"I thought I hear music," he said, sitting down.

"If you close your eyes, you're not in Brooklyn anymore," I said.

"Many people."

"The whole block is over there."

"You not go?"

"I just came back," I said, opening my eyes.

I looked over and saw Mr. Chen had closed his eyes, and I wondered where the music had transported him. I closed mine again and was taken to a land I've never experienced. To a land that was once inhabited by the Sumerians, a people that invented the written language, the wheel, farming, to name a few—all of which laid the foundation for the evolution of our society. I see it all in my mind's eye, yet I'm experiencing the sounds, smells, and harmonious atmosphere all in my Brooklyn neighborhood. Are these the same people I'm told every day to judge and fear?

Opening my eyes, the scene before me didn't match the corporate and religiously manipulated conflicts that the media and politicians have imbued on my psyche. What I saw was a quartet continuing to jam in the universal language we all understand, and the only conflict I saw was a small Jewish boy, still wearing his Borsalino hat, trying to score a goal on a man who looked decidedly like the disciple John.

"I like the neighborhood like this," I told Mr. Chen, who eyed me taking out a Winston. "I think this is how we are supposed to be. The power should go out once a year just to shut off all the noise that tells us how we're supposed to think and feel. We need to breathe for ourselves, you know?" I put my cigarettes back in my shirt pocket without lighting one. "Know what I mean?"

"Yes," Mr. Chen said, looking back across the street. I couldn't tell whether he understood me or not, but it didn't matter. We both sat there listening and watching the jubilee before us.

"Maybe power come back tomorrow," Mr. Chen said after several minutes. "Then back to normal."

"How sad," I lamented.

There was a click, and we both turned to see Mrs. Chen push the screen door open with her back. Turning to face us, she looked right at me, holding a large bowl and a spoon.

"Oh no!" I protested. "I couldn't possibly eat…"

"Shoup!" she said, smiling. I looked over at Mr. Chen and back to his wife, whose smile only broadened as she extended the bowl closer, nodding. "For you!"

Mr. Chen was right, the power did return by Sunday night, and the TV was once again debating the bombing of yet another Middle Eastern country, proving the majority of politicians are mouth-breathing imbeciles who, with their mediocre personalities combined with their monumental greed, really need to be stripped of their powers to wage war. Major US General Smedley Butler nailed it when in 1935, he wrote his book entitled *War is a Racket*. The majority of politicians are thrown away like an old shoe once they've served their usefulness to the corporations. Only the great ones who stood up for humanity are ever truly missed or quoted. This leaves the vast majority of politicians who spend their careers acting in the corporate interests to rarely be remembered, while even fewer will ever be mourned. They will not even warrant an asterisk in the footnotes of history. They will simply be forgotten.

Anyway, that brief weekend, without a doubt, was one of the major highlights from my ten years in New York. It's the racially and ethnically diverse nature of the big city that attracts me. It is, for me, an intense study in the laboratory of humanities.

An Orchestrated Mistake

We now join our regularly scheduled book already in progress…

In the village of Halifax, even during rush hour, I rarely had a problem finding a seat on a bus should I chose to sit. But I found it was much easier to remain standing near the front of the bus rather than winding my way through the other passengers in search of a seat. I just didn't have the balance for such a venture, and once the bus started moving, forget about it, I was back to doing my drunken sailor routine.

My therapy sessions began the moment I stepped out of my apartment to attend my rehabilitation programs, and those bus rides to and from were often just as challenging as the actual therapy sessions themselves.

Heading over to Dartmouth to the Heart and Stroke Program, I got on the wrong bus one day and had to change midway at Summer Street. The temperature outside was sub-zero, and a snowstorm had recently dumped another foot of snow, so with the windows steamed over from the heat of all the passengers inside, I couldn't tell if I was nearing the correct stop.

"Excuse me, miss," I said to a young college-aged girl seated in front of me. "Would you mind wiping the window beside you and tell me if we are near Summer Street?" I don't know whether she thought I was trying to make conversation, but she turned and looked up at me with such a disgusted look on her face I thought she just sucked the fart out of a lemon.

"What?" she scoffed.

Before I could repeat my request, the man seated behind her wiped a small patch off the window and peered out. "It is Summer Street. Would you like me to pull the bell?"

An Orchestrated Mistake

"Please," I said, shooting Miss Congeniality a look of indifference, who instantly rolled her eyes before returning to scroll through her phone.

The bus lurched to a stop, but there was nothing even mildly like summer or even a street as I exited the bus. As my foot hit the icy sidewalk, I did an immediate face plant into a snowdrift.

"You ok?" the driver yelled down to me.

"Swellegant!" I responded, pulling my face out of the snowbank. The driver closed his doors and pulled away, and as I pushed my toque out of my eyes to sit up, I saw Miss Congeniality had wiped her window to peer out and enjoy my show.

"You sure you're alright?" another young university girl standing at the bus stop asked me.

"Ya, thanks," I said, struggling to my feet. "Global warming!" I sneered. "Whatever!"

"Hmmm," The girl mused. "You won't be so cynical when you see a polar bear sitting under a palm tree."

"Miss," I lamented, finally getting to my feet, "this is Canada. If I see a polar bear sitting under a palm tree, I'm pouring myself a drink and joining him." I should have also added that if I'm ever lucky enough to get my life back, I'm certainly moving to a warmer climate and won't even Skype with a Canadian during winter.

I could have made my journeys to and from rehabilitation much less arduous by simply enrolling in Access a Ride, a provincial government program that provides a minibus to ferry people with health challenges to and from their medical appointments. Of course, I had about as much interest in utilizing this service as I had in using a cane. It would just signify a further eroding of my mobility and independence. So, if I had to do the occasional swan dive into a snowbank to hang on to the illusion of freedom, so be it. I was diving headfirst.

For the most part, I enjoyed attending the Heart & Stroke Program. I wasn't happy I *needed* to attend such a program, but I was learning a lot, and I enjoyed the company of my fellow participants. They all had a good sense of humor, which is something I strongly recommend to help anyone going through any health crisis, and after almost nine weeks in the program, I got to know quite a bit about each one's story. I only volunteered that I had recently moved to Halifax from New York because of a stroke. That was all they needed to know.

I took my usual seat for attendance and saw Mickey Rooney over in the corner having an animated discussion with Phyllis Diller. I'm not sure about what, but I did hear Mickey claim he now eats it instead of smoking it.

Moments later, Bea Arthur took a seat beside me, reeking of cigarettes, yet proudly declared she hadn't smoked since her heart attack four months ago.

"Really? Not one cigarette?" I asked her, wrinkling my nose.

"Not even a puff," Bea stated, chewing her gum madly. "I don't even miss them!" she added.

I thought this woman is more delusional than I am. I refrained from congratulating her on her achievement for fear the guilt may trigger a second heart attack. I felt sorry for Bea. Although I hadn't struggled to give up smoking, my neurologist had asked me if I had returned to the nasty habit, stating a high percentage of people return to their old destructive ways within one year of a health crisis. Poor ol' Bea had fallen into that high percentile after only four months.

As a warm-up, Janet, the physiotherapist, would often have us walking around the perimeter of the large rec room to some

An Orchestrated Mistake

70s disco hit. I always seemed to be getting lapped by other participants who would often slow just long enough to engage me in a brief conversation before speeding on. Estelle Getty sashayed up next to me wearing those damn shoes, offered me a few words of encouragement, and then strut off to Gloria Gaynor's 1979 hit, "I Will Survive." I looked directly opposite across the room and caught Borgnine's eye, who immediately put his forefinger to his temple and pulled the trigger.

"Nicholas, you need to settle a bet," Ruth Buzzi said, pulling up on one side of me while Bud Abbott flanked the other. "We all bet you are the youngest one in the program, so how old are you?"

"I'll be forty-five in a few months," I said.

"Forty-five?" Bud said. "I had you not yet forty."

"Even so," Ruth interjected, "a stroke, and you're only forty-four. That's young."

It crossed my mind to tell them about Robbie, who attended rehab with me, who at only nineteen had suffered two strokes. Robbie moved with the help of his father, his therapist, and two canes, but before I could mention him, Ruth and Bud sped off while Gloria Gaynor continued to survive.

I didn't mind the stationary bike as an exercise in the program. I could hang on to the bike and pedal slowly for fifteen minutes. However, I hated every moment when I was expected to use the treadmill in those early days. Even though the treadmill was only about eight inches off the ground, the mere thought of me having to balance on one leg, even for a millisecond while I stepped on or off, would have me completely paralyzed in place.

"Here, use my shoulder," Janet would say, appearing at my side. I'd put my hand on her shoulder and push myself up onto the treadmill, and then Janet would hit the buttons to get me walking at an extremely slow pace. "Hang on," she would say. "But try to relax. You're just going to go nice and slow."

For the next fifteen minutes, no one else existed in the gym, and other than quick glances at the clock to see how much time I had left, I never took my eyes off my feet. When the machine stopped, I'd wipe the brow of sweat that had formed on my forehead—not from physical exertion, but from the concentration it had taken to put one foot in front of the other on that slow-moving rubber belt.

The gym we used for our program was a public gym, so it wasn't just full of old-time movie stars nattering away while they rode exercise bikes and strolled on treadmills. The gym would be energized by an infusion of youth who would really give the machines a workout.

A young lad got on the treadmill in front of me and immediately began stretching while he walked at a rather fast pace. Straddling the moving belt, he bent over, swiveling his torso from left to right before jumping back on the moving belt and continuing in a light jog. A wave of sadness washed over me at the realization even those light jogging days may be behind me.

The lad quickened his pace before sprinting on the machine. I watched and was instantly taken back to my early twenties running up the San Gabriel Mountains north of Los Angeles. Not caring about the smog because I was young and healthy, I would do this five-mile run twice a day as a break from sitting and writing in my Burbank apartment. If I got bored running in the hill's winding roads, I'd turn and run backwards, watching the sun reflect off the glass buildings in the San Fernando Valley. I'd sprint backwards up the hill as long as I could before turning and finishing with a strong sprint to the top. Fitness was a part of my life for those two years I lived in LA. I went to the gym daily, but fitness was the only part of my life in balance back then. The rest of my life was out of sync, and I could never seem to find the right balance between body and spirit. I kept running every day then like I was chasing the synchronicity between body and soul until the enthusiasm of my youth wore out and I returned to Vancouver. No longer desiring that chase, I settled for being out of balance, out of synchronicity, and by my late twenties was greeted with a more sedentary lifestyle.

The young man on the treadmill was still sprinting long after Janet had lent me her shoulder to step off.

It wasn't just the physical part of the program I struggled with. I also struggled to understand the dietary aspects of the program.

"What's a legume?" I whispered to Borgnine's wife, who, like so many spouses, attended the dietary lectures.

"Nicholas, you have a question?" Danielle, the dietician, asked, turning the focus of the room uncomfortably towards me.

"What's a legume?" I mumbled, trying to ignore the multiple sets of eyeballs staring at me over bifocals.

"Can anyone tell Nicholas what a legume is?" Danielle asked, sounding like a third-grade teacher.

"They give me gas!" Mr. Magoo announced and was promptly elbowed in the ribs by Mrs. Magoo, resulting in his eyes opening for the first time in I'm sure sixty years.

"Well, true. Introducing too much fiber too quickly can cause bloating and gas. So, what's a legume? Beans, mostly, aren't they?" Danielle said, answering her own question.

"Explains the gas," Cloris Leachman told Magoo.

"Black beans, kidney beans, lentils are all good sources of fiber and protein we need in our daily diet, aren't they? Can anyone tell me why fiber is especially important for diabetics? Nicholas?"

Why is she asking me? I didn't even know what a legume was.

"Gives you a lot of regular bowel movements!" Buddy Ebsen hollered from the back. Dang! I love a good fart joke as much as anyone, but these old celebrities seem obsessed with the human plumbing system. I hadn't heard this much talk about gas since the energy crisis of the 70s.

Perhaps I would have been a little more familiar with a legume had it been listed as a topping at Dominos, but now given the description by my classmates, I wasn't sure a legume would be finding its way onto my dinner plate anytime soon.

Danielle thanked Buddy for his insight and went on to say some diabetics with adult-onset diabetes may even be able to lower their insulin requirements by adhering to a high fiber diet, but added that adding fiber to your diet should always be done gradually, as Buddy Ebsen had pointed out.

The dietary discussions were always interesting to me, mainly because I knew nothing about proper nutrition before entering the program. Up until those discussions, I thought 'buying local' meant buying at your local Safeway. I had no idea the contents of the average dinner plate travels arguably fifteen hundred miles before it gets to your dining room table. Or that a few teaspoons of organic apple cider vinegar a day can help improve blood pressure and diabetes and even support weight loss. Who knew apple cider vinegar is an amazing healing compound?

I may have been learning a lot about the benefits of proper nutrition, but I continued to struggle to put them into practice. Intellectual knowledge is useless until it makes its way to the heart and stimulates real change.

An Orchestrated Mistake

****

"You can't be serious?" I said to Ken after running into him at the checkout line at the supermarket.

"What?" Ken asked, taking the box of chocolate hearts out of my hand and throwing them back into his basket.

"Chocolate valentines!" I said, pointing into his basket. "You don't even have a valentine."

"I have an ex-wife," Ken said, breaking into a toothless grin. "Besides, Valentine's Day is over. These are fifty percent off, and it was either the valentines or the ice cream sandwiches."

"You shouldn't be having either!" I stated.

"Look at you!" Ken said, reaching into my basket. "What's this?" he asked, pulling out a box of cookies.

"No sugar added!" I stated defensively.

"Sugar alcohol! Eight grams!" Ken said, reading off the nutrition label.

"Eight grams. That's nothing. What does eight grams matter?" I asked.

"It matters when you eat the whole box!"

"I don't eat the whole box," I said, snatching it out of Ken's hands.

"You're the only person I know who eats a box of cookies and calls it lunch!" Ken scolded.

"That's such an exaggeration…"

"What's this?" Ken asked as he reached inside my basket again, pulling out another box like it was a dirty diaper. "Frozen pizza! My God! Not a fresh ingredient in sight," Ken lamented, reading from the box.

"Hey, it's topped with all the major food groups," I replied. "Even the US Congress voted pizza a vegetable."

"Leaving no doubt they're total morons!" Ken sneered. "I thought you said you were studying nutrition and supposed to be some kind of expert!"

"We are, and I am!" I proclaimed, snatching the pizza from Ken.

"Some expert!"

Looking down at Ken's basket, my eyes widened in shock and disbelief. Ken followed my gaze, and when he saw I was staring at his box of ice cream sandwiches, he tried to cover them with a package of hot dogs.

"You hypocrite!" I said. "Chocolate valentines *and* ice cream sandwiches. And let's not overlook that package of hot dogs!"

"You two actually want to buy anything?" the checkout lady asked. "Or you want to go away and work this out?"

Ken stared at me defiantly as he began handing over his items to the cashier. Diabetic or not, what Ken and I were buying was not only completely destructive to our bodies, but such a basket full of processed and sugary food goes a long way in promoting a condition that marches a person down the path towards diabetes. A condition that is at the core of diabetes is known as insulin and leptin resistance.

I won't bore you with all the science behind these two major hormones that mainly deal with metabolism and hunger, as there are much more qualified writers to speak on this subject than me. However, I will try to give you a brief idea, only because they're so darn important to the health of our bodies whether you have diabetes or not.

I told you earlier that insulin is needed to help open the cell doors for glucose to nourish the cells in our bodies. What is insulin resistance? This is when the body becomes resistant to the effects of insulin. The insulin has little or no effect in opening the cell doors for the glucose to nourish it. A diet full of innutritious empty calories, such as soda and processed foods to name a few, along with a sedentary lifestyle, will have the body developing insulin resistance over time. The body will then need more insulin to regulate blood sugar, and high insulin levels are the first sign of a problem. Most doctors don't check your insulin levels, they check your glucose levels, or your A1C, and the high insulin levels will lead to an increased appetite and weight gain, which will have you telling yourself, "No, I wear sweatpants and elastic jeans because they are trendy."

Eating healthy, avoiding processed foods, and getting regular exercise can help you avoid this condition, and vitamin D is also very helpful in increasing insulin sensitivity. I should also mention insulin resistance might lead to diabetic complications without you ever being diagnosed with full-blown diabetes.

Leptin is another hormone that affects eating habits. Leptin wasn't discovered until about the mid-1990s. It's made in our body's fat cells and communicates to the brain how much fat is stored. When leptin works properly, our levels rise and tell our brain we have excess fat and no longer need to eat or store more fat. In other words, we've eaten enough and are no longer hungry. The brain then speeds up the metabolism, beginning to burn fat more efficiently, and when leptin levels drop, it tells the brain we're hungry and we need to eat. When we let our leptin levels get out of balance due to poor eating habits, obesity, and even stress, we become leptin resistant. When we're leptin resistant, the brain thinks we're starving, increasing our appetite and slowing our metabolic rate way down, leading to low energy, further

An Orchestrated Mistake

weight gain, and often insulin resistance. Once we've opened the door to leptin and insulin resistance, we've opened the door to a whole series of health complications, including diabetes.

Insulin and leptin resistance often comes into play with menopausal women, contributing to their weight gain, and they experience further difficulty shedding the pounds because the fat storage switch is left on. You can see the merry-go-round here. The more resistant we become to these two hormones, the more we eat to satisfy our hunger, and the more we eat, the more obese we become, furthering the resistance.

How do we get off this merry-go-round? By eating well-balanced, healthy meals, getting up off that couch, and getting regular exercise.

My mother was constantly telling me at the dinner table, "Slow down and breath!" Did Mom know it takes time for leptin to travel from the fat cells to the brain to signal that I'm full? No, she didn't, but it does take time, and she was right to tell me to slow down. Our stomachs are only the size of two fists, so when we eat quickly we are more likely to overeat as the leptin has not made its way to the brain. Of course, everything will spike when we overeat—our sugars, insulin, leptin—and the nasty cycle continues. It's no wonder uncle Bert hits the couch after Thanksgiving dinner.

These two hormones are not just affected by our eating habits. Our overall lifestyle will significantly influence their ability to work effectively. We may be eating properly, but if we're chronically stressed out for whatever reason, or not sleeping well, or not getting any exercise, these two hormones will be thrown out of balance.

So just like weeks earlier with Ken at the supermarket, I once again found myself at the checkout with a basket full of items that would keep me nutritionally starved yet overfed. This time I

An Orchestrated Mistake

didn't have boxes of cookies or holiday chocolates, just packages of food whose colorful images exuded far more nutrition than its contents ever would.

It was spring, but there was still a real winter's bite in the air when I left the supermarket for the long two-block walk home. Even though I had been attending my sessions faithfully at the Heart and Stroke Program and rehab with Lori, I felt frustrated because I wasn't getting the desired results. I especially enjoyed my time at rehab with Lori because she had this talent that not only pushed me hard but made me laugh at myself, sometimes hysterically. She also knew exactly when to push me and when to back off. Most importantly, Lori had my trust completely. Perhaps that's why I was feeling a little frustrated. I felt I was letting Lori down, therefore letting myself down. I felt that all our hard work should have yielded better results by now, but I didn't really feel that much stronger or mobile than when I started. I felt I was working hard, but I wasn't working smart. I knew in my gut I needed to refocus my efforts, but I wasn't sure on what or even how to do it.

****

I was about a third of the way shuffling home from the supermarket when I felt a tapping on my left heel. "Excuse me," a voice said from behind. I was already all the way over on the right side of the sidewalk and was about to turn and snap at that speedster to just go around me when I turned and couldn't believe who asked me to step aside.

Walking past me with a spring in his step was a man at least twenty years my senior with his seeing-eye dog and white cane.

"Thank you," he said as he passed me.

"Sure," I mumbled, completely frozen as I watched this man and his dog pass. My soul began to drain inside as I watched him continue briskly moving down the sidewalk, his cane swinging from side to side.

I wanted to run up to the man and tell him I, too, can walk as fast as he or challenge him to a foot race, but there was no way I could catch him or even win such a race.

I stood there, unable to move or pry my eyes off the man as he and his dog turned up a side street at the end of the block. I tried to swallow, but the lump in my throat wouldn't let me, just as the water in my eyes wouldn't permit me to focus.

I continued to walk home, even slower than before, the image of the man and his dog burned in my mind. "Excuse me," another voice said, and I realize I'd been staggering like a drunk as I moved over to let a woman hurry by.

When I got up to the street where the man and dog had turned off, I looked, but the street appeared exactly how I now felt—empty.

Once through the front door of my apartment, I dropped my bags and caught my reflection in the bathroom mirror. I saw an image of weakness. An image that was broken beyond rehabilitation.

My health was a series of tomorrows. I'd quit smoking tomorrow. I'd start eating healthier tomorrow. I'd start exercising tomorrow. I'll take control of my diabetes tomorrow. I'll deny what I can today and deal with it tomorrow. There's an obvious problem with that approach. You eventually run out of tomorrows.

I felt trapped. I needed to get out. I grabbed my keys and iPod and exited back out into the cold.

I had no idea where I was walking to. I found myself staring up the street that the blind man and his dog had walked to, but there was still no sign of life. I wondered whether I had imagined them, or did they just walk into and out of my life?

It began to snow as I set my iPod to full volume, hoping it would be loud enough to drown out the noise in my head. I walked further than I had at any one time since the stroke, and crossing the deserted field of the Halifax Commons, I struggled to carry on against the flurries and the blowing, cold wind. I could tell I was getting tired after crossing the Commons because my left leg was thumping against the sidewalk, but I kept walking until I reached the old fort atop of Citadel Hill that kept watch over Halifax and the harbor at the center of town.

I sat down at the top of the hill to rest and watched a freighter battle the elements while exiting the harbor before it completely disappeared into the flurries. I must have sat for the better part of an hour with the music from the iPod cranked at full volume. Music clears my mind, and it struck me that my worst fear was being realized. My recovery had hit a wall, and I was far from being whole again. I needed a new plan and approach if I had any hope of regaining my life back. The goal to get my health and freedom back was far too general and vague. I needed a narrower target, an attainable short-term goal. I needed to see and touch a moment of success I could build on. But what?

I got up and walked down the hill, but instead of turning right and heading home I absentmindedly turned left, and in a few blocks found myself standing in front of the Lord Nelson Hotel. Maybe it was because of the weather, but the city was mercifully deserted. For once, I was grateful for the size and peacefulness of Halifax and was drawn inside the hotel.

I abhor war. In spite of this fact, Admiral Nelson had been a hero of mine since I found myself standing on the quarterdeck of the HMS Victory in Portsmouth, England, at the age of thirteen. Since that youthful moment, I have devoured every book I could get my hands on about Nelson. As a captain, he had lost an arm

An Orchestrated Mistake

and an eye in earlier battles, and it is often said he needed a nurse more than he needed a mistress. But even with his physical challenges, he managed to defeat Napoleon at the battle of Trafalgar in 1805. This battle played a huge role in stopping Napoleon and prevented an invasion of England, but sadly cost Nelson his life.

I walked into the Victory Arms Pub inside the hotel and was drawn right away to a small painting of Nelson accepting the sword of surrender from an enemy captain. The painting reminded me of a story about Nelson when as a vice admiral at the Battle of Copenhagen, the signal flags were flown to retreat. Nelson, putting the telescope up to his glass eye, said, "I see no signal." He went on to defeat the Danes, and I understood why I admired Nelson so much. He never gave up or shied away from life's battles.

As I stood staring at the painting, the Irish band Hothouse Flower's song "This Is It" played on my iPod. "*...and you've tried all the quacks, all the doctors, and all you really need, really need, is a healing sound. But just listen to the waters, find the answers on the streets, because now it's time to listen, now it's time to meet...your soul.*"

The universe provides the answers when we quiet ourselves long enough to listen, and as I stepped outside back into that cold spring air, I knew exactly what I needed to tell Lori to refocus my efforts.

"Lori, I need to run."

CHAPTER FOURTEEN

Every health professional I had met since my return to Canada, whether the cardiologist, endocrinologist, ophthalmologist, or any other kind of 'ologist,' always asked me the same question: 'What does neurology have to say?' I refrained from asking them whether they were referring to neurologist number one or two. We all know neurologist number one was like God in the Old Testament, a bit of a judgmental prick, while number two was like the God in the New Testament, kind, helpful, and encouraging. Either way, whether he liked it or not, neurologist number two took on God-like qualities, as I and all the 'ologists' were standing by for that MRI so we could find a way forward and cling to his every word.

Over a year and a half after the stroke and almost one year since my return to Canada, I finally received notice of a date for my MRI. It wasn't long after I arrived at the hospital I realized by the paintings on the wall of Winnie the Pooh and Tigger they had scheduled my MRI at the children's hospital. By this point, I didn't care if Piglet was performing the procedure. I just wanted the information an MRI would provide so I could at least feel like I was making some progress. If knowledge is power, I needed to know exactly what had happened to my brain that afternoon in New York.

"Why am I at the children's hospital?" I asked the technician after changing into a hospital gown.

"We're trying to get rid of the backlog of MRIs," she said, appearing annoyed she had to slow down with my questioning. She began sifting through some papers before she asked, "You had the stroke eighteen months ago?"

"Bout that."

"I don't see a record of a previous MRI?"

An Orchestrated Mistake

"This is my first one. Well, first one in Canada."

She looked up at me with her head cocked to one side.

"Don't ask," I said with a shrug.

Following a head shake, she motioned me with her hand onto the machine.

A few short weeks later, my neurologist walked into his office holding under his arm my medical file that now resembled a draft of *War & Peace*.

"How are the programs going? Heart and Stroke, rehab?" he asked, closing the door behind him.

"Fine, I guess," I said, shaking his outstretched hand. "I only have a few weeks left with the Heart and Stroke folks."

"Finding the information practical and useful?"

I wasn't quite sure if he was joking. My colleagues in the program may have resembled the Hollywood stars of old, but I, too, was well on my way to resemble a Tinseltown actor of yesteryear—Fatty Arbuckle. Of course, I didn't see myself that way, but I did know I had no business wearing stripes in any direction.

"Useful, yes," I said, "but I seem to be having a little trouble putting their whole exercise and nutrition thing into practice."

"Keep at it," he said. "Perseverance always wins out."

I admired his enthusiasm, but I was struggling to believe that of late. Recently, it seemed the harder I worked, the more I was falling apart.

"How's rehab?" he inquired, opening my file.

"Good." I lied. Truth was, I had been less than enthusiastic about rehab for several weeks, but after the incident with the blind man and his dog, I had raced into rehab with my new attitude to tell Lori what I needed to do. I was excited to see her face when I would tell her that I wanted to run.

Waiting for Lori in the waiting area, I was flipping through a magazine when a young woman approached me. "Nicholas? I'm Sara," she said, extending her hand. "I'll be taking over your file."

"But I'm waiting for Lori," I said, standing.

"Yes, I know. She's not with us."

"Oh, you mean she's out sick today?"

"No, she's not with us anymore," Sara said.

"What? But I need to talk to her. When's she coming back?"

"I don't know that she is coming back. I'll be taking over her caseload."

I stared at Sara. She had kind eyes, but I looked down the hall towards Lori's office. The door was open, her chair empty.

"She couldn't have just left. Could you find out?" I asked, turning back to Sara. "Maybe tell her I need to talk to her."

"Nicholas, Lori's gone. You can talk to me now."

"But I trust Lori," I said, looking back down the hall.

"But you'll be working with me now, and probably a therapist named Sherry. You can trust us. What is it you wanted to tell Lori? You can tell me."

An Orchestrated Mistake

I looked back at Sara then back at the empty office, biting my lower lip. "I wanted to tell her," I said, turning back to Sara, "I wanted to tell her I want to run."

"Ummm, oh, Nicholas," Sara said, her face failing to conceal her shock and disappointment at hearing my statement. "I've read your file, and I don't think…" She looked down at my file, shaking her head before looking up to meet my eyes. "Nicholas, I don't think you're ready to try running." I looked away, not knowing what to say. "Look," Sara continued, "maybe if we work really hard, maybe one day you'll run, but I just don't think you're ready to try that now. Okay?"

I felt like I had just taken several hard blows to the stomach. "Yeah," I said, nodding in agreement at the empty office. "You're probably right." Sucking in a deep breath, I turned back to Sara.

"So, let's get started."

I liked Sara, but I wasn't thrilled to continue my rehab with a new therapist. Lori had known how to push my buttons to get results. It was like she had a sixth sense when it came to my motivation. There were countless times I would be frustrated by my inability to execute an exercise at the level which I felt I should, and Lori always found a way to communicate that I was progressing and exactly where I should be in my rehabilitation.

After telling me one afternoon my test scores had shot up by twenty-one points since my first day, I twirled my finger in the air, saying, "Big deal. I still can't accomplish shit."

"Come here," Lori said, walking over to the parallel bars. She threw a wobble board down between the bars. "Stand on it," Lori commanded.

"We already did this," I lamented. "I suck at this too."

"Stand on it, and when I tell you, let go of the bars." I stood on the board, holding onto the bars for support. "Let go of the bars," Lori ordered. I let go of the bars as Lori clicked her stopwatch. I immediately started wobbling, coming close to falling off, but somehow managed to stay on the board. "Stay on!" Lori urged, glancing down at her watch. My arms started twirling in the air as the board wobbled back and forth beneath my feet. "Come on! Hang on! Three more seconds!" Lori encouraged. "Two seconds, one second," and I fell forward, catching myself with the bars before I hit the floor. "Ten seconds!" Lori announced triumphantly. "Ten seconds!" she said again as I pulled myself back upright. "Do you remember how long you stayed on that board the first time?" I shook my head no. "Zero! You couldn't even stand on the thing!" I couldn't suppress the smile that broke across my face, and I noticed that Lori, too, couldn't hold back hers.

It was this belief in me and her ability to point out my little victories that kept me motivated during the bleak days, and for a generally upbeat guy, there were many bleak days. I knew I would miss Lori, but her departure was yet another gift, as it forced me, despite Sara and Sherry's professionalism, to search within my attitude for positive motivation.

"Follow me," Sherry said, spinning on her heel, sending her blonde ponytail dancing. For the last half hour, I had been doing the same exercises Lori had prescribed: the Delorme Boot on my left foot to build up the strength in my left leg, along with the stairs for stamina and strength, and of course the wobble board and parallel bars, amongst others. It was tiresome and tedious, so I was eager to follow Sherry down the hall to try something new. "Do you know what a Wii is?" she asked as we rounded a corner to enter a small room.

"Yes," I said. "My nieces have one. It's a kid's video game."

An Orchestrated Mistake

"Right, but we use it in therapy to work on your hand-eye coordination and sensory motor skills. I'll show you. We'll try the hula hoop first," Sherry said, stepping up on the sensory pad.

"Hula hoop?" I questioned. "I don't do hula hoops. Actually, I don't do games."

"I'm going to show you," Sherry said, ignoring my statement.

"Point the controller at the TV and use the buttons to throw the hoop around your waist." Sherry 'throws' the hoop and starts swiveling her hips, and the little video man's hula hoop starts swiveling around his waist. "See, it's easy. Just like when you were a kid."

"I didn't play with hula hoops when I was a kid."

"Now you try," Sherry said, again ignoring my mood and stepping off the sensory pad.

It's just by the grace of the sky gods I can work a TV remote, so when she handed me the controller, a look of terminal confusion spread across my face.

"It's not that complicated," Sherry said. "Like you said, your nieces can use it."

"They're smarter than I am."

"Just step on the pad and give it a try."

The pad is barely two inches off the floor, but the fear of lifting one foot and balancing on one leg, even for a millisecond, had me frozen in place.

"Here," Sherry said, seeing my hesitation. "Use my shoulder."

"I can do it," I said. But after several more attempts, Sherry stood beside me so I could use her shoulder. I listened to Sherry's instructions again, but I could not get the hoop on the screen to swivel around my waist.

"You need to swivel your hips," Sherry encouraged.

"They don't swivel."

"Yes, they will. Try again."

"They didn't swivel before the stroke. If we have to play a game, let's play frozen tag. You tag me, and I'll freeze."

Sherry realized it was not about moving my hips that had me frozen in place but the fear of losing my balance and stumbling off the sensory pad. Even though the pad was barely inches off the floor, my perception was much higher, which threw my sense of balance way off.

"You're not going to fall," Sherry said. "I can get you a harness if you'd feel better."

"I don't need a harness! I'm barely off the floor!"

We abandoned the hula hoop to try skiing, but again, I couldn't control the man on the screen, and he ended up resembling the crashing skier in that opening of the *Wide World of Sports*.

We abandon the mountain for the tightrope, but again, my little man couldn't make it across the rope.

"Try again," Sherry said, and I felt her grab my belt at the back of my pants. That time I was finally able to complete the crossing on the tightrope. "Wow! You did it!" Sherry exclaimed with more enthusiasm than my comfort level appreciated.

Not wanting to burst her state of euphoria, I said, "Yeah, I'm a regular Wallenda."

An Orchestrated Mistake

"Who?"

"Before your time." I shrugged.

I did improve with the Wii, but I didn't have the temperament for games, especially games that I can't do well. I really wanted to run, but Sherry and Sara were completely resistant to this idea.

Many times over the next few weeks, I came into those rehab sessions and announced to Sherry or Sara I wanted to run.

"I want to run today if we could," I'd tell them. Each time I was met with friendly opposition.

"I have an extra patient today, so I can't be with you. Let's put it off until Sara or I can be there with you."

"I'm only running on a treadmill. It's not like I'm asking you to supervise me running a marathon."

"I don't think you are ready for it," Sherry said. I looked away, shaking my head. "Let's see what Sara says during your next session."

Sara's assessment of my capabilities wasn't any different than Sherry's. "Nicholas, I just don't think you're ready to try running today."

In the weeks ahead, I would tackle the Wii every session with varying success, do my exercises in the gym, then approach whoever was assigned to me and ask them if I could try and run on the treadmill. I always got the same reply: "I don't think we should try it today." I didn't understand why they weren't letting me at least try to run. I'd ask every time I came to a session, so they had to know it was important to me. Each time they said no, I got more frustrated and more determined to try.

When did I ever need permission to run before? Running was just something I did. I ran for the subway, ran across 6th Avenue, and ran to get to an audition. I was always in a hurry, so I always ran. I never needed someone's permission, nor did I need someone to hold my hand. I would just run.

One day while preparing to step on the treadmill, near the end of a session, I looked over and saw Robbie, the now twenty-year-old double-stroke survivor, barely mobile even with the assistance of two canes. My heart sank as I watched him struggle. He fought just to walk a few feet then get onto a padded therapy table where he would lie down and a therapist would manipulate his body into positions that it no longer had any desire to do. His father, who collected him every morning from the seventh-floor residence of the hospital, watched the determination on his son's face, completely unaware of the sense of hope etched onto his own. I watched Robbie battle for inches, resisting the urge to run over and help him. The mere thought of me running anywhere left the therapy gods laughing hysterically and me standing there empty, broken, and void.

"You okay, Nicholas?" Sherry called out from across the gym where she was helping another patient, breaking my trance. I waved back to her. Looking back to Robbie's fight on the therapy table, I pulled myself up on the treadmill.

I looked over my shoulder at Sherry, who had her back towards me as she worked intensely with her patient. I decided then what I was going to do. I was going to run.

The sweat of anticipation was already rolling down my temples as I hit the start button on the treadmill. I was walking slowly. I looked down. The death grip I had on the handles of the equipment was turning my knuckles white. I knew I was overthinking. I just needed to hit the damn button and speed up that belted monster to start running. I knew I wanted to, I had to, but fear had my hands frozen to the handles. My brain was not sending the signal to my legs to run. I thought about tricking my brain. Pretend you're late for an appointment back in New York.

An Orchestrated Mistake

Don't use the railing, fly down the stairs two, three at a time to the subway platform. *'Hey, buddy, coming through! Excuse me!'* Dart left then right, through the crowded platform, just make this train! There's the door chime, the subway doors are closing, one final sprint with a leap, and I'm on! The doors slam shut behind me. Was there ever any doubt?

As long as I remain walking, I know I won't have failed in my attempt. I can live without knowing if I can run again. I can. I'm safe as long as I'm walking. Adults only walk with a destination. Children are the ones who run without a destination. I'm not a child, therefore I don't need to run.

I began to breathe easier, but my breathing became shallow and intense as I looked back over my shoulder at Sherry. She still had her back to me and was heavily engrossed with her patient. I stared back down at my feet, walking slowly. I tightened my grip with my left hand and loosened my right. Be that child again. Let yourself run with no destination.

I tasted the salt on my top lip. My hand let go of the right railing to wipe the sweat from my face, but I didn't return it to the handle. My need to know if I could run far outweighed my fear of failure. My right hand hit the button and sped up the beast. I did it! I wasn't running, but I was walking fast. I kept walking to let the signals to my legs synchronize to this faster speed.

I glanced back at Sherry, who was still with her patient. I glanced at Robbie, who was attempting to stand up again with the help of his therapist and those two canes.

I let go of the handle with my right hand and stabbed at the power-up button. The monster sucked more energy from the wall and came to life. One more stab of the button and I'd be running like a child without a destination! My brain had found the connection to my body. I punched the button again, and I swear I heard the monster laugh. *'Yes! Let's do it!'*

An Orchestrated Mistake

Gulping in air, I tried to keep up with the whirling tread. I didn't take but a stride before my left toe scuffed the belt and I stumbled. My left leg went out from under me, and my right leg buckled under the added pressure. Instantly both legs were no longer supporting me. I tried to pull my legs back underneath me, but they wouldn't obey my brain's commands to support me, and I knew I had to hit the kill switch.

With my legs flopping behind me, I reached up and slammed my hand down hard on the kill switch, silencing the monster, and in doing so, silenced my dream. I had my answer.

On my knees and still holding on, head down between my arms, I heard the voices and sounds of the gym over my gasps for air. Turning, I saw Sherry still engaged with her patient. Robbie was still struggling with those canes, and I bit my bottom lip as the gymnasium got a little greyer.

Shaking, I pulled myself up and saw an older lady sitting in a wheelchair staring at me. Our eyes connected, and she smiled. I knew she saw the whole thing. She had seen me fail. But that's not the message I read in her eyes. Her eyes twinkled. *'You tried.'*

"Sorry I wasn't able to spend much time with you this session," Sherry said, walking me to the gymnasium door. "I hope you were able to manage on your own."

"Yes."

"Good," Sherry said, stopping at the door. "I know you want to run. We'll try running soon. I promise."

"Don't worry about it." I shrugged, not making eye contact.

"I thought you wanted to run."

"I'm sort of over it. It was just a phase."

"No, seriously, we can try. That is if you still want to?"

"I don't know. Kids run, adults walk."

Bewildered, Sherry nodded. "Okay, I'll see you next week then?"

"Yeah, next week."

****

"Are you happy with your progress in rehab?" the neurologist asked, looking through my file.

"I wouldn't use the word 'happy' to describe my feelings for rehab."

"Well, you know what I mean," he interjected.

"Yeah," I said. I thought about telling him about my attempt to run, but I still hadn't processed my feelings with that whole episode, so I just said, "I think I'm a little steadier on my feet than when I started."

"Good, good. I see here you took your driver's exam and passed, so you have to be happy about that."

"I guess," I said with a shrug. I also thought about telling him the examiner thought long and hard about failing me. During the driver's test, I was making a left turn through an intersection with a crosswalk. I waited for a man to cross the street, but fifteen or so feet behind him, a woman entered the crosswalk talking on her phone. She was more interested in her conversation than crossing the street, so I stepped on the gas to shoot through that fifteen-foot gap.

"Wait! Wait!" the examiner screamed, hitting the break on his side of the car.

"What? I had plenty of room," I protested as both our heads snapped forward.

An Orchestrated Mistake

"There is a pedestrian in the crosswalk!" he said, pointing at the woman still sauntering across the street.

"She wasn't crossing the street, she was strolling, and I had plenty of room to scoot by."

"That may be how you drive in New York, but here in Halifax, that's an automatic fail."

I shook my head in disgust. He did pass me, so I got to keep my license, but only after a long lecture on pedestrian etiquette.

Apparently, the stroke hadn't affected my ability to drive, but living in New York had.

"So, what happened to me?" I asked the neurologist, uncertain.

"You've had an ischemic stroke," he said, turning the computer monitor towards me so I could see it. With a few clicks of his mouse, the image the MRI took of my brain appeared on the screen.

"One of the arteries that feeds blood to your brain became clogged and cut off blood and oxygen, causing all these little infarcts here." Pointing at the screen with his pen, he continued, "See all these little white spots, like little white snowflakes scattered on both hemispheres of your brain?"

"Yeah. Looks more like a blizzard than a few snowflakes."

"Yes, well, those infarcts, or dead brain cells, are a result of the stroke."

"Looks like it affected both sides of my brain," I said, examining the image.

"Yes. See this area here?" he said, circling the image of the front of my brain. "That's the anterior frontal lobe, and it looks like you've had some volume loss from an earlier head injury. Did you have some sort of head trauma previously that you can remember?"

I actually could remember a head injury when I was sixteen or seventeen. During a hockey game, I took a slap shot to my head, which was so hard it knocked me off my skates, cracking my mask. I was dazed, but I stayed in the game. It was only after the coach realized I could no longer even stop a beach ball that I was pulled for the backup goaltender. I had headaches for months after that shot. I did continue to practice and play, albeit very inconsistently, but it was the late 70s, so there wasn't as much awareness paid to concussions in sports. Back then, you just grabbed your balls and spat, shrugging off any notion that you would come out of a game. It's only in recent years that professional sports are beginning to understand the real effects concussions have on player's lives.

"Yeah, I took a slap shot to the head when I was a teenager," I told the neurologist.

"Some slap shot. Well, it's definitely an old brain injury."

"Explains my career in show business. What about MS that I've heard bandied around?"

"No. You've had a stroke. Think of all these little infarcts as roadblocks, and these are what's stopping you, say if you want to retrieve information from your memory or want to give your body the signal to run. You're hitting one of these little roadblocks. What we're trying to do in therapy is rewire your brain. Find a way around these roadblocks."

"So, I may run again?" I asked. "Get my balance back?"

"Sure, it's possible. As I said, we don't know how far the brain can succeed when it comes to repairing itself. But it doesn't do it alone. You have to help it. Mental and physical exercises are going to challenge you to improve and rewire your brain around these roadblocks."

"How long?"

"That's up to you. How hard do you want to work? For each person, the results are different. How far can you go? We just don't know."

We chatted about the effects the stroke had on me, my *expressive aphasia* being one of them. "Sometimes, I just can't say what I mean. I struggle to articulate my thoughts clearly. It seems like I'm constantly searching for the right words." He began to write in my file. "While I'm at it, sometimes letters seem reversed, or things are weirdly spaced. I don't know."

"You're struggling with your visual-spatial," he offered.

I stared at him with only an idea of what he meant. "Yeah, yeah, my visual-spatial seems off," I said.

"What do you think about seeing a neuropsychologist?" the neurologist asked.

"A what?"

"Neuropsychologist."

"You mean a shrink?"

"Not really." He chuckled. "A neuropsychologist will run you through some tests, ask some questions, talk to you about these issues, help you figure out your strengths and weakness in order to refocus your efforts. They can get a good assessment on where your head's at."

"I'm not sure I want to know where my head's at. I mean, I do know, but I spend almost every waking minute trying to forget."

"I think it would be good for you."

"I don't know."

"I can't force you. It's just a suggestion."

I had trusted my neurologist's treatment so far, so why was I balking? Probably because I didn't trust myself to tell the psychologist the truth about what I was feeling. I stared at the brain specialist across from me for a moment.

"Okay. I'll see the neuro…"

"psychologist."

"Yeah, him."

"Her," the neurologist corrected, writing in his notepad.

CHAPTER FIFTEEN

"I know you just sit here in the dark chain-smoking, eating ice cream sandwiches, making shit up," I accused Ken, who sat in his chair scrutinizing the pages I printed off the Internet.

"I'm tellin' ya, I heard it on TV!"

"You believe everything on the propaganda box?" I asked.

"I read it in the paper too!" Ken said.

"Oh, well, if you saw it on TV and read it in the paper, it must be true. That seals it then," I teased Ken.

"It does!"

"Ken, there's no way the batting champion in Major League Baseball would sign a two-year contract for two million. Baseball players don't get out of bed for anything less than thirty."

"I heard what I heard!" Ken argued.

I was surprised Ken heard anything at all since he talked over everything, including the television at full volume. Ken forced me to become quite adept at lip-reading, which was rather a science when you consider he hadn't any teeth and was constantly gumming a cigarette. Quite often, I'd just nod and agree—it was much easier than arguing over the television—but not that time. I could be just as stubborn as the old curmudgeon who sat opposite me. I wasn't really sure who was more pathetic, Ken for completely making up his own facts or me for printing three pages from the Internet to prove the old seadog wrong.

"All right," Ken finally conceded, "maybe I was off by a few million."

"*A few million?* Try five years and sixty million!" I said, turning in the screws.

An Orchestrated Mistake

"Look! There's Ethel!" Ken said, pointing to the TV, changing the subject. "The old girl has an ice cream sandwich! Look! She's talking to Fred! She's going to eat his too!" Ken shouted, almost coming out of his recliner.

"You're just jealous."

"Of course!" Ken said, sitting back down.

When Ken and I weren't arguing moot points, this was the second pathetic thing we did: Watch Toronto Blue Jays home baseball games and make up stories about the fans behind home plate and analyze their eating habits. There was a regular old couple we dubbed Fred and Ethel, and both Ken and I could tell you who ate what and during what inning. For example, the seventh-inning stretch always included a box of ice cream sandwiches passed around amongst the fans in those choice box seats. The only time Ken would shut up during the game was when the sandwiches made an appearance.

"Look at that! The lady in the purple dress took two! Oh, that's going to piss off Ethel!"

If those fans behind the plate only knew that a thousand miles away a couple of diabetics were watching and clinging to every bite of their hot dogs and ice cream, they might have opted for the nosebleed section.

"Look at Ethel talking up that guy on her left," Ken said.

"She's trying to talk him out of ice cream," I added.

"No. She's making plans to meet him at the Four Seasons after the game."

"Four Seasons?"

"Yes, the Four Seasons!" Ken said. "Check out those sequins. That ol' girl ain't slumming it at a Motel Six."

"Ethel wouldn't cheat on Fred."

"Sure she would, if Fred ain't putting out. And I don't think the ol' boy is given 'er up. Why else would Ethel be wearin' sequins to a ball game?"

"She's going ballroom dancing with Fred after the game."

"Oh, she's goin' dancin' alright," Ken said. "But it ain't the dancing you or I know, and it ain't with Fred."

Ken watched the attendant in the box seats hand Ethel a Diet Coke.

"I could use one of those," Ken said, getting up.

"It's nice to know the power of suggestion is alive and well," I told him.

"You want one?" he asked, walking over to the fridge.

"No, I don't drink that shit anymore."

"What shit?"

"Diet Coke, Diet Pepsi, diet anything."

"What? They find a cure for diabetes, so you drink the real deal now?"

"No, but diet drinks have aspartame in them."

"So?"

"So, aspartame is a chemical, and I don't want chemicals pumping through my body."

"A few chemicals aren't going to hurt anyone." Ken chuckled, returning to his chair with his Diet Coke.

An Orchestrated Mistake

"Did you know at high temperatures aspartame breaks down into formaldehyde?"

"Huh?"

"Formaldehyde. The same chemical used to preserve dead bodies," I said. "You're drinking it now."

"Well, I could use a little preserving," Ken said, hoisting his soda.

"The Splenda you think is a healthy sweetener that you put in your tea is chemically related to the pesticide DDT."

"You're just a ball of good news, aren't you?" Ken said, sipping on his Diet Coke.

"Diet soda also robs the body of calcium."

"Well, that explains my osteoporosis," Ken lamented.

"Let me put it to you this way. You know who the CEO was of the company that lobbied the FDA and the Reagan administration to get aspartame approved in the 1980s? Donald 'there are weapons of mass destruction' Rumsfeld. I don't know about you, but I wouldn't trust anything that guy says, let alone want to put it in my mouth."

"Maybe he's like me. He just sits in a dark room making shit up," Ken said, chuckling.

"Apparently."

In truth, artificial sweeteners are used in thousands of food and beverage products, and the key word to these sweeteners is *artificial*. They contain manmade chemicals so they can be patented and turned over for a huge profit. Some estimates say the makers of Splenda profit to the tune of $1.5 billion a year on that one product alone.

An Orchestrated Mistake

Numerous studies have linked these sweeteners and the chemicals in them to cancers, autoimmune diseases, migraines, and other health problems. While formaldehyde and methanol are two naturally occurring by-products of our body's metabolism, drinking and eating products with aspartame in them exposes us to excess amounts of these toxic chemicals, which over time leads to the destruction of cells and the breakdown of organs.

Artificial sweeteners stick themselves to cells, where they add free-radical damage and literally excite the cell to death. That's why scientists have classified them as excitotoxins. These excitotoxins attach themselves to cells in the brain, exciting them to the point where the cell dies, in effect punching tiny cell-size holes in the brain. From the moment excitotoxins attach themselves to a cell to the point of the cell's death takes about an hour. We don't know this is happening in our bodies because millions of healthy cells have to die before the target organ malfunctions and we find ourselves at the doctor's office asking, 'How did this happen?'

When enough of your brain cells are killed off in this way, neurological disorders can move in. Both the US Air Force magazine, *Flying Safety*, and the US Navy magazine, *Navy Physiology*, published articles warning about the many dangers of aspartame, including that the ingestion of aspartame may render pilots susceptible to seizures and vertigo, recommending pilots abstain from the use of such products. Off the record, flight surgeons in Washington DC acknowledge the problem with aspartame but claim their hands are tied until the FDA (Food and Drug Administration) addresses the issue. It's argued the FDA will never acknowledge the problem with artificial sweeteners because of the billions of dollars at stake, and those that are thrusting these degenerative chemicals upon us have the FDA and the politicians in their back pocket.

There are many natural sources of sweeteners that can replace refined sugar, such as coconut sugar and muscovado sugar, but for diabetics or those wishing to lose weight, Stevia wins the sweetener contest hands down. Stevia is harvested from the leaves of the stevia rebaudiana plant, which is part of the sunflower family native to South America. It is naturally 200 to 300 times sweeter than refined sugar and completely free of calories.

Stevia won't spike your glucose levels. In fact, it seems to improve glucose tolerance. The plant has been used by the Guarani people of South America for medicinal purposes for over 1,500 years, as well as a sweetener for teas and dishes in South American countries like Paraguay and Brazil.

As more and more people are becoming aware of the dangers of artificial sweeteners, Stevia is finally finding its way onto supermarket shelves.

****

"Why do slightly cooked vegetables have more nutrients than raw ones?" I asked Danielle, the dietitian at the Heart and Stroke Program. I drove the dietitian at the diabetes clinic batty with the same question. I would ask anyone, including the waitress serving my dad and me at a Greek restaurant. I was beginning to sound like Holden Caulfield from *Catcher in the Rye*. "Where do the ducks go in the winter?"

"I don't know that they have more nutrients," Danielle said after giving it some thought.

"Yeah, they do," I said. "I read it in the chart you gave us."

"Nicholas, I'm impressed." Danielle laughed. "You actually read one of the handouts."

"Of course," I countered. I didn't have the heart to tell her I couldn't help it. I was using it as a placemat under one of my TV dinners.

"Well, let me get back to you on that one," Danielle said. "I honestly don't know."

It turns out slightly cooking your vegetables can make the outer cell walls of the vegetable less rigid, making them easier to absorb and digest. As for where the ducks go in the winter… If they live in Canada, to Mexico if they had any sense.

In the last few days of the Heart and Stroke Program, I tried to do and learn as much as I could. I had worked hard throughout the program but didn't feel I made as much progress as I should have. Turns out, months after the program would end, I would find out why.

In those closing days, I was finally stepping on and off the treadmill without the assistance of Janet's shoulder, and while my sugars had come down, they were still twice as high as they should be. Pam, the nurse for the program, had sent me to the hospital for a stress test, but again, I couldn't perform well enough for the results to be conclusive.

Janet had asked me weeks earlier if I wanted to participate in a study for Capital Health, the health organization for Nova Scotia.

"All you have to do is wear a pedometer on your waistband and it will measure how many steps you take in a day. They want to see the effects of activity on recovering heart and stroke patients."

I wasn't sure I wanted a record of how many steps it was from my chair to the refrigerator, but after I saw Estelle Getty clip one to her designer Sears track pants and march around the rec room in those white shoes, I agreed to clip one onto me. I looked down at my pair of white shoes and vowed to get a new pair so Estelle and I would no longer share the same footwear.

An Orchestrated Mistake

"Okay, you guys! You know what to do!" Janet hollered, putting on the 70s disco classic, "Do the Hustle." We all stood in front of our single portable steps and began stepping up and down. I looked around, and almost all were wearing pedometers. I looked to my right and saw Mickey Rooney wasn't wearing one.

"No pedometer?" I asked.

"I don't need one to tell me how far I'm not moving," Mickey replied.

To my left, Borgnine was stepping on and off his step to the music with his pedometer. "Why do I always feel like an asshole?" He asked when our eyes met.

I did go out and buy new runners the next day. Discarding those old lady shoes did wonders for my soul! I did get out and walk more with the pedometer, but I would often stop at sheltered bus stops to have a seat and rest.

During one particularly long walk, I found myself stopping at Tony's Pizza to wolf down two slices of pizza. Feeling guilty for inhaling so much pizza, I continued on.

I noticed a group of rather tubby mourners standing outside having a cigarette as I passed a funeral home. It was as if there was an intermission in the service. As I passed them, a line from the Indian epic *Mahabharata* came to mind. *The most wondrous thing in the world is that all around us people can be dying, and we don't realize it can happen to us.*

During another walk, I stopped at a bus stop to rest and check my pedometer when I noticed that the numbers would increase if I shook the pedometer. I instantly had an image of Borgnine sitting at home in his recliner sipping beer, shaking his pedometer while watching a football game. Next time he bragged about walking five thousand steps in a day, I replied, "Sure ya did."

An Orchestrated Mistake

After completing the Heart and Stroke Program, I attended my final consultation with the health practitioner.

"We weren't going to let you into the program," Pam, the nurse, told me during our chat. "We thought you weren't up to the physical challenges of the program and weren't going to make it."

"Yeah, well, surprise!" I replied smugly.

"You surprised us all."

"You thought I'd have to choose the color of my cane?"

"Quite frankly, yes. But before you get too full of yourself, I still have a few concerns."

"Like?" I questioned.

"Your sugars are still twice what they should be, and your blood pressure is still over-target at one-forty-seven over eighty-six."

"I can work on those," I told Pam. "Anything else?"

"You still have that dry cough."

"Yes, but it's gotten better, I think," I replied optimistically.

"We still need to know what's causing it. I'm going to mention it to your doctor in my report," Pam said.

"Sure." I shrugged.

I thought Pam was going to nail me on my weight gain, but she never brought it up. Even my doctor and the diabetes clinic hadn't said anything about my weight gain. Instead, they just suggested we up my insulin doses and blood pressure meds.

An Orchestrated Mistake

Many of my celebrity friends in the Heart and Stroke Program thought I had made the biggest improvements since the program had started, but realistically that was only because I had the farthest to travel. I knew nothing about nutrition when the program started, but at least I learned what a legume was, even if I didn't know how to prepare it. I still had a lot of work to do to improve, but I now had a starting point. The program was never the magic blue pill I had hoped for that would cure my ills, but what it did do was open the door. Now it was up to me as to whether or not I went through it.

In the closing weeks of my rehab, I was about to pull myself up on the belted demon when I heard a familiar voice call out to me across the gym. "So, I hear you want to run!"

I turned around and was so surprised I couldn't speak. Like an over-excited dog, I could only walk in circles. "Well?" the voice asked. "Is it true?"

"Lori?!" I said, finally stopping in mid-circle.

"Yeah! Who did you expect?" she replied, walking over.

"You're back?"

"I've got you now. The party's over."

"Aw, man," I said, finishing one more circle.

"So, is it true? You want to run?" Lori asked, standing beside me.

"Well, I…"

"Let's do it," Lori said.

"Well, I… Really?"

"I'm game if you are," Lori announced.

An Orchestrated Mistake

I looked at the belted dragon now roaring with laughter and wondered if I should tell Lori about my humiliating defeat only a few short weeks ago. "I don't know," I said. "I really didn't expect to run today."

"Good, then let's face the unexpected together," Lori said, walking over to the beast.

"Are you sure you want to do this?" I asked Lori but was wondering if my psyche could take yet another humiliating defeat.

"Don't you?" she questioned.

"Yes, but…"

"Then let's do it. I'm here with you," she added, taking a position beside the monster.

My heart began to cantor while the butterflies swirled in my stomach. I wanted to tell Lori I had tried to run, it didn't work, I've moved on. Instead, I just stared at her, speechless.

"Okay, step up," Lori said, offering her hand.

"I got it," I said, stepping onto the treadmill. I stood on the beast, staring down at Lori. It was as if I was expecting her at any moment to break into fits of laughter, exclaiming, 'Psyche! Kidding! How funny! You actually thought that you could run?!'

But she didn't. She was calm, her look serious. I had never seen her that serious before.

"I want you to hold on," Lori said, tapping the front handlebars.

"I'm going to work the controls for you. We're going to do this together. We're going to start off nice and slow and build up to it, okay?"

"Yup," I said, wiping the sweat from my forehead with the back of my hand.

"You okay?"

"Of course," I replied, thankful my voice didn't betray me.

"Okay, here we go," Lori said, holding down the start button.

"That's it. We're just going to walk nice and slow for a few minutes."

I could feel my body temperature rising with every step. "That's it," Lori said. "Remember to breathe, try and relax into it."

After a moment, she added, "I'm going to increase the speed a bit. At any time, you can tell me to stop and I'll stop it right away, okay?"

"Yup," I replied, concentrating on my white knuckles.

I was walking quickly, and the image of me falling a few weeks ago made my left leg stumble. "You okay?" Lori inquired.

"Yup!"

"You're doing great! We're almost there. Just a little faster, and you're going to be running."

"Yup!"

"Breathe."

"Yup!"

My left leg thumped louder as Lori increased the speed. "Okay, I'm going to turn it up now! I want you to hold on! You're going to tell me when you've had enough and want to stop, okay?"

"Yup!"

The thumping I heard was no longer that of my left leg but my heart drowning out the monster's laughter.

"Here we go!" Lori cheered.

The monster screamed to life, spinning below me. I stumbled but quickly recovered, gaining speed. The monster attempted to throw me again, but I kept up, hanging on, one foot after another, thump, thump, faster and faster! The beast roared and sped up yet again in a final attempt to throw me, but it was of no use. My feet were moving swiftly over the beast's back, and for the first time since the stroke, I was running! I was running like a child without a destination!

"Nicholas!"

"Yup?" I replied.

"You're running!"

"Yup!"

"You've done it!" Lori said. "You're running!"

"Yup!"

"You want to stop?"

"No!"

"Tell me when you want to stop!"

"Yup!"

"You want to stop?"

"No!"

"Thirty seconds!" Lori said.

"Tell me at a minute," I told Lori.

"Okay. You want to stop at a minute?"

"Maybe!"

"Okay…forty-five seconds."

My breathing became more labored.

"You okay?"

"Yup!"

"Almost there! Fifty-six, fifty-seven, fifty-eight, fifty-nine, one minute! Stop?"

"Not yet," I managed to huff out.

"Tell me when."

"Yup."

I ran for another few moments before I managed to blurt out, "Okay!"

"Stop?" Lori questioned.

"Yup!"

Lori instantly reduced the speed. The treadmill quickly slowed, and I was walking for a moment before Lori cut all the power and I came to a stop. Breathing heavily and still holding on, I stood there stunned, staring straight ahead. I finally turned my head to face Lori.

"Well, how was that?" I finally managed to ask.

An Orchestrated Mistake

Lori's eyes were full of emotion. Swallowing hard, she said, "Nobody runs in this room."

I stared at her, bit my bottom lip, and then looked past Lori to Robbie, who was sitting on his therapy table staring at me. Looking back at Lori, I smiled. "They do now."

"Yeah," Lori replied, blinking away tears. "*You* do now."

After running with Lori, my confidence grew and I progressed with my exercises. However, while the Wii did teach me to compensate and anticipate my moves, even with Lori's help, it continued to be a major source of frustration.

"Oh, come on! I jumped!" I blurted out after my little man crashed for the third time on the ski jump.

"I think your little guy needs a thicker helmet," Lori said, laughing.

"Or more athletic ability," I retorted.

"Maybe we should just forget the ski jump," Lori said. "There must have been freezing rain or something last night. The ski slope is a sheet of ice."

I looked over at Lori like she'd lost her mind. "Yeah, that's it, freezing rain."

"Why don't we try the wobble board," Lori said enthusiastically after she took the remote and switched the program. "You're good with that one. Here, try this."

The wobble board moved on the screen according to how I moved and leaned my body on the Wii sensor pad, and the object of the game was to roll the little balls into the holes without sending them crashing over the edge. I managed to get the first few balls in the holes quite easily, but then one went over the edge, followed by another, and I began to get frustrated.

An Orchestrated Mistake

"Ah!" I yelped as another one went over the edge.

"You're not concentrating," Lori offered.

"I am concentrating!"

"Just relax, take your time. Breathe," Lori encouraged.

"I am breathing!" I said as another ball tumbled over the edge.

"Relax. You're not relaxed," Lori said.

"I am relaxed! Here, you try!" I told Lori as another ball fell off the screen.

"I don't need to try. You have to do it, not me," Lori responded.

"I want to see you do it. I need to see how it's done."

Lori glared at me, took the remote, and stepped onto the pad. She immediately started to wobble, and her first ball flew all over the screen and fell off the edge.

"I wasn't ready," she said.

"Sounds familiar," I commented.

She started moving her body on the pad and got a ball to go down a hole.

"There!" she said, looking at me triumphantly.

"You don't have time to gloat," I said, pointing to the screen.

Lori started moving her body, and a ball went over the edge.

"Okay! Okay, I got this one," she said, but a moment later, that ball, too, went over the edge. "Arrrgg!"

An Orchestrated Mistake

"Breathe!" I encouraged.

"I am breathing!" Lori snapped as another ball went over the edge. "Arrrrrgggg!"

"Relax, you're not relaxed!"

"I am relaxed!"

"No, you're not, I can tell."

After another ball went over the edge, the game ended and the word "Rookie" flashed on the screen.

"Rookie?" Lori said, exasperated.

"Well, you only got one ball!" I explained.

"You put it on the hardest setting when I wasn't looking," Lori accused.

I took the remote and flashed the setting. It read, "Beginner."

"Oh," Lori said, staring at the screen.

"Oh," I echoed. "No need to be glum," I told her. "You did get the wobbling part down."

****

The warm spring weather had come, and Lori got special permission to take me to the park to run with her new Golden Retriever pup, Molly. Molly was at that stage where she wouldn't bring the ball back after fetching it but would expect you to run around and chase her until one of you got tired. That was usually me, but that's what Lori wanted, me running around chasing Molly. I eventually did find a way to get her to bring the ball back so I wouldn't have to run so much.

"Well, don't bribe her!" Lori yelled onto the field.

An Orchestrated Mistake

"I'm not bribing her!" I hollered back while bribing Molly with a treat. "Drop it," I told Molly. Molly dropped the ball at my feet and gobbled down the morsel from my hand. "See! She was hungry!" I yelled to Lori.

"She's a dog! She's always hungry!"

Running in the rehabilitation center was safe. No one even expected you to move quickly, never mind run, so style and appearance never mattered. But while at the park, I couldn't help feeling all eyes were watching and judging, and people were whispering, "Check out the running style of that guy! Ten bucks says he shit himself!" That's what I told Lori anyway when I ran for the second time on the treadmill: "I run like I crapped my pants."

I picked up the ball, threw it again, and Molly took off across the field after it.

"Bring me the treats!" Lori hollered. "You're supposed to be chasing her, not tricking her with snacks." I turned and walked the short distance back to Lori. "Hand them over," Lori said, extending her hand. "How are you supposed to practice running if you keep enticing her with snacks?"

"I don't need to run," I said, smiling. "I'll just leave for everything earlier."

"Yeah, sure," Lori said. "See how well that works for you."

"You know what I did today?" I said, taking a seat beside Lori on the bench.

"What?" she asked.

"Sat at the back of the bus."

"Really?"

"Even walked to the back when the bus was moving," I said proudly.

"That's really great," Lori commented. "You know we can probably think about discharging you from rehab."

"You think?"

"I do. You've improved a lot since you first started. But it would be useful to retake the tests you did and compare the results."

"Sure."

"You comfortable with being discharged from physiotherapy?" Lori asked.

"I'll miss you teasing me, but yes, I think I am."

"Great, then let's do the test in our next session and see how it goes."

Standing at the top of the staircase during the Community Balance and Mobility test, or CB&M, and looking down, I wasn't quite as confident as I was on that walk home. It's the damn vertigo that throws my balance.

Watching me staring down the stairs, Lori said, "We can pass on this part of the test if you'd like."

"And have you put down a zero? No way."

I stepped down on the first step, then the second, and then just resting my hand on the railing, I slid it down with me each step—three, four, five steps, faster now. Reaching the bottom of the staircase, I turned and looked up at Lori. "Well?"

"Not bad," she said, looking at her stopwatch. "Now come up."

An Orchestrated Mistake

No longer pulling myself up the stairs with two hands, I slid my hand up the railing with each step.

"Looking good," Lori said when I reached the top.

"I still need the railing."

"A lot of people do, even those who haven't had a stroke."

"I suppose."

Lori put me through the paces of the CB&M test during our next session, and any result I wasn't happy with, I told her I wasn't ready and had to do it again. She perfected her eye roll during the tests but didn't let me cheat, paying particular attention to my technique, making sure I was doing the exercises correctly.

Sitting on the bench in the gymnasium, Lori totaled up my score on her clipboard. "Do you remember your score the first time you took the test?" she asked after a series of calculations.

"No," I replied. "But I remember it wasn't very good."

"Five months ago, your score was 36 out of 96."

"Ouch. And this time?" I asked.

"72 out of 96."

"Hmmm."

"What do you mean, hmmm? 72 is great! Some people are lucky if they go up ten points."

"I just felt like I did better."

"You did do better," Lori exclaimed. "Thirty-six to seventy-two? That's a lot better, and you looked better too! You're not running like you crapped your pants anymore."

"Oh, now I know you're lying."

"So, you run like you've had a little accident. Who cares? You're running! You have to remember it's not about style. Sometimes it's about the effort you give. Some people come in here thinking we can do it for them, but we can't. They have to put in the effort if they want to improve, and you improved. Forget about style. I'd rather run like I crapped my pants than not run at all."

"Yeah," I said, nodding.

"I'm going to recommend you be discharged. I don't think there is anything more you can accomplish here. Keep doing your exercises, and who knows how far the brain can go in repairing itself, but I don't think you need us anymore."

"A little scary," I said, looking at the floor.

"What? Not needing us?"

"Yeah."

"You've made a lot of improvements with us around, so you're used to us, but you'll make improvements all on your own. And we're always here if you think you need a refresher. Well, I won't be here. I start my new job in a few weeks."

"What new job?"

"Physio over at the ICU with liver transplant patients. I'll help them come off the ventilators and focus on their mobility and what they need to accomplish physically so they can go home."

"Don't beat them like you did me."

"I'll just cut off their air."

"You're evil."

"Yeah, but I get results. So, the next session will be our last?"

"Sure. Our last," I said, nodding.

Walking to the elevators after our final session, Lori said, "You know, for someone who claimed he didn't need rehab, you sure have used it to travel a long way."

"I stagger around a lot, but I usually manage to find my way." Hitting the elevator button, I turned to Lori and handed her a card. "This is for you."

"Aw, thank you, how sweet," Lori replied, taking the card.

"You don't have to read it now. I just wanted to say thank you. You did a lot for me."

"You did all the work. I just supervised."

"You did more than supervise. You listened to and trusted me. That means a lot."

"I'll concede I listened to you, but you trusted you, and that's what meant a lot. Trusting yourself, that's when you start to make real progress."

"I guess."

"Thank you for my card."

"You're welcome," I said, giving Lori a hug. "I guess I was wrong about not needing rehab."

"Yeah, you were." Lori chuckled. "But you were right about one thing though, Nicholas."

"What's that?" I asked, stepping onto the elevator.

"That you didn't need a cane," Lori said, flashing her smile as the doors closed.

CHAPTER SIXTEEN

"It's sad when two fat people can't pass each other in a hallway without turning sideways," Bill, the fat superintendent of my building, said as we rounded the corner, passing each other. I chuckled and continued the ten paces to my apartment door. Wait a minute, I thought, looking back down the hall for Bill, but he had already disappeared. Did he just call me fat?

My dad had told me that I was looking a little tubby during lunch a few weeks before, but I blew it off, thinking I was just starting to look my age, middle-aged. No one had ever used the adjective *fat* in describing me before.

I put my key in to open my apartment and stepped inside. Closing the door, I went to the bathroom and stood in front of the mirror. "Shit," I said out loud. "When did this happen?"

There was no question. I was fat. I had graduated from tubby to fat—okay, morbidly obese—and hadn't even noticed.

When the programs ended some six months ago, I figured I had done all that I could, so that was that. This was how I was going to be for the rest of my life. Lori and the Heart and Stroke Program had taken me as far as I was going to go. Balance issues will forever challenge me. I will struggle to find words at times to communicate, and, at times, my thoughts will seem to stutter. This, along with a laundry list of diabetic maladies, may very well be my new world.

Once the programs had ended and I had turned in my pedometer, the only real exercise I was doing was walking—when I felt like it. Waking up tired every morning, I didn't often feel like walking unless there was a sale on some package of processed food, the staple of my diet. I knew intellectually I needed to make a lifestyle change, but the uncertainty if it would make any

An Orchestrated Mistake

difference in my physical abilities or cognitive function left me paralyzed, deflated, and unmotivated.

I had seen the old gang from the building sitting out back when I had walked up, and after Bill's jab, I decided to amble outside and join them.

Bobby, the retired postal worker, was regaling the gang about his mastery of the curveball that would have taken him to the majors, maybe even a World Series if only he could have put it over the plate. When Bobby finished, the group all nodded in agreement and sipped their beers, saying it was just bad luck he didn't make it to the majors. Denise, the hard-luck, middle-aged woman, offered some extra words of encouragement: "Don't worry, Bobby," she said, attempting to roll a cigarette, "you'll show 'em next time."

"Christ, woman!" Bobby snapped. "I'm seventy-five years old! There ain't going to be a next time!"

"Oh," Denise said, stunned. "Well, never mind then."

Ken leaned over towards me and mumbled, "Do-wacka-do."

I sat there listening to the group's stories of their youth, but really, I was thinking of how I could take control of my health. I wasn't entirely sure how. The programs had given me the tools, but I didn't know how to leverage them. What good is acquiring knowledge if you don't use it? I believe my tombstone will read, "He actually knew better."

"I grabbed the steel cable and pulled myself to the front of the ship," Ken said, pausing only long enough to take a sip of beer. "You should've seen it! The wind was blowing, the ice on the deck was six inches thick, and I had to smash it to bits, or we'd capsize! I'm telling ya, the North Atlantic is colder than a whore's heart in the winter, but I fought 'er and cleared that deck!" he said, chugging the last gulp of his beer before looking in his empty cooler for another one.

"Maybe she doesn't want to be a whore," Denise said across the table.

"What?" Ken groused, annoyed at the empty cooler and the interruption.

"I said, maybe she doesn't want to be a whore, and that's why her heart is cold."

Ken looked at the group that was staring at him, then looked at me. I shrugged my shoulders. "Okay!" Ken snarled at Denise. "It was colder than a witch's tit! Happy?" Ken looked around, his gaze finally settling on me.

"Well," I said with another shrug, "apparently you just need some part of the female anatomy to tell your story."

"Jesus!" Ken growled. "It was fuckin' cold, alright? Now stop interruptin'!"

"Who cares," Bobby interjected, reaching into Dave's basket to grab a beer after Dave had nodded off. "We've all heard the damn story a thousand times!"

"We have to listen to your damn baseball stories!" Ken snapped back.

"I think I was right," Denise said. "I don't think she wants to be a whore."

"Oh, for Christ's sake, forget it!" Ken bellowed. "I'm going inside!"

"Abandon ship!" Bobby mocked. "Tell us again how you sunk the fucking Bismarck!" Bobby yelled as Ken walked across the parking lot.

An Orchestrated Mistake

The banter and griping between the gang in the back parking lot was no longer a playful distraction but a reminder of how short life really is and how quickly broken dreams and aspirations can be snapped in two and left abandoned along the pathways of our lives. We are the writer/director of our own story, and it's up to us how the hero will live and how our movie will end. I knew that, but for some reason, I didn't yet feel the writer of my own life.

In the months after the programs, not only had my weight increased, but also my need for more medication. I was up to almost forty units of insulin a day, and the diabetes clinic suggested I needed additional fast-acting insulin to take with every meal. Roberts, my doctor, was prescribing more blood pressure pills as my blood pressure and weight increased. I had forgotten the taste of success I achieved by running with Lori, and in many ways, it was like I was still waiting for that magical pill, or maybe just someone to do the work for me. I felt lost and unfocused in the months immediately following the programs.

I thought long and hard about my situation and what I needed to do. First off, I knew no one would do the work for me, so it was up to me to take responsibility for my own health. Secondly, I knew there were three areas I needed to work on and improve to get my health back.

The biggest hurdle was my diet—no more processed food. I was going to have to make an effort in the kitchen beyond taking some prepackaged crap out of a box and throwing it in the oven.

I needed to find a proper diet, but there are so many diets out there, and I wouldn't know the difference between gluten or paleo or any other diet if they were doing a jig on my dinner plate. I didn't want to go on a diet. I would just start it, fall off or stop, and then go back to my old routine. No, I didn't need a diet. I needed a lifestyle change, including how I ate. I needed a way of eating that I could easily adopt and make my own. There would be time down the road to make adjustments or modify my nutritional habits, but for now, I wanted simple and immediate. I thought my head was going to explode when I was reading about food and nutrition, but one diet that stood out for me was the Mediterranean diet. It contained all the foods I enjoyed, was easy to prepare and understand, and was something I could adopt quickly. In my search for a nutritional lifestyle, I learned I needed to cut out refined, processed products like sugar and white flour.

Refined sugar is an addictive poison that permeates our society. Numerous studies have shown it speeds up aging, and in men, even drops their testosterone levels. Refined sugar affects the brain negatively in many ways, including brain atrophy. Forget just diabetics, refined sugar is a toxic poison to all our bodies. I love jams. Jams of all kinds, but jams are made with copious amounts of sugar. There are numerous reasons to cut this poison out of your life, and it's not hyperbole in calling refined sugar a poison.

As I was writing out my lifestyle plan, I was excited but also scared. Scared I couldn't make the changes that I needed to, and most importantly, make them stick.

The other two areas I needed to work on were obvious to me. I needed to exercise—and not just a walk to the store or a walk of a mile or two a day, but I needed to join a gym and get serious. I saw one down the street from me, about a ten-minute walk. Half the battle about committing to a gym is just getting there, and with this one being so close, I made a note to go in and sign up.

The third thing I needed to do was improve my word recall and use of language. I was hit with a mild form of expressive aphasia, although often it didn't seem very mild to me. Caused by a brain injury, expressive aphasia is the loss of understanding or expressing speech.

There are obvious signs of expressive aphasia that most people associate with a stroke patient, like slow speech and the slurring of words. There are also patients with this disorder that may not display these obvious outward signs. Nevertheless, the internal battle to find the right words rages on. I fell into this latter category.

I didn't have a problem keeping up with simple conversations, but anything above that, I'd switch into listening mode and lob easy questions if I wanted to remain engaged.

Keeping up in a detailed, fast-moving conversation was akin to driving the Autobahn in second gear. I'd eventually get there, but I had to over-rev my brain to do it.

After the stroke, searching for words and ways to articulate my thoughts was, and remains, exhausting. I was far more likely to fall back on my expletive vocabulary because it's easier to find and say, 'fuck it' or 'screw this' rather than trying to engage in a polite response.

This also significantly affects how I write. If I was trying to write the sentence, "It's a beautiful blue sky," but wrote *bleu*, I might stare at the word bleu and know it was spelled wrong, but if all the various technological spell checks couldn't correct it, I was screwed. The sentence then became, "It's a beautiful *green* sky." Not exactly what I wanted to say, but it's all I had. My only other option was to drop the sentence altogether or perhaps write, "No one gives a shit about the fuckin' sky."

To overcome this malady, I knew I needed to do two things. I first needed to focus on words, their meaning, correct usage, and spelling. I found a wonderful way to do so by volunteering at the Halifax Public Library teaching English to immigrants new to Canada. There I found myself immersed, challenged, and motivated to strengthen my use of language.

An Orchestrated Mistake

Secondly, I had to do something I had put off for years. It was a part of the dream that took me to New York in the first place. I needed to write again. I began by rewriting my play.

It is a two-act drama based on the relationship between a father and a son, which I had written when I was around thirty. It was produced and first performed in Vancouver, and after the show one night, a psychiatrist came up to me and asked for a copy of the script to use in his practice with his patients. I told him I intended to rewrite it, and when finished, I would send it on to him.

I never did get around to that rewrite, and in New York, I got preoccupied with working on other people's projects. My writing got put on the back burner.

I now know why. It all flooded home to me while I was working on the rewrite in Halifax. I'm terrified of writing. I'm passionate about it, and I love it, but it also scares the hell out of me. Intellectually I know each keystroke or phrase can't be perfect, but my passion says it better be. Starting that rewrite, it wasn't just that desire for perfection that handicapped me. It was also the expressive aphasia.

Shortly after I began the rewrite, I had a realization that knocked me over and stopped me cold. During the press interviews during the original production, I said the show was about a father and a son. It was a fictional family relationship and not about my relationship with my father. At the time, I truly believed it.

I was right. It had nothing to do with my father and me, but the show had everything to do with my mother and me. The backdrop was completely different, masking who those two main characters were, but there was no doubt in my mind when I was rewriting the play it was, and remains, my mother and myself in those pages.

An Orchestrated Mistake

My old high school staged the show for a week and invited my family and me to attend the final performance. Someone asked me after the show if I was going to write another play. My mother heard the question and chimed in immediately, "Oh, probably. I'm sure the next one will be a comedy." We all laughed, but thinking back on it, though she would never admit it, I think she recognized herself up there on the stage.

The whole play was autobiographical. A point I aggressively had denied to the press. I couldn't believe I had been so willfully blind to the fact the show came from my family, and more so, my most personal relationship with my mother.

In my mind, the play was conceived in a strip club in Vegas when I was in my late twenties. I didn't even recognize until I was doing the rewrite in Halifax that the female love interest was based on a stripper I had met at that club.

"So why are you here?" she asked me, abandoning her stool and taking the one next to me.

"Drinks are seventy-five cents," I replied, stirring my drink.

"Not here at the club. Vegas. You said you're not a gambler, so why are you here?"

"It's not L.A. You?"

She nodded and took a sip of her beer. "It's not Aberdeen, South Dakota either."

It was my turn for a knowing nod.

"You see my show?" she finally asked, resting her head on her hand, waiting for the review.

"No," I replied. "I watch strippers about as often as I gamble."

"You don't like strippers?"

"It's not that I don't like them," I said. "I just never know where to look."

"What do you mean you don't know where to look? When you go to a movie, you look at the screen, don't you?"

"Of course."

"Well, think of us as an action movie."

"Hey, Janice!" the bartender called from midway down the bar. "You want another?"

"Yes, but make it a Greyhound this time," she shouted back. "And don't make it a seventy-five cent Greyhound. You want another?" she asked, turning back to me. But before I could answer, Janice yelled, "And another…"

"Gin and tonic," I said.

"Gin and tonic! A real one!"

"Thanks," I said, draining my glass.

"Thank me if it's not piss water," Janice replied. "Probably should have stuck with beer."

"Why is American beer like making love in a canoe?" I asked her.

"I don't know," she replied with a puzzled frown. "Why?"

"It's fucking close to water."

"Oh, Jesus, that's lame."

"Old Canadian joke," I said.

An Orchestrated Mistake

"You Canadian?"

"Yeah, between failed stints in L.A."

"Oh, an actor," Janice said with an eye roll.

"Only between rejected screenplays."

"So, L.A. spat you out too, and you thought you'd try Vegas?" Janice asked.

"I wouldn't use the word 'spat.' I was more like thrown up."

"Hey, you haven't lived until L.A. has thrown up on you at least once."

"True," I said. "So, your name is Janice?"

"Yes," she said, extending her hand. "You?"

"Nicholas. My dad wanted to call me Shane. You know, after the Western movie."

"What movie?"

"Shane."

"Never saw it."

"Neither did my mom. So, my mom won out and named me Nicholas."

"Good," said Janice, "you don't strike me as the bronco-busting type."

"Well, I did get bucked off a horse once," I replied.

"Nah, I'm guessing you like cats."

"I do like cats," I said, staring into Janice's deep blue eyes. "You know, the first girl I went out with at sixteen was named Janice."

"Got your heart broken at sixteen, did you?"

"Who says I got my heart broken? Maybe I broke her heart."

"I don't think so," Janice said, studying my face. "I think the relationship just ended, and you were just as confused about it as to why you are here tonight."

"You think so?"

"I do. You see," Janice said, turning on her stool towards me, "there are three kinds of guys in the dating game. Those that break hearts, 'snap!' And those that get their heart broken, 'boing!' And those that are too distracted to know the difference. I think you're one of those."

"Too distracted?" I questioned.

"Exactly. Distracted guys just don't get it. Relationships are secondary. They'll never have a wife or a serious lover. They'll only ever steal a night."

"I see," I said after mulling over her words.

"No, you don't," Janice replied. "That's the problem with distracted guys. They don't see."

The next morning, I walked back from Janice's apartment to my motel. The guy in the next room had blown his brains out, and the cops had yellow tape everywhere. The motel manager told me he would move me to a room at the opposite end if I wanted to stay another night. I told him I wanted to stay in the same room.

An Orchestrated Mistake

"You don't understand, kid," the manager, an ex-Vietnam vet, said. "Death stinks. It's hot. This is Vegas. I'll give you a new room."

"I want to stay in my room," I said. "And I want to stay for a week."

That memory of my trip to Las Vegas came flooding back as I struggled to rewrite the play in Halifax. I had forgotten about Janice, yet Janice was the name of a character in my play. She was even from Aberdeen, South Dakota. I realized that Janice was right all those years ago. I was, and remain, distracted. I had been distracted by my quest for success in the entertainment industry, and in so doing, I had forgotten to be good to myself. I look at life, and I just see a series of stories: short, long, some happy, some sad. In a way, I guess there is nothing wrong with that—unless, of course, the stories distract you from what your reality truly is. Case in point, I'm diabetic. I ignored it and walked right into another story.

While I was working on the rewrites, I was still blogging. I also joined the gym down the street and signed up to teach English at the public library. I needed to keep busy to distract from my crumbling peace of mind.

On my first day as a volunteer teacher at the library, Francis, the ESL coordinator, told me about my two students. "They've only been here a few weeks, so their English is very limited. The daughter understands a little more than the mother, so you're really going to have to start with the basics and work on their conversational English."

I had only taken one weekend workshop to become a volunteer, and other than working with the interns at Three Walls Productions, I had never formally, or informally, taught anyone. I learned new immigrants who don't speak their adopted country's language could often feel overwhelmed by the simplest tasks, such as setting up a home phone and Internet or even just going on a trip to the bank. Communicating in person is a little easier because the newly arrived immigrant can pick up on body language or gestures. On the other hand, communicating over the phone in a strange language is nothing short of a total nightmare.

Francis introduced me to the mother and daughter, the beauty of their Arabic features instantly striking me. It turned out the daughter was a fashion model in Tehran, and by all accounts, the mother could have been on the runway as well.

"Are you a model too?" I asked, turning to the mother after we had introduced ourselves.

"No, no," she said bashfully, looking down at the floor. "Bank," she added, pointing to herself.

"She mean she a bank manager in Tehran," the daughter chimed in helpfully.

"Ah, you work with money? We like money."

"Yes!" Both ladies giggled in stereo.

"Well, let's start with the basics," I suggested, opening up the Farsi-English Pictionary.

"No! No!" the mother said, putting her cell phone in my hand. "You must call."

"Call?" I questioned. "Call who?"

"Um, doctor," the mother responded.

"Oh, you want me to call your doctor?"

"Yes!" she responded, handing me a slip of paper with the number.

An Orchestrated Mistake

"And say what? You want me to make you an appointment."

"No, no," the mother said, frustrated. She looked around the room at the other students and tutors, and then grabbing and bouncing one of her rather buxom breasts with both hands, said, "I need you to call doctor."

"Oh shit," I mumbled, looking around for Francis.

The mother started conversing with her daughter in Farsi, and finally, the daughter turned to me, grabbing her own set of what had to be at least 38 DDs.

"Jesus," I mumbled, wondering where the hell Francis was.

"She had test," the daughter said while jiggling her pair. "She miss call from doctor."

"I got it. I got it," I said, raising my hands to get her to stop shaking her breasts. "She had a mammogram, and you want me to call to get the test results."

Both ladies looked at each other. I looked around, and all seemed oblivious to our little game of erotic charades. "Mammogram," I said, grabbing my own breasts. "Call the doctor for the mammogram test results."

"Yes! Yes!" both women shrieked.

I dialed the number, wondering where the hell Francis had disappeared to, and also wondered if any of the other tutors in their first five minutes on the job ever had to play a game of such charades.

I got the receptionist on the line, and after explaining the situation and who I was, the receptionist stated she couldn't give out test results over the phone. She would need to make an appointment to see the doctor.

"She needs to go in to see the doctor," I said to the daughter, who translated to her mother.

"When?" the daughter asked, turning back to me.

"How soon can you get her in," I asked the receptionist. "Tomorrow morning at ten?" I asked the ladies after getting the receptionist's reply. Both women nodded 'yes.' "Fine, she'll be there at ten tomorrow." I looked across the table at a frightened mother and a hopeful daughter. "Look," I added to the receptionist. "I'm more than a little familiar with your policy on giving out test results over the phone, but you're not staring across the table at two frightened ladies. Can you at least give me a hint so I can tell them something to ease their minds?" The receptionist fell silent for a moment. "Please," I added.

"Tell her that everything is just fine," she finally said.

"Thank you," I said, hanging up. "She said everything is just fine." I smiled to make sure they understood. The two turned and hugged each other for a moment. When they turned back to me, they both had huge grins. Instantly, the mother's eyes began to water as she put her hand up to her mouth, and I honestly couldn't tell whether she was laughing or indeed crying.

In the weeks prior to teaching ESL, I did waddle on down the street to join the gym. I had also decided to adopt the Mediterranean diet lifestyle. I hadn't yet begun my dietary regime when I got a bit of a shock on my first day at the gym.

Waiting at the gym for my trainer in my cut-off sweatpants, Mets t-shirt, and ball cap, I resembled Spanky from *Our Gang* way more than someone searching for the path to wellness.

I spotted a digital scale just outside the changing room door. It had been almost six months since the scale at the diabetes clinic groaned, "A hundred and eighty-seven pounds, fatty, now get the hell off!" At five-foot-eight, at that weight I already looked like I was with child, perhaps twins, and I was definitely rocking the man-tit thing.

Stepping on the scale, I looked down as the numbers flew by and soared like the debt clock in Times Square. When they finally stopped, it read 198.9 pounds. "This can't be right," I said out loud, staring down at the numbers. "Gyms never have working scales," I said to a guy exiting the changing room while stepping off.

Intrigued by my comment, he jumped on the scale, looking down at his weight. "Yeah, this one works," he said, stepping off.

I stepped back on the scale after he was out of sight, and peering down with one eye shut, the scale now read 199.0. Jesus, I've gained an ounce in less than a minute. What happened? Did I forget to exhale?

I walked over and plunked my now fat ass down in a chair to wait for the trainer and thought, *I really do need to change my eating habits. Immediately.* As long as I continued to trade convenience for healthy eating by consuming processed crap out of a box, my body was going to reflect what was really going on inside. I would look overfed, but in reality I was nutritionally starved.

"So, you said you've worked out before?" Dustin asked after introducing himself.

"Yes," I replied, trying to sound enthusiastic about being back at the gym. I told Dustin about my days working out with Sonya's ex-husband, who was an amateur bodybuilder. My then brother-in-law put me through the paces and had me bench pressing my body weight, a muscular 180 pounds. "Yeah, I've worked out before, but it was a long time ago," I added with a shrug.

"That's fine," Dustin said enthusiastically. "Muscles have memory."

"Mine have short-term memory," I lamented.

"Why don't you tell me what you hope to get out of the gym?" Dustin asked.

"Well, I want to lose weight," I said sheepishly.

"Okay."

"Maybe ten or fifteen pounds," I continued as Dusty stared blankly back. "Okay, maybe closer to twenty or thirty pounds," I said as Dustin's brow involuntarily furrowed. "Okay, fifty pounds," I finally confessed. "I'd like to lose about fifty pounds."

"Okay, what else?"

I launched into a short monologue about all my health issues, which ended up sounding more like a manifesto as to why I should *not* be at the gym but rather splayed out on the couch eating chocolate bonbons.

"Don't worry," Dustin said after my monologue. "I'll design a good workout for you."

Damn. I was hoping he'd just tell me to forget it and send me home with that box of bonbons.

Dustin and I both were surprised by my lack of strength and coordination. It had been twenty-plus years since I had last worked out and well over ten years of uncontrolled diabetes ravaging my body.

"Here, let's try the two-pound dumbbells," Dustin suggested after I had dropped both the ten and the five while attempting simple deep knee lunges. Again, my balance wouldn't permit me to lunge at all, never mind trying to do so while holding two-pound dumbbells. Exercises I had performed with ease years ago were now destroying what little ego I had left.

An Orchestrated Mistake

Whistling happy tunes between sets of exercises, it finally became evident I couldn't lift and control the lightest free weights, even to Dustin, the quintessential optimist. He was going to have to relegate my exercise program to fixed machines. Dustin designed a program for me on the Nautilus machines that relied less on coordination and balance and focused more on developing strength and stamina. However, I knew exactly what I would be shooting for, and that was picking up and utilizing those free weights.

Resting after using a machine, I didn't realize I was staring at a woman some twenty-five to thirty years my senior working out on the leg press.

"Are you waiting for this?" she asked, standing up.

"Oh, no. Sorry, whenever you're finished. I was just standing here catching my breath."

"Well, I'm finished, so it's all yours. Would you like me to remove my weights for you?"

"Oh, no, no. I was thinking of adding more, but I'll just use your setting for a warm-up," I said, sitting down on the machine. Pushing the leg press, an involuntary guttural groan escaped. I was able to push the weights no more than two inches before they came crashing down. I tried again, repositioning myself, but this time the weights barely rose an inch before slamming back.

The woman reappeared by my side. "Here, honey, let me remove some of those weights for you."

"Thanks," I mumbled.

"That better, dear?" she asked after leaving just two small weights on each side of the press.

But after a brief push, I sighed. "I think you should take one more off."

There have been many times during my recovery my fingertips have slipped off the mantle of pride. But as Lori had said on my first day of rehab, there is no room in recovery for ego.

Like most things, I get obsessed with achieving my goals, so in those early months when I wasn't tutoring or working on my literacy skills, I often attended the gym up to three times a day.

I also started my Mediterranean lifestyle in my small kitchen, and for the first time I could remember, was actually looking forward to preparing and eating meals. Between the gym and the healthy eating, I lost over twenty-five pounds in three months, and Roberts, my doctor, cut my medications way back. I eventually went off insulin completely. I was feeling great, but recovery was waiting in the wings to give my ego another body slam and show me life still required me to fight.

****

It had been well over a year since I had seen Jan and Geoff, who I had met days after my arrival in Halifax. It was probably even closer to two years before I saw them again—not because I didn't want to, but because in those early days I was on such an emotional rollercoaster I didn't feel much like socializing.

After we reconnected, Geoff called me up to tell me about a job opportunity at the National Film Board of Canada in Halifax.

"You could do this job in your sleep," Geoff said. "It's a production coordinator position."

Geoff gave me the number to the woman at the NFB, and I called her, and she said she had heard about me through Geoff. Unfortunately, the job had been filled, but she asked me to send my resume anyway. I didn't have a resume. I hadn't needed one in decades. So, I got my friend Rosemary, another tutor at the library and a few years my senior, to help me put one together.

"I can't believe you've never had a resume." Rosemary laughed, saving her creation in my computer.

"Never needed one," I said, pulling my laptop closer so I could send the CV to the Film Board. Rosemary was always quick to laugh, and as a newly retired editor/reporter from a Saskatchewan newspaper, she was always willing to read and offer me help for my blog.

About a month after sending in my CV, I got an interview at the NFB. "You're actually overqualified for the position," the cheerful woman said after I took a seat in her office. "Reading your resume, you're also overqualified for my job."

"Well, I wasn't sure when you called what exactly you were looking for."

"It's really only a temporary entry-level position, so I'm not sure if you'd like to be tested for it, but I thought it was a way to at least get you in here and meet you. Seriously, I feel kind of silly testing you for this position," she added.

I looked at it as an opportunity to reenter the industry and as a way to meet others and make contacts. "Well, I'm here now, so we might as well do it," I said.

The test was remarkably simple. She showed me their computers and software in a vacant office and asked me to look up an item, identify the quantity in stock in their Montreal office, and email her the information. She added that she needed a green screen and wanted to know where to purchase one in Halifax and how much it would cost.

An Orchestrated Mistake

I'd done these simple tasks a million times before at Three Walls, and a green screen is just what it sounds like. Any flat or green surfaced material used to project digital images on. Simple.

My problem began immediately when she closed the door to my office. "You've got fifteen minutes."

The simple instructions I'd jotted down were now not only a jumbled mess on paper but also a jumbled mess in my head. I couldn't remember how to log on to look up the codes. The simple data entry system she demonstrated only moments before looked like a foreign language, and none of her instructions made any sense. After almost ten minutes, I finally accessed the database, but I'd accomplished nothing else.

"How's it going?" she asked, poking her head in.

"Getting there." I lied.

"Five more minutes," she said, closing the door.

Abandoning the database, I was able to look up a vendor in Halifax that sold green screens, but their descriptions of the products and their website had me confused. I was able to write down the price for some green screen software before she opened the door and asked me to return to her office.

"Well, how did it go?" she asked.

"I think you're right. I think the job is more suited to a film student or someone wanting to break into the business," I said, almost to the floor.

"You weren't able to look up the item and send the email to Montreal?" she asked, checking the database on her computer.

"No," I replied.

"Were you able to get a price on a green screen?"

"No."

"Did you find anything out about them? What kind we should purchase, anything like that?"

"No."

"Do you know what they're made of? What they're used for?" she asked, puzzled by my replies.

I looked around her office for an answer. Unable to find one, I searched the chasm of my memory but saw nothing. "I have no idea," I finally whispered.

Crushed, hurt, and humiliated, I walked halfway home before I realized it was pouring rain and I was drenched through to my marrow. How could I have failed this simple test so miserably? I emailed the woman at the NFB and withdrew my application. Having thought about it on the way home, I added some tips for using a green screen, suggesting material and storage options. I hit send and just stared at my computer, still in my wet clothes.

A few minutes later, the building-entry buzzer snapped me out of my trance. Moments later, there was a knock on my door, and I opened it to find Rosemary standing there. Her mouth dropped open. I had forgotten we had made plans to work on my blog.

"What the hell happened to you?" she asked.

"I walked home."

"Why didn't you call? How did the interview go?"

I couldn't find any words to say to Rosemary, and she instantly started blinking away tears. "It's not that bad… Really," I said. Rosemary bit her bottom lip. I stepped in to hug her. "I'm fine, really," I repeated. "It's all good," I whispered. "I just need to work harder."

CHAPTER SEVENTEEN

Roughly seven or so weeks after my disastrous interview with the National Film Board of Canada, I received written notice the appointment to see my neuropsychologist was only days away. This was one appointment that had me scheming about what to say to my neurologist to get out of it. I did think about telling him the truth: "Hey, I was just going to lay on her couch and lie anyway, so really, what's the point?"

That wouldn't have been far from the truth. I have known most of my life I struggled with social anxiety and bouts of depression. In kindergarten or grade one, I came home in tears when I was given an invitation to a classmate's birthday party. I did everything in my power to get out of it, including trying to convince my mother she should attend for me. Surprisingly, that didn't work, so I just told her I was sick. In my final year of high school, I attended many parties because I felt I should, but I struggled to get through each of them. When a friend of mine heard that my parents were both out of town one weekend, he talked me into throwing a party, but when about three hundred people showed up, I welcomed the cops busting it up before midnight and sending everyone home.

My rounds of depression have broken countless relationships and kept me less than honest with friends. Humor has always been my passport to get through the day in a social situation, and when that fails, it can be booze. I need to know there is an exit strategy. If I feel trapped, whether it's a social situation or a relationship, it's game over. I have no idea how I'm going to react. I need to know that I can go home alone.

I cannot define the feeling of depression. I'm just unmotivated, unfocused, and all over the map. I can go months and never experience it. When it hits, it may last an hour, a week, or even months. Or maybe it's just there all the time. I really don't know. But what I do know is that because I was unwilling to talk about it to anyone, the moment a partner would ask me, "What's wrong?" I was looking for the exit. How do you answer that question when you, yourself, are unable to define what you feel? You can't, so you walk away.

I don't know how you combat social anxiety, I'm not a psychologist, but I know I was happiest when being true to my authentic self. I need to create. I loved working on other people's movies at Three Walls Productions, but even that was not being completely true to myself. I needed more than that. I've always known I've needed to find and tell stories. But not any story; stories that enlighten and entertain. They needed to be stories that, when finished, go beyond the question, 'So where are we going for pizza?'

I knew after the NFB interview I had to step into the ring in a big way. I needed to put my doubts and fears into a headlock and squeeze until they cried *uncle*. I knew, and was certain, there was only one way out. I needed to do something I should have done thirty years ago. Commit to my authentic self and write my way out. I knew in my heart, but my heart was not speaking to my brain, and I didn't have the courage to write anymore.

"Rosemary, I've decided I'm not writing the blog anymore," I said, weeks after the NFB interview. "We don't need to work on rewriting any more chapters."

"What?" Rosemary choked, almost dropping her coffee.

"I don't want to do it. It's just an exercise in frustration," I replied. "I can't spell. When you read it out loud, it always sounds awkward, and right now, my head is just not in it."

"So, when will your head be in it?" Rosemary said with a bite of sarcasm.

"No idea."

An Orchestrated Mistake

Rosemary stared me down for a moment, then looked away.

"Look," I finally said, "I thought I was at least ready to return and work on other people's films. But I can't even do that. Forget about a return to New York. I can't even get an entry-level job in Halifax. And writing? Forget it. I can't even sort out the thoughts in my head."

"So, what? You're quitting?" It was my turn to break her glare and look away. "Well?" Rosemary asked.

"Yeah, I suppose I am," I whispered.

"That's not the Nicholas I met and worked with these last few months."

"Yeah, well…"

"Well, what?" Rosemary asked. "One interview goes sideways, and you throw in the towel? Are you just going to give up? Are you quitting the gym too?"

The truth was the gym had been my lifeline. It was the only way I was able to tread water. Exercise is well known to be a way to get the body to release endorphins and serotonin, which have a positive effect on the mind, body, and spirit. I became obsessed with the gym. That, along with my Mediterranean eating habits, had me shedding fifty pounds in under six months, off insulin completely, and cutting my blood pressure meds down to next to nothing. I started Pilate's classes for my balance and was probably in the best shape of my adult life. Despite these achievements, I couldn't shake the feeling that one engine had flamed out and the other was on fire and I was going down.

"No, I'm not quitting the gym," I mumbled.

"Just writing," Rosemary snapped again.

"Yeah."

"Well, if you're not going to write, I'd sure like to know what the hell you're going to do," she quipped.

"Me too."

"I'm not letting you give up, you know."

"Sadly," I replied. "I know that too."

Life is not the sole pursuit of happiness, but the pursuit of life experiences, some joyful, others dark. Both make up the human experience that is revealing of self. You must experience the yin and the yang, the light and dark, for the true pursuit of self. The contrast pushes you to the edge of self-examination, revealing the characteristics that make up your soul. Darkness is a great learning tool, and you should not shy away from, but embrace it as part of the human experience.

An unexpected dark moment hit me a few days later after meeting with Rosemary. At four thirty-six in the morning, my eyes snapped open. As I stared at the digital clock beside my bed, I instantly knew I had an exit strategy.

I had become obsessed about a way out for months. Even though I was in excellent physical shape, emotionally I was a wreck. Since the NFB interview, I felt my situation was hopeless. At four thirty-six that morning, I finally had an answer. No pain. No blood. I would simply go to sleep and never wake up. It would just look like I miscalculated with my medications and made a fatal error. An idiot right to the end. Everything would look like an honest mistake.

It had been no secret I've never had any fear of dying. I clearly remember at age six, one day while my mother was helping me put on my boots to drive me to kindergarten, I asked, "What does reincarnation mean?" I have no idea where I heard this word or even why I asked.

An Orchestrated Mistake

My mother stared up at me, stunned by the question, before finally answering, "It means that you've lived here before."

"Oh," I responded as she slipped on the last boot and stood up. "Well," I said, looking up at her, "if we've lived here before, why are we still fighting in Vietnam?"

My mother stared down at me for a moment before she finally said, "Get in the car."

Over the years, I had moments like that with my father as well.

I knew exactly what I would do. Go for lunch with Dad and have one of those conversations about how at peace I am with death. It would just be ironic that it happened a few days later.

That morning at four thirty-six, I got out of bed and went into the bathroom to open my medicine cabinet.

On the second shelf staring back at me was my ticket home. My exit, my way out. I stared at the bottles. It was numbing to know I could do this. I know suicide is a permanent solution to a temporary problem, but I was tired, and this just seemed simple. I was tired of the struggles with anxiety and depression. While my struggle with diabetes had been barely two decades, my struggles with anxiety and depression had been a lifetime. I was just tired and without hope.

I started to feel guilty the longer I stared into that cabinet. Only days before, I had watched the documentary entitled *Blood Brother* about AIDS orphans in India. The last twenty-five minutes of the documentary showcased a young boy clinging and fighting for his life. It was particularly hard to watch. I paced in front of the screen with tears streaming down my cheeks as the little boy waged his battle to live. Staring into the cabinet that morning, I felt the tears again on my cheeks. Not because of the memory of the boy, but because of the guilt I felt for giving up on my own life. The boy fought to live while I struggled to understand my want for death. My two arms supported me as the tears of weakness and hopelessness dripped into the sink. I looked back up at the open cabinet, unable to look at those medications anymore. I closed the cabinet door and saw a completely shattered man staring back at me in the mirror. I didn't recognize him. I thought about the boy. I also thought about my mother's courageous thirteen-year battle with leukemia. As I stared into my own image, it came to me in a flash. I had my way out. It takes great courage just to incarnate into this world. The darkness and the light must both be embraced and experienced to reassure us we are indeed a part of this universe.

The emotional pain and conflict began to recede like a tidal wave returning to the ocean. In the cabinet was an exit door, but I knew at that moment I didn't need to take it. I just wanted to know it was there. Knowing that gave me an illusion of control over my own life, and thus I could control my future. I could control whether I lived or died.

I stood there for some time in the bathroom, numbed by the whole experience, and eventually made my way back into bed. I lay there exhausted but unable to sleep. I read years earlier Ernest Hemingway and his father, Clarence, in addition to their mental health issues, suffered for years from devastating health complications brought on by diabetes. Sadly, as we know, both took their own lives. I'm in no way a mental health expert, but as I lay there staring at the ceiling, I wondered if the effects of diabetes played some role in exacerbating their already fragile state of mind.

It was my impulse to walk to that edge that woke me at four thirty-six that morning. And an hour or so later, it was the acceptance that we are all the writers and players in our own story that walked me back from the edge.

An Orchestrated Mistake

This was my state of mind when I received the notice to meet with the neuropsychologist. I knew I would be truthful with her. I would be honest about my self-destruction. After all, I brought all this hardship upon myself. My bitterness was directed at myself because I knew the stroke was completely avoidable, and I'd known it long before it ever happened. I was solely responsible.

I didn't want to discuss the 4:36am episode. I needed more time to process that. Also, I knew I was much too male to delve into that. Besides, I had been deflecting truth and questions my whole life, so I was sure I could do it for two days of testing with a neuropsychologist. I just had to make sure I picked a suitable mask to wear.

"Do you know why you're here?" the neuropsychologist asked, taking a seat opposite me.

"Because my neurologist thinks I'm a loon?" I replied, looking around her office for the infamous couch.

"No, that could be a separate matter," she replied, smiling. "We're going to assess any changes that may have occurred, neurologically speaking, as a result of your stroke. Things like your memory, concentration, language, spatial skills, and things of that nature."

"So, you want to see what lights are still turned on?"

"In essence, yes," the doctor said. "There will be three parts to your assessment. This morning's interview, the testing, which will take the better part of the day tomorrow, and a feedback session in a few weeks to review your results. Okay so far?"

"Let's get started."

I felt comfortable with the doctor, but when she got around to asking me about the day of the stroke, I was completely caught off guard by my strong emotional response.

"It's fine," the doctor said, pushing a box of tissues towards me.

"I don't need those," I said, wiping my eyes with the back of my hand. "I've told the story a hundred times before, but I've never really heard it, ya know?"

"But it's your story," she stated.

"I know," I replied. "I've just never listened to it. I guess I'm a little emotional. I'm sorry."

"A stroke is an emotional event."

"No, you don't understand. I don't do emotional."

"I see," the doctor said, nodding.

"Well, I lie. Ever since the stroke, happy makes me emotional."

"Are you happy now?" she asked.

"No," I responded, looking out the window. "Just fragile."

I felt safe with this doctor, but I wasn't about to elaborate on my fragility. Instead, I chose to tell her about the ticking clock that had been in my head since that September afternoon in New York.

"The ticking just got louder that afternoon. I mean, I'm sure we all are aware of the clock, but it's digital. We can't hear it. But now it's right here," I said, holding an imaginary clock to my ear. "It's just so loud, and now more than ever, I feel desperate to get on with it. On with what, I don't know. But on with something."

"You always hear the clock?" the doctor asked.

"Since the stroke, yes," I said. "Sometimes it's louder than other times."

"What do you do about it?"

"Get angry," I said.

"Angry?"

"Yes."

"About what?" she questioned.

"Wasting so much time."

The next day the neuropsychologist's intern spent the day with me conducting tests. After asking me to repeat back a series of words in a certain order, I got so frustrated after my third attempt I finally said, "Let's forget it and just move on."

Games of connect the dots always bored me as a kid, but now I was concentrating like a brain surgeon to complete the task. At one point, I was so inept at utilizing my short-term memory I burst out in uncontrollable laughter. Trying to pull it together, I couldn't stop laughing, and before long, the young intern was giggling right along with me. The two of us had to take a timeout and leave the room before we could pull it back together. The rest of the day's testing was pretty much hit or miss, but I did manage to muddle through.

I went back to see the neuropsychologist a few weeks later, and subsequently, she sent her final report to my doctor. Dr. Roberts called me in to go over the results.

Her report stated: *His visuospatial skills were an area of weakness.* This may be why I can stare at a word, know that it's spelled incorrectly, but I cannot sort out the letters to correct the spelling. *His concentration and processing speed were consistent with weaker visuospatial skills, and there was a mild relative weakness in visual attention* span. *Auditory working memory was also somewhat lower than expected given his good basic attention span. There were subtle findings of very mild difficulty monitoring responses on a word list, learning task...*

The report went on to state: *He uses humor frequently, but in a self-report questionnaire, Mr. Alexander showed subclinical dysphoric symptoms such as mild decreased interest, loss of pleasure, guilt, increased crying, and reduced energy. He also endorsed the item, "I have thoughts of killing myself, but I would not carry them out." However, his responses did not suggest clinically significant depression, and when asked about it in our feedback session, he stated he did not think he was depressed.*

Wow, so glad I chose the right mask that day. I certainly didn't recall endorsing the item that I have thoughts of killing myself, and I would think I would remember endorsing such a statement. I guess I must have if she put it in her final report. Her line about *subclinical*, as I understood it, meant a disease without signs or with symptoms that are undetectable by physical examination. *Dysphoric* is the opposite of euphoria, or an emotional state characterized by anxiety, depression, or unease.

I did my best at masking my inner truth and emotional state of mind at the time, but when it came right down to it, she saw right through me. When Dr. Roberts was reading the report to me in his office, he snapped his head to look at me after reading the comment on suicide. I scoffed, shrugged my shoulders, and said, "Well, that's total bullshit." We both had a nervous chuckle and moved on.

The dark times are there for a reason. They may seem long at the time, but they are brief. Most importantly, they must be embraced if there's going to be any hope of returning to your light.

My cousin Michael in Australia had taken to calling me every few months just to say hi and let me know he was thinking about me. Other than the call when he told me our grandmother had died from complications of diabetes, our calls were usually light and wandering in scope. We would take jabs at the secrecy and sometimes lunacy of our mothers. After that, though, I said, "You know, all I really know about my mother and your mother's side of the family is that they are direct descendants of Thomas Moore, the Irish revolutionary poet."

Michael roared with laughter. "Who told you that, mate? That is funny, crikey! Thomas Moore!"

"Mom told me. I remember her reading me one of his poems in the laundry room when I was a small boy."

"That's a good one," Michael said, laughing harder.

"Ask your aunt next time you call her. Ask her if she is a descendant of Thomas Moore!"

Michael was finding this way too funny. "What the hell is so damn funny?" I finally asked.

"Mate," Michael said, "Thomas Moore had five children, all of whom died very young. I think the oldest died at twenty-seven. So, you tell me, how did he have any descendants?"

"Oh," I said.

"Oh!" Michael roared. "That was a classic story by your mother. Crikey, I needed that laugh."

"Glad blowing our family history out of the water could help."

"Yeah."

"Well, Mom gave me my last name," I said.

"I know," Michael responded.

An Orchestrated Mistake

"Alexander," I said. "After our uncle, Vivian Alexander."

Michael laughed so hard I briefly moved the phone away from my ear. "Now what the hell is so funny?" I snapped.

"Nicholas, Nicholas," Michael said, pulling himself together. "Call my mum in Vancouver and ask her where your name comes from. She'll tell you."

"Okay, I will."

I knew Aunty Vivian was weak, so I figured I better call soon if I wanted to learn the truth.

I never could identify with my father's side of the family growing up. Their religious hypocrisy was too much for me even as a child. I couldn't stand constantly hearing about how 'today's kids' have it so good. I respected them for being hard-working, but I loathed their societal opinions. Although I've always respected my father, I could never get past his side of the family, and that's what led me to change my name.

Coming home one night, I plunked down in the chair opposite my mother and said, "That's it! When I turn eighteen, I'm changing my name!"

My given name was Nigel Nicholas Vryenhoek.

"Changing it to what?" my mother asked.

"Moore. Nicholas Moore."

"Oh, no, you're not," Mom said.

"Why not? You've always said I'm not a Vryenhoek. Your maiden name is Moore, like that poet guy, so I am too."

"You're more an Alexander than a Moore," my mother stated.

An Orchestrated Mistake

"Alexander? Who is Alexander?"

"You are. I've always known that."

"Family name? I haven't heard of the Alexanders," I said, sitting up expecting a family history.

"You're more like Uncle Vivian."

"I'm not changing my name to Vivian. I'm dumping Nigel and keeping Nicholas."

"Of course, keep Nicholas," Mom said, picking up her book. "You'll just be Nicholas Alexander," Mom said triumphantly.

When I turned eighteen, I legally changed my name to Nicholas Alexander and got my Australian passport. Some thought I changed my name because I entered show business, but I did it for personal reasons, and it was Alexander because my mother had given it to me, and it was a family name. Or so I thought.

When I phoned Aunty Vivian the next day, she sounded in good spirits. She confirmed what Michael had told me previously, that my grandmother, her mother, had died from complications of diabetes.

"Yeah, she had some health problems," Aunty Vivian conceded. "We all do sooner or later, ya nut."

"Yeah, but I just wonder why Nanny's health was downplayed, even ignored, especially when Mom knew I had the same disease."

"Oh, come off it, Nicholas, it wasn't ignored."

"It was never discussed."

"So? That would have made a difference to you?"

An Orchestrated Mistake

"We'll never know."

"We couldn't tell you children anything," Aunty Vivian snapped. "You knew it all."

I could tell it was deteriorating into one of those generational conversations that lead to nowhere. I figured I might as well put the *Thomas Moore* issue to bed once and for all.

"You know Thomas Moore outlived all his five children," I told Aunty Vivian.

"What?"

"Thomas Moore. He had five kids. None of whom lived very long."

"Yes, I know," Aunty Vivian replied.

"So how can we be direct descendants if none of his children lived?"

"We're not."

"Mom said we were. She read me his poems in the laundry room. Even admonished me because I had never heard of him."

"Your mother told a good story, didn't she?" Aunty Vivian laughed.

"So, for my whole life I've been telling people I'm a direct descendant of a dead guy whose statue stands outside Trinity College in Dublin, and we're not even related?"

"Not a strand of DNA." Aunty Vivian chuckled.

"Mom made the whole thing up? I can't believe she made this up!"

"You believed her, ya dope!"

An Orchestrated Mistake

"I'm not sure what I believe," I told Aunty Vivian, feeling duped by my own mother. "So, are you and I really named after the same uncle, Uncle Vivian Alexander?"

"*I* am."

"What about me?" I asked. "His name was Vivian Alexander?"

"No, ya dope!" Aunty Vivian said through fits of laughter. "His name was Crockett. Vivian Crockett."

"Crockett?"

"Yes! Vivian Crockett!"

"Then who the hell is Alexander?"

"I thought you knew," Aunty Vivian said, trying to compose herself.

"I haven't clue."

"Alexander was a storyteller on the radio in Australia that your mother adored as a child. She loved his stories, and even as a little girl, used to say that if she ever had a son, she would call him Alexander. Hello?"

"I'm here," I said, stunned.

"So your mother gave you the name she always wanted, Nicholas Alexander, after her first love, the love of story."

"Jesus!"

"No, that was taken," Aunty Vivian said, laughing. "So, you have Dutch, some Scottish from your father's side, and Irish from your mother's."

"I'm a real mutt."

An Orchestrated Mistake

"You know what Vryenhoek means?" Aunty Vivian asked.

"Yeah, Dad told me."

"Street corner," Aunty Vivian said.

"So, I'm an Irish mutt on the street corner," I said.

"Pretty much!" Aunty Vivian laughed.

That was one of the last conversations I had with her, as she passed away shortly after.

When I told my family about my call with Aunty Vivian, they said they knew Uncle Vivian's last name was Crockett but didn't know the origins of my name, Alexander.

"I just never questioned Mom," I told my dad one night. "Ya just didn't, ya know?"

"Oh, I know," Dad replied, sighing. "She's probably up there right now with your aunt enjoying a cup of tea and a good laugh."

It wasn't just the name change I had to get my mind around with my mother. I also had to get it wrapped around the last thirteen years of her life.

Growing up around my mother was a constant lesson in acceptance and understanding unless, of course, that lesson made an appearance in her own backyard. My mother had progressive social values and was very understanding and accepting unless those values came into question in her own backyard. Unfortunately, I resided in her backyard.

****

"I don't want you to miss our lunch tomorrow," my mother had said to me over the phone. "I need to speak with you."

An Orchestrated Mistake

"Mom, when have I missed one of our Friday lunches," I quipped. "Besides, I need to speak to you too."

A play, a comedy, was opening that Friday night at the Arts Club Theater in Vancouver, and I had one of the lead roles. I already had a lot of nervous energy pent up when Mom had called to remind me about our lunch.

"I'm sorry," my mother had said when I sat down at the table. "I had forgotten you were opening tonight."

"No, it's fine," I said. "I thought you didn't like Thai food," I added, looking around the restaurant.

"It's Indian food I don't like. Finding that long black hair put me off."

"Mom, not all Indian food comes with black hairs."

"I'll never know."

After the waiter came and took our orders, I asked, "What is it you want to tell me?"

"No, you go first. What is it you want to tell me?" Mom questioned.

"Okay," I'll go first I said. "Mom, for the past two years, I've had girlfriends and boyfriends, and right now I have a boyfriend."

She stared at me a moment before saying, "I've just been diagnosed with leukemia and have been given three years to live."

We both sat in stunned silence, digesting each other's news.

"Oh boy," she finally said.

"Shit," I mumbled into the table.

"Yeah, shit," she echoed. "Don't tell your father! And for Christ's sake, don't tell your sisters."

"What do you mean don't tell them?" I asked. "They have a right to know. Mom, you can't keep something like this a secret!"

"Oh, yes, I can!" she snapped.

"They have a right to know!"

"Keep your voice down," Mom said.

"Mom, you can't expect to go through something like leukemia and not have Dad or the girls learn the truth."

"Of course I know that. Don't be stupid," she quipped.

"Then what are you saying?"

"I'm saying your father and your sisters don't need to know about you. They won't understand, and it will only disappoint and hurt them."

"Mom, now who is being stupid?"

"Excuse me?" Mom shot across the table. "There are more important things to discuss than five minutes in a bedroom."

When our food arrived, we both just pushed it around our plates.

"So, what are you going to do about it?" I finally asked.

"Nothing," she said. "It will be like you never said anything at all."

"Not me. You."

"It's not me I'm worried about," Mom said. "What about all the girlfriends you've had?"

"So, I've had girlfriends," I replied. "You can be seventy-thirty women or ninety-ten guys. Everyone thinks bi is fifty-fifty, well, it's not."

"Oh, God, you're bi!"

"You know I really didn't expect you to react this way. I thought you, of all people, would not think sexuality is a big deal."

"You've just told me you've got a boyfriend. Of course it's a big deal."

"And you just told me you have three years to live."

"Well," Mom stated, looking around the restaurant, "isn't this the ultimate lunch."

Neither one of us touched our food. Standing on the sidewalk outside the restaurant, Mom said, "And you don't need to tell your friends either."

"Are we talking about my news or your news?" I asked.

"Yours," Mom snapped. "I don't care who you tell about me." Briefly embracing me like a chimpanzee holding its deceased young, she suddenly pulled away. "Good luck tonight," she said and spun on her heels and walked back to work.

I thought, *There goes the loneliest woman in the world.*

That lunch marked the beginning of our tug of war regarding my sexuality. My mother religiously followed Edgar Cayce's readings and treatments for leukemia, beat the odds, and lived thirteen more years. While she was alive, I kept my promise and didn't speak about my intimate relationships. Anytime my sexual identity came up privately between my mother and me, the conversation would always leave me feeling the same way: with incredible deep shame.

An Orchestrated Mistake

There were times during those thirteen years the leukemia would bring her very close to death. During those times, my mother would say quietly to me she could care less who I dated, but as she would rally and gain strength, she would then question my choice in partners.

Two years after my parents had settled into their new home in Nova Scotia upon leaving Vancouver, I got a call from my dad telling me that I better come quick. It didn't look like Mom was going to make it.

She lost consciousness shortly after I arrived, and my sisters and I took turns staying overnight with her in the hospital room. Standing beside her bed in the middle of the night, with my eyes closed, a nurse entered the room and startled me. "Sorry," the nurse said. "You thought you just saw God, and she was wearing white?"

It was around the tenth night I fell asleep beside my mother with my hands on her stomach. I fell asleep mumbling, "Out with the bad and in with the good," as I tried to draw out the negative energy and transfer positive energy into her. My own voice woke me an hour or so later. "Out with the bad and in with the good." Opening my eyes, I saw my mother was awake and staring at me.

"Good morning, love," she said in a weak voice.

"Good morning, Mom," I said, choking on my emotions. "Welcome back."

My mother lived for one more year. Long enough to see me swim with a beluga whale in Chedabucto Bay, Nova Scotia, and just long enough to see my sister Deirdre get married in New York. After that lunch in my early twenties, the war over my sexuality was civil both inside ourselves and outward between each other. The war was ugly at times, but it forced me to focus on my career, which enriched my life, and I loved it. Perhaps I wasn't meant to explore life with another in this lifetime but learn through my mother's shaming the greatest lesson of all: love of self.

We never talked about my sexuality in the last year of her life, but I feel we were getting close to a truce. I wanted to have one more conversation with her, maybe even a laugh about our stupid war, but sadly she passed away before I could fly across the country to be by her side. I will remember her for the wonderful qualities she had, the mother who drove me to hockey practice at 3am, who gave me my love of words and my sense of understanding and acceptance of others, even if our relationship left me struggling to accept myself.

She did get one final poke at me in death, which I had to laugh about. Driving my dad back from the funeral home after collecting her belongings, my father said, "Here, hold out your hand."

I held out my hand, and my father dropped my mother's wedding rings into it. "Your mother wanted you to have these."

I looked down and saw the gold rings in my hand. "Do you think you'll ever get married?" Dad asked.

"Maybe," I said, looking back up to the road. "But let me tell you a story about the last thirteen years…"

I used to tease my mother that maybe one day I'd write a movie based on that lunch and those thirteen years, and I'd call it *One Foot Out*. It would have to be a comedy. However, truthfully, you'd find it listed under horror.

****

A few weeks after I had received my final report from the neuropsychologist, I was at home looking at my blog, figuring out

An Orchestrated Mistake

how to shut it down when I saw an email. I read the email at least five times before I picked up the phone to call Rosemary.

"Rosemary," I said after she picked up, "I was just shutting down the blog when I saw an email from some guy in Naples, Italy."

"What does it say?"

"Please don't stop writing because I know you're helping people because you're helping me."

We both sat in silence for a moment before Rosemary finally said, "Let me grab my laptop. I'll be right over."

CHAPTER EIGHTEEN

Walking through the waiting room at the hospital, I saw something that made me stop dead mid-stride. I was just leaving a meeting with my neurologist where he informed me I was ready to be discharged from neurology, a few months short of three years since my return to Canada.

But the excitement of that news isn't what stopped me in my tracks. It was the sight of Robbie, the now twenty-two-year-old double stroke patient, walking without the assistance of his two canes. Just paces behind, his father followed. Spotting me out of the corner of his eye, his father came right over.

"Nice to see you, Nicholas," he said, extending his hand.

"You too. Robbie just walked by without his canes?" I said, stunned.

"That's right."

"That's incredible," I said. "I'm so happy for him!"

"Yes," the father said. "We all are. He's been working very hard. You know he watched you run that day on the treadmill. That was quite a moment."

"Ya. I guess."

"It was. Well, I better go catch up to him," Robbie's dad said, shaking my hand. "It was nice to see you again, and you're looking pretty good too."

"Thanks. Tell Robbie congratulations," I said as he smiled and disappeared around the corner.

I didn't think Robbie would ever walk again without the assistance of those two canes, so to see him walk by so confidently without them was incredibly moving. I, too, had made a lot of progress in the close to three years, but I never really thought about that. However, seeing Robbie sure sent a message loud and clear. With hard work, the brain *can* rewire and heal itself.

I was going to the gym twice a day, once in the early morning and then again for cardio after dinner. Sometimes I would even go down in the middle of the day just to get that exercise rush. I was going so much Rosemary often teased me, telling me I suffered from obsessive-compulsive disorder, or OCD.

"You're going to love this," I told Rosemary at one of our writing sessions. "When I told the nurse at the Diabetes Clinic I go to the gym twice a day she told me I was OCD and sent me over to the clinic shrink."

"I've told you, you are OCD." Rosemary laughed.

"Wait, it gets better," I said. "When the clinic's psychiatrist looked at my file and saw where I was and where I am now, he asked me why I needed to see him. I told him the nurse said I go to the gym too much and I'm OCD."

"I'm sure he agreed." Rosemary laughed.

"No. He said everyone should take their health so seriously and threw me out of his office. First time I've ever been thrown out of a doctor's office for the right reason."

"I still think you're OCD," Rosemary said.

"Even the shrink's assistant commented when I left the office that it was the fastest she'd ever seen a patient enter and leave the psychiatrist's office."

Rosemary sat there rolling her eyes.

"Hey," I continued, "I told her when you don't have issues, you don't have issues."

An Orchestrated Mistake

"Oh my God," Rosemary roared. "You are just so full of it!"

I did have to concede a little to myself that, yeah, I can be a little obsessive about things, but I enjoyed working out, and it remains one of the stabilizing factors in my life. The gym is just a fun, positive atmosphere to be in. I learned a lot by watching the other members and would incorporate parts of their regime into my routine. But some exercises were quite simply to be admired but not tried.

"Turn it up full blast," one jock said to the other. His friend put the incline all the way up on the treadmill and increased it to maximum speed. The jock then took two steps and leaped on, and immediately his feet and legs became a blur as he sprinted on the machine. Ten seconds later, he jumped off and the second jock jumped on and sprinted. These two repeated this cycle for several minutes before both stopped to rest.

Seeing me staring at them and the machine, one of the jocks goaded me. "Want to jump on and give it a try?"

"If I did, you'd be scraping me off the back wall," I said.

"I don't think so," he responded. "I figure you'd just shoot right through it."

Oh, I thought, *what I would give just to be thirty years younger, just for five minutes, to show this punk I could sprint with the best of them.* Instead, I just walked away mumbling, "Yeah, you're probably right."

The gym, tutoring, and of course, my Mediterranean diet were very instrumental in my recovery. In many ways, it built the house on the foundation that hard work and dedication had laid.

My friends Geoff and Jan are incredibly caring and thoughtful people, so it goes without saying all their friends are exactly the same way. The countless dinners, laughs, sailing trips, hockey

An Orchestrated Mistake

games, and just the stimulating conversations went such a long way to bring me and my chronic disease in from the cold. Love is the biggest source for healing.

Shortly after rehab, Jan and Geoff asked me to take care of their purebred Standard Poodles while they vacationed. I thought, *Sure, how hard can that be?*

That first afternoon, nine puppies soon to be ready for their new homes and six adult dogs took off down the beach. As I watched them all take off out of sight, I thought, *Shit! There goes twenty-five grand worth of dog!* It took me over an hour to catch them. Carrying the puppies two by two up the hill, I eventually got them all back into the kennel. As I collapsed on the couch in the living room, the phone rang. Their neighbors, Michael and Cathy, were kayaking in front of the house, and it was Cathy calling from her cell.

"Nicholas," Cathy said. "You left the gate open to the kennel and all the dogs are out!"

"Perfect," I replied before heading back outside.

Healthy activities are the cornerstone for the mind, body, and spirit. They transform us. Even for an introvert like myself who is more secure in his solitude, having meaningful social interaction is vital to long-lasting health.

To further enhance my speaking and vocabulary development, I began teaching English online to a young Sri Lankan man named Asanka. The best way to learn a language is to speak and write it as much as possible, so Asanka would send me emails about his life in Sri Lanka, and I would correct them and send them back. Not only did I get to know Asanka very well, I also got to read about a culture I knew very little about. Our emails quickly developed into English lessons on Skype, and those sessions grew into a strong and connected friendship. No matter how frustrated or down I got about things, I always looked forward to my Sunday morning Skype sessions with Asanka. Witnessing Asanka's growth, both personally and professionally, is without doubt one of the highlights of my recovery.

Things at that time really couldn't have been much better. I was discharged from neurology, my cough had subsided, and my lungs were given a clean bill of health. Besides my time spent tutoring or at the gym, interesting, loving friends surrounded me. I still held doubts about the course my life would take, but with every writing session with Rosemary, my confidence grew, and it became abundantly clear I had to follow my instincts and write my way out of life's stalemate.

My confidence in my day-to-day activities was growing so much that when my friends said they were going skating at the outdoor Commons Ice Rink in the center of Halifax, I decided to join them. I didn't give much thought to my balance issues, and since I had been working hard at the gym with the balance ball and Pilates, I didn't give the balance required for skating a second thought. I was aware, however, that I hadn't skated in over twenty years. Having spent the majority of my youth on skates, I thought I might be a little rusty, but I'd just pick up where I had left off.

After lacing up my skates, I was walking to the ice when my friend chuckled. "I thought maybe you'd just watch."

"Why would I just watch?" I frowned.

"Well, I thought maybe you'd lace up the skates, but I didn't think you'd actually follow through and get out here and do it."

"I'm Canadian," I said. "We take to ice like ducks to water. Watch this. You might learn a move or two," I added, stepping onto the ice.

An Orchestrated Mistake

"Excuse me, sir," a little five-year-old girl said as she skated up behind me. "Can I get by?" This was the second time this preschooler had lapped me since I'd stepped on the ice.

"Yeah, sure," I said, stopping and pressing myself against the boards to let her by.

"Thank you!" she said as she whizzed by. I never wandered too far away from the support of the boards, and that little girl must have lapped me at least four or five times. I may have done okay with my balance on land, but that didn't translate to skating on ice. So, my speedskating days were over, but I did enjoy doing something I never thought I could do again.

The next day I went to the gym in the morning, as usual, hit the organic store to pick up some veggies, and then went home to write in my blog.

After an hour or so, I felt I was having trouble focusing and thought maybe I should just lie down for a moment. Unable to concentrate or sleep, I got up and went over to sit in front of the computer.

There was so much red highlighting on the screen, and words were not even forming cohesive sentences. My breathing was shallow and in staccato bursts. I tried to ignore the heart hammering in my chest by opening my eyes wide to try and make sense of the gibberish on the screen.

I thought to myself, *This feeling in my body is familiar. It can't be happening again.*

I pushed myself up out of the chair and stumbled as I walked into the bathroom. I told myself I just needed to slow down and breathe and I'd be fine. Turn on the water and just listen to the water. Why did I turn on the water? Do I need to shave? Brush my teeth? Why am I even in the bathroom? Where is logic? Oh shit, I need to lie down. I staggered out of the bathroom and collapsed face down on my bed. Why is this so difficult? Why can't I just admit what is happening and pick up the phone and call 9-1-1?

TICK TICK TICK…

I had gone to dinner at Windows on the World atop of the World Trade Centre with friends less than forty-eight hours earlier. Now our location on the Lower East Side rumbled. "Don't tell me that's another blind pilot," I said to the director as he looked through his viewfinder.

I was down eating breakfast at catering some fifteen minutes earlier when we heard a distant explosion. You often heard loud bangs and noises in New York and never gave it a second thought. Minutes later, one of the teamster members stuck his head out of his truck and said, "Fuck! A plane just hit the World Trade Center!"

"Probably one of those traffic planes," someone commented.

On September 11, 2001, we were shooting a film, but because of a mix-up in permitting, we were on location on East 8th Street rather than outside the downtown courthouse, only blocks away from the World Trade Center. We were a little behind schedule, and as a freelance crewmember at the time, I was eager for us to finish so I could move on to the next gig that I had lined up.

The director took the viewfinder away from his eye and looked at me as we heard someone running frantically down the stairs. Moments later, the apartment door flew open and a winded crewmember bolted inside. "The second tower was just hit! They're both burning!"

"Another small traffic plane?" I questioned.

"That wasn't a small plane," he said, still gasping. "There is a ton of smoke. It had to be something much bigger."

"Where are you watching this from?" the director asked. "Where is everyone?"

"We're all on the roof," the crewmember said, exiting. "It's fucking crazy!"

The director of photography, the director, and I all exchanged looks.

"Maybe we should go up to the roof," The DP finally said.

TICK TICK TICK…

I know I'm standing at my apartment door with my coat on because I want to go out. But why is my phone in my hand, and where the hell am I going? Confused, I drop the phone and then realized where I wanted to go, to the drugstore. They have blood pressure pills at the drugstore, and I'm sure that's all I need, blood pressure pills.

Standing on the street outside my apartment, I leaned on a telephone pole and stared at the signal across the road that had a hand up. I looked both ways and stepped off the curb to the immediate long, loud blast of a car horn. Staggering back onto the curb, I wondered if I could make it the few blocks to the store.

I used fences for support to ricochet down the side streets, but when I stumbled and almost did a face plant, the realization of how much trouble I was in hit me. I needed help.

Leaning on a fence, I spotted a teenage girl talking on her phone, walking towards me on the sidewalk. I could ask her to call 9-1-1 for me. I started to stumble towards her but only made it a couple of steps when I fell against the fence. I thought I would wait for her to approach me, but she spotted me and stopped too.

We were staring at each other, separated by about thirty paces, and after a brief moment, she darted across the street with her phone in her hand. I tried to call out, but no sound emerged. I couldn't blame her. I, too, would have avoided what appeared to be a drunken middle-aged man in the middle of the afternoon. I watched her staring back at me as she disappeared around the corner like a rescue ship disappearing over the horizon.

Using fences and trees for support, I eventually made my way to the shopping center parking lot. Spotting an abandoned shopping cart, I commandeered it for support to cross the short distance to the drugstore.

"Can I help you?" the pharmacist asked as I leaned on the counter. I tried to answer right away, but nothing came out. "Are you alright?"

"I think my blood pressure is low," I slurred. "Or high."

"I recognize you. What's your name again?" she asked, stepping in front of her computer.

"Nicholas Alexander," I finally mumbled.

"That's right. Tell me what's going on, Nicholas," she said, quickly reading my history. I shrugged my shoulders.

"What's your address, Nicholas?" I shrugged again. "What's today's date?"

"June. July. No, January. January something."

"Next of kin?" she asked, glancing at her computer.

"Dad."

"His phone number?"

"No clue," I said after a moment. "I best just go home."

"No, you're not," the pharmacist said. "I'm calling 9-1-1."

An Orchestrated Mistake

"No!"

"You're going to the hospital!" she insisted, dialing.

"No, wait, wait. Fine, I'll go, but just call me a cab."

She stared at me, and I'm sure the terror I saw in her eyes was once again the reflection in my own. She redialed and spoke into the phone.

"This is Shopper's Drug Mart on Qinpool. I need a cab right away. We have a medical emergency!"

The pharmacist walked me outside and joined me, sitting on the curb. "Try to relax, Nicholas," she said. "The cab will be here any second."

After a moment, a cab pulled up to the curb, and the pharmacist helped me get into the back. I fell over on the back seat as she slammed the back door and opened the front. "Get him to Emergency right away," she yelled to the driver. "He's having another stroke!"

TICK TICK TICK…

Out on the roof of our location, I instantly thought I had stepped onto the set of the *Die Hard* movie franchise. The Twin Towers were burning before my eyes, and my ears were filled with the sound of sirens and roars of fighter jets circling out of sight, high above. A radio tuned to a news station blared at one side of the roof, giving a play-by-play of events as they unfolded along the Eastern Seaboard.

As I stood staring at the burning towers less than a mile away as the crow flies, a crewmember came up and stood beside me. "Do you think that helicopter is going to try and land on the roof?" he asked after we had watched the chopper circle above the South Tower for several minutes.

"No way," I replied. "There's too much smoke."

"But there are people up there," he said.

"I know, but what can he do? Maybe we should go down there," I suggested.

"And what can we do?" he asked.

Shaking my head, I conceded, "I don't know."

"We can confirm another hijacked aircraft has hit the Pentagon moments ago," the excited announcer on the radio said. "There could be as many as eight other hijacked aircraft at this time. We don't know if these aircraft are on their way to Washington, New York, or where, but it does appear we're under attack!"

Looking across the roof, I spotted my friend, Verna, a large black woman in charge of craft service, physically engaged with several of the crewmembers in a group hug. Beside them was another small group kneeling in prayer. Looking back at the towers, I could see the helicopter had given up any attempt to land on the roof and pulled back, hovering, relegating itself to the role of witness to the wounded and dying.

"We should get the hell off the roof before we're a target," a fellow beside me said.

"Why?" I asked. "We're not a target, but they would be," I said, nodding toward the Empire State Building.

Some of us on the roof watched the chaos before us in agonizing isolation, while others found solace in being physically connected with others. Many searched for service on their cell phones so they could call loved ones. Surprisingly, my cell rang in my pocket, and it was my brother-in-law Jay calling to check up on me. Perhaps worry just isn't in my DNA, or I'm just too full of denial, or maybe it's just a little bit of both, but I told Jay I was fine and he needn't be concerned. It was the souls in those towers we needed to pray for.

A low rolling rumble emanated from downtown, and with it, the smoke thickened and spread. A silence fell over the roof. A moment later, I noticed a hole in the smoke, and through it, blue sky was visible.

"What the fuck was that?" a young crewmember said beside me.

"It just collapsed," I said, relaying my thoughts.

"No," another person said.

As the smoke dissipated slightly, it was obvious to all the South Tower had disappeared. Heartbreaking screams on the roof drowned out the distant rumbles of grief, and a moment later, a veil of stunned silence enveloped the city.

"Holy fuck," the guy beside me whispered. "It's gone."

"Yeah," I murmured. "All those people."

TICK TICK TICK…

"The hospital is just up the street," the driver said in a Filipino accent. "We be there in couple minutes."

"Good," I said into the backseat.

"Stroke, huh? That's bad," he said, making a sucking sound on a tooth. My brother had stroke back in Philippines."

"Sorry," I slurred.

"Yeah, it was sad," the driver continued. "It killed him."

"Oh," I groaned.

"He brought it on himself. I told him, but no. He did what he want, ate whatever he want, bad. He was diabetic."

"Oh," I moaned louder, pushing myself upright in the backseat. "You're not even out of the parking lot," I complained, looking out the window.

"It's busy. Soon there," he said.

A cab? What the hell was I thinking? I let my body fall back down to the seat.

"Yeah," the driver said a moment later. "That diabetes will kill you." Sucking his tooth, he repeated, "Kill ya."

"Oh, please," I groaned.

"I'm lucky. I don't have it!" he said cheerfully.

"I'm glad," I slurred. "Now, can you just drive?"

Lying on the seat, I began to drift in and out of almost a dreamlike state, and my impulse to let myself drift was countered by my will to stay conscious. I focused on the smell of the dirty carpet.

"Stroke," the driver said after a few minutes when he was obviously completely bored with the silence. "You seem young to be having a stroke."

"I have diabetes."

"Oh, that's bad. Just like my brother!"

"Yes! Like your dead brother."

I felt the car come to a stop. "We're there?" I asked, pushing myself up.

"No, no." the driver said. "Pedestrian."

"You're kidding me," I snapped, watching an older woman step off the curb. "Just remove my body when we get there," I said, falling back down to the seat.

True to Canadian politeness, I tipped him before staggering through the emergency room doors. A young medic spotted me right away and helped me over to a chair.

"I think I'm having a second stroke," I managed to get out as soon as I was seated.

I gave him my name, and he picked up the phone while asking me, "When did this start?"

"Hour ago. I'm not sure."

"Out of the way," the medic yelled at a nurse who'd stepped out from a side hallway. The young medic pushed me, slumped over in the wheelchair, through the corridors of the hospital at breakneck speed. "It's okay, Nicholas," he huffed, "we're almost there!"

Making a hard left turn, we burst through the emergency room doors, and there was a doctor and two nurses waiting.

The medic helped me stand up, and the doctor, taking one look at me, said, "Get him on the table." Once I was placed on the table, he began examining me while two nurses helped me out of my shirt and into a gown.

"Are you cold, honey?" a nurse asked as I faded in and out. I shook my head no. "You're going to feel two little pricks," the other nurse said. "One in each arm. Just relax."

With my arms extended out to each side, I was staring up at the bright emergency room light. I could hear the medical team, but it sounded like they were off in the distance. For the first time since the ordeal started, I began to wonder if this was it. My body wouldn't stop shaking, but I wasn't cold. I wasn't even scared. With each arm still extended straight out, the bright light above me began to go in and out of focus. Is each thought going to be my last? What do I want my final thought on Earth to be? I thought about Rosemary and the book we were working so hard on. Then one thought consumed me, and I mumbled, "This is really going to fuck my ending."

TICK TICK TICK...

Thirty minutes after the South Tower collapsed, the North Tower followed suit. Just before it fell, the radio issued reports of people jumping to their deaths. The vaporized towers emitted a dark smoke that engulfed all of lower Manhattan, and sobs were the only sounds clearly heard that permeated an otherwise silent soundtrack to a dark reality. Members of the crew stood holding one another, but I couldn't share in a united grief.

I took the stairs back down to the vacant set and sat down in a director's chair. Noticing the video monitor was left on, I leaned over to shut it off. Did I just witness the murder of thousands of people? And if I did, why am I not up on the roof grieving with the rest of the crew? Why am I down here on a vacant set feeling alone and spiritless? The answer was too painful to examine.

Later, down on the street in front of the apartment building, I asked the line producer, "What do you mean we're wrapping?"

"We're wrapping," Cindy responded.

"We can't wrap," I said. "We're behind schedule, and it's barely noon!"

"Nicholas, no one is in any condition to continue."

"We need to continue!"

"You were up there. Didn't you see what just happened?"

"Yes," I said. "And that's exactly why we need to carry on."

"Nicholas, you can't be serious," Cindy lamented.

"Of course I'm serious. You work through tragedy. Wrapping isn't going to bring all those people back!"

Speechless, a voice over Cindy's two-way radio asked her what she wanted done with the production vehicles. "Lock 'em up," Cindy said, staring at me. "We're wrapping and walking away."

"Alexander! What are you doing?" Verna hollered, walking towards me.

"We're wrapping," I spat.

"I know, honey, but what are you going to do?"

"Go home, I guess," I said, looking for the F-15 fighter jets that roared overhead.

"To Brooklyn, baby?" Verna asked. "There's no subway service."

"I'll walk."

"Baby," Verna said, "no one is getting in or out of Manhattan. And even if you could," she chuckled, "you think you're going to walk your white ass all the way out to Coney Island? You won't even make it off the bridge."

"We shouldn't be wrapping."

"Of course we should. No one can work."

"I can."

"With everything that's going on? Have you lost your mind, child?"

"I'm fucking angry."

"We're all angry."

"Yeah, well, I'm really fucking angry. This whole thing is fucking insane. It's all total bullshit!"

"Honey, people died."

"I know that! You think I don't know people died? Of course I know people died. That's exactly why we need to keep working!"

"Baby, come here, give me a hug."

"I don't want a hug!"

"I do," Verna said, wrapping her arms around me. My shoulders immediately began to rise and fall. Verna held me tighter.

TICK TICK TICK…

After I returned from the CAT scan, I was given a series of motor skills tests, and after all was complete, my neurologist was the doctor on call and entered the emergency room.

"Fancy meeting you here," he said.

"Surprise," I said, sitting up on the table.

"Indeed, it is. But the good news is your CT scan didn't show any acute abnormalities, but we'll do an MRI on Monday just to take a closer look. I'd like to keep you in over the weekend until then," my neurologist said. "Keep an eye on you and get some more blood work done."

"Can I go home?"

Slightly taken aback by my question, the doctor said, "Well, I can't force you to stay, but I strongly recommend you do. I'd like us to keep an eye on you."

"I'd like to go home."

The neurologist stared at me a moment, then finally said, "Okay. I'll give you a prescription for blood thinners, and this is my direct line to my office. You start feeling uneasy or anything I want you to call and get yourself back here right away."

"Sure."

"And Nicholas, don't take a taxi. Call 9-1-1."

I took a taxi back to the drugstore to get the prescription filled. Waiting for the prescription, I heard the pharmacist's assistant whisper, "That's the guy that was having the stroke this afternoon."

"Yes," the pharmacist said.

"What the hell is he doing back here and not in the hospital?"

"He's a fucking idiot," the pharmacist replied.

I was going to speak up to tell them I could hear them, but I couldn't argue with the truth. Like I've said, sometimes I act like an idiot. Other times I am one.

I got back from the pharmacy shortly past 10pm, and I did take it easy that night. But the next morning, I found myself at the gym working out. Yeah, even I had to shake my head at that one.

The following week I met with the neurologist to get the results of the new MRI. He confirmed that I indeed had a second stroke, and had I not lost the weight and taken my health seriously, this could have been the one to put me under. This stroke was very near to my brain stem. My balance did take another hit, but I didn't feel more rehab would be beneficial. There wasn't anything more I could do in rehab I couldn't already do at the gym. I'd follow up with the neurologist in a few months.

TICK TICK TICK…

"What the hell is that?" Rosemary asked as we sat around my kitchen table with our laptops open.

"That's my new neighbor," I said. "Bill, as his last act as superintendent, decided the old lady upstairs would be better off on the ground floor."

"What the hell is she doing?"

"If you asked her, she'd tell you she's rehearsing for her church choir. If you ask me, I'd tell you she's in there skinning a live cat."

"Oh my God." Rosemary winced. "What a horrific noise."

"Wait till she starts pounding on her keyboards."

I had been over numerous times to tell the old lady it was an apartment building, not a music hall. She always responded the same way, putting her hand up to mouth and saying, "Oh, I didn't think anyone could hear me." I used to think she was looney-tunes until someone told me she translates Latin into English for her church. No fewer than seven tenants moved in and out of the apartment on the other side of her. I would have moved out, too, if I could have afforded it. At any rate, Rosemary and I decided to move our writing sessions to a local coffee shop.

We were making real progress. I was almost finished with the blog, and we had nailed down a first draft of the first seven chapters of the book.

An Orchestrated Mistake

I was to meet Rosemary at our usual time, 3pm, at our favorite coffee shop. Rosemary was ten years my senior, always impeccably dressed and organized, and she ran about ten miles a week. When she hadn't shown up by 3:30, I sent her an email to tell her I was waiting for her. When it was 4:30, I sent an email saying I was heading home and she should call me. That night I tried her cell. She didn't answer. I called several times on Saturday, and on Sunday, I sent her an email asking her when I should start calling hospitals and police stations.

Rosemary finally phoned on Monday, all apologies. She stated a good friend was ill, so she stayed the weekend with her at the hospital. I didn't buy it, but I didn't want to say anything. We had a chuckle, as I was usually the irresponsible one, but we did make plans to have another session for the coming Friday.

On Thursday, I sent Rosemary an email as a reminder just before I headed out to meet Jan and Geoff for coffee in the North End. I heard back almost immediately.

I entered Jo's coffee shop and sat down opposite Jan and Geoff.

"What's wrong?" Jan asked immediately as I sat down.

"Rosemary's dead," I uttered. "Her daughter just emailed me," I explained. "She was in the hospital last weekend, and they discovered her body was full of cancer. She died two days ago."

We all just stared at each other in stunned disbelief. I took Rosemary's passing pretty hard. My friends were very supportive, but I didn't let on how hard her death hit me.

I tinkered with the blog at best. I stuck to my gym regime and healthy eating, but my writing fell by the wayside for over three years. Anytime anyone asked how the writing was going, I would just say, "Fine." That was much easier than explaining I'm in an uncontrolled tailspin. I eventually did finish the blog, but I never touched the book past chapter seven, exactly where Rosemary and I left off. I know people only ask because they want to be encouraging, but unless you yourself have sat in front of a computer and bled, or you're an agent, publisher, or perhaps even a muse, never ask a writer when their book is going to be finished. You're only giving them an excuse to put another bullet in the chamber.

Over two years after Rosemary's passing, I still hadn't sat down and done any writing on the book. The absence of any meaningful work and goals led me into more cycles of depression. Some months it was almost paralyzing, but some months weren't so bad. However, it did take an enormous amount of energy to be social and not reveal what I was truly feeling inside. I knew my only way out was meaningful writing, but I just couldn't get myself to sit down and do it.

I would nap up to five times a day, and I would often wake up exhausted. I told Dr. Roberts this, and he sent me for a series of blood tests that landed me with a specialist of internal medicine. That doctor ordered more tests and a bone marrow biopsy.

I didn't know if all my sleeping was just a side effect of my state of mind or there was something going on.

Finally, all the test results were in, and the specialist called me into his office. "Well, we know what's going on with you and why you're feeling so fatigued. You have diabetic anemia."

"Perfect," I said. "What's that?"

"Your bone marrow is not producing enough oxygen-carrying red blood cells," he explained. "If your red blood cell count drops much more, we may be looking at a blood transfusion."

"Nice."

"But there is a hormone shot we can try first. But you'd have to be monitored closely because too much of this hormone could bring on another stroke."

"Wonderful," I said.

The doctor was a little perplexed by the tone of my one-word responses.

"I have some more bad news," the doctor said.

"Good," I answered. "Let me have it."

"The anemia," the doctor said, taking a breath, "is brought on by kidney disease."

"I see."

"Stage three," the doctor added.

"Stage one being the worst," I asked.

"No," he responded. "Five is the worst."

"Well," I said, "I'm over halfway to somewhere."

"We'll get you under the care of a nephrologist. Keep tight control of your diabetes, and hopefully we can slow down its progression."

I nodded. "Great, another ologist. Is there a cure?"

"No," the doctor said. "You'll be under the constant care of the renal clinic."

I looked out the window and watched a leaf fall to the ground. I looked back to the doctor and chuckled.

An Orchestrated Mistake

"What?" the doctor asked, puzzled. I looked back out the window and started to laugh louder. "What is it?" the doctor asked again.

"Kidney disease!" I laughed louder. "Stage three!" I tried to suppress my laughter, but the harder I tried, the more laughter burst out of me. Eventually, the doctor started to chuckle and was momentarily unable to control his composure. We finally got it together and stopped laughing, but then both began to smirk before breaking out in more laugher.

"This is not funny," the doctor managed to get out.

"Level one just wasn't good enough for me," I said. "I had to go straight to level three." I finally pulled it together and thanked the doctor, who apologized for laughing. "It's fine," I said before I left. "It's good to laugh."

Walking down the hall, I thought of a movie Neil Simon wrote years ago. In it, the daughter, Polly, is nursing her mother, Georgina, back to health after an unfortunate incident.

"Does it hurt much?" Polly asked.

Georgina responded, "Only when I laugh."

TICK TICK TICK ... TOCK

CHAPTER NINETEEN

Currently, over 422 million people are living with full-blown diabetes. It's safe to say it is a worldwide pandemic, and the number is growing each year exponentially. The Center for Disease Control in the United States estimated the cost to treat a patient with type II diabetes at approximately $14,000 per patient per year. The CDC also states 100 million, or one-third of the population in the US, are living with diabetes or are pre-diabetic. The numbers in India, Canada, and, indeed, worldwide are staggering. The direct cost to national healthcare programs and global economies is astounding. Not to mention the loss of productivity by the individual due to the effects of this physically debilitating and emotionally devastating disease.

There are numerous articles and books written on this subject, so I won't venture down this rabbit hole. Even with a genetic predisposition to type II diabetes, it is still mainly avoidable. It is the disease of an unhealthy lifestyle. Simply put, it's a poor diet combined with a sedentary lifestyle.

While the costs to our healthcare systems are enormous, the costs incurred by the individual can be financially crippling. I wouldn't wish this disease on my worst enemy. Well not quite true... Maybe just on that old singing banshee next door... I'm kidding... Well, not really.

The Canadian doctor Frederick Banting, along with his partners, discovered the lifesaving drug insulin in 1921. Banting sold the patents for one dollar in 1923. He did this so the drug could be affordable to everyone. Our pharmaceutical industry and its monumental greed have priced many lifesaving drugs out of reach for many individuals. I also believe governments should make gym memberships and gym equipment 100% tax-deductible. There is obviously a lot more that can be done, but that's for better-qualified individuals than me to write and speak about. But I will add we are ultimately responsible for our own health, and it is up to us to respect our bodies and take care of them. The body does not work itself out, nor does it feed itself a healthy diet. Those responsibilities ultimately fall on us to make those healthy decisions.

I eventually did finish the blog after Rosemary passed away, but I couldn't bring myself to sit down and seriously continue with the book. Every writer has his or her muse, and without Rosemary, I didn't feel the confidence to continue. I would only sit down to work on the project when the pain of not writing exceeded the pain of struggling with writing.

Around this time I got an email from Heather, who was the head of development for Three Walls Productions. They had decided not to renew the option for *Thaddeus*. This was no surprise at all. I had written to Mike throughout the option period, telling him *Thaddeus* needed a serious rewrite. My suggestions were always rebuffed, that he, Mike, was the word artist and I should stick to what I know best, fucking a moose.

Predictably, the day Mike received the news Three Walls would not renew the option, I got an expletive-laced email, blaming everyone but himself for the project's demise. The email was shallow and childish in its tone, and although a small part of me felt sorry for Mike, there was nothing to do but shut off the light, close the door, and walk away. I don't know if it was the second stroke, the news about my kidneys, Rosemary's passing, or what, but I just didn't need to be around negative energy. It's best just to walk away.

When a close friend of mine of thirty-five years turned fifty and was going through his mid-life crisis, I listened and offered friendly advice for months. Finally, losing patience with the whole episode, I said, "You know you're a walking cliché? Turning fifty, the new fast car, the younger girlfriend, the lamenting about the girlfriend, all of it."

"I know," my friend said over Skype.

"For months, we've been going around and around. I'll be honest," I said, "I'm as bored as fuck with it."

"I just can't stop thinking about her," he said, choking back more tears.

"Oh man," I said, annoyed. "Let's change the subject and talk about something different. Anything as long as it's not your perceived crises."

"Oh," my friend said, "I just can't get her out of my mind."

"Well," I said, "maybe this will do it. Last month I was told my kidneys are failing and I have stage three kidney disease."

"Oh," he responded, looking shell-shocked.

Right away, I regretted the way I had told him. I saw my friend begin to tear, and I began to feel guilty for being so abrupt. I was about to apologize when he said, "I just feel like she's playing with my emotions. I can't help it, but it hurts."

I was stunned. I just told a friend of thirty-five years I had a potentially life-ending disease, and he said he hurt because his girlfriend's pelvis didn't trick or treat. This was self-absorbed beyond even show business standards. I didn't recognize this guy anymore. I had no comeback at all for that reaction. I shut off the light, closed the door, and walked away.

Sometimes you need to step away from negative energy, either permanently or temporarily, until there is positive change. This may include backing off from your own family, as I did. Luckily for me, my sisters aren't as stubborn as I was, and we talked through our differences and became much closer in the end. I still don't agree with a few of June's societal opinions, but does it matter? No, it doesn't. I respect her for her kindness and the love she shows towards her family, especially my father. On an individual basis, perhaps she loves everyone. The trouble starts for all of us when we slip into that protective tribal mentality. That's when human ugliness shows its head.

Sadly, shortly after his retirement, Jay passed away from brain cancer. I was saddened for my sister and my nieces. He was an emotional bully, but he was their bully.

I even learned through Christmases on St. Margarette's Bay with Jan and Geoff and their neighbor, Scott, to embrace the yuletide and give Christmas a chance. All right, I still struggle with it just a little, but I no longer receive Scrooge toilet paper. And that is a huge step forward for me. Gathering with friends on St. Margarette's Bay will always be special and important to me. I still can be a loner, but St. Margarette's Bay requires me to be a more social loner. I think I can handle that.

Dad is 89 now and has stood by me to lend a hand in every way. I could not have made it through without his unconditional love and support. He is, however, the only known senior with a hat who drives like he's still qualifying for the Indy 500 every time he gets behind the wheel. We both still reach zero gravity when on occasion he does nail a curb.

I continued at the gym, taught English at the library for three years before giving that up, and just overall, I was in a much better place. The only thing I wasn't doing was writing with any earnestness, and that did bother me, even hurt. However, that, too, was about to change.

I got an email from Andre almost six years after my return to Canada. In the email, Andre asked if I remembered that night in New York where I had told him about a story idea I had about organized crime and an undercover operation. He said he'd been thinking about it, thought it was a TV series, and then asked me what I thought about the idea now. The story idea came from my friend Sam who was an undercover cop in the Vancouver Police Department. It was incredibly interesting and unique. Nothing like it had ever been written.

I wrote back to Andre and said if Sam agrees to feed me the material, which is based on a true story, I'll write the script.

A few days later, I was able to track Sam down, and I called him. We re-connected over the phone like we had just hung up yesterday, not twenty-five years ago. Sam had retired a few years previous as the commander of the Vancouver Police Major Crime Unit, culminating a distinguished twenty-five-year career. I brought him up to speed with my life as Schmucky the Clown in Vancouver, New York, and now Halifax. The conversation was freewheeling, honest, and fun.

Finally, after a couple of hours on the phone, I asked Sam what he thought about using his undercover story as the backdrop for a TV series. Whether it's music, theatre, or film, Sam had always been on the fringes of the art scene, so I knew the idea would have some appeal to that artistic muscle. Sam mentioned that some of the crime figures are still active, so he'd like to think about it.

I emailed Andre and told him Sam was a little cool to the idea but that he'd give it some serious thought over the next few days.

Sam and I did enjoy reconnecting, and I spoke to his second wife of the last fifteen years, Sidney. It was all just a comfortable fit. Sam's career had taken him all over the world, including a diplomatic posting, and I just loved listening to all the adventures. We were speaking a few days later day when there was a brief silence.

"Nicholas, I've thought about it. And I'm willing to do it."

"Great. You know what will set this series apart from all the others is that we use the uniqueness of that undercover operation. It's already written for us."

"Okay," Sam replied. "Where do we start?"

That marked the beginning of Sam and I spending two years going down rabbit holes, developing characters, plots, arcs, and themes for the show bible. The bible is what writers use as a road map for the show. It felt good to be seriously writing again, and it was wonderful to work with such a creative old friend. It was also refreshing not to be told to go fuck a moose every time I had an original thought or a suggestion.

Jan and Geoff had given me a free airline ticket with their points, so I decided to fly to Vancouver to see Sam. I saw some old high school friends, and it was great to stay with Sam and Sidney to put the finishing touches on the show bible. The last night I was there, Sam and I were having a glass of wine while Sidney cooked my favorite meal, Indian curry.

When we had the show bible to where we wanted it and Andre signed off on it, Sam asked me, "What do we do now?"

"Well, Andre will have to offer us a contract at some point here, and we stand back and see if he can get any traction with a network."

"We just wait?"

"Well, I think it's about time I got back and finished my book," I mused. Working with Sam for two years had been a great experience, both creatively and personally. "Why don't you work on the book with me? I'll write the chapters, email it to you for any thoughts and tweaks, and then we'll read through each chapter on Skype or Facetime."

An Orchestrated Mistake

I then began a page one rewrite. Sam kept me focused, and he turned out to be every bit of the muse that Rosemary was. We made progress over the next seven or eight months, and then Andre emailed me to tell me he was coming to Halifax for a film forum and it would be great to get together.

Seeing Andre in Halifax was a lot of fun. Our relationship picked up right where it had left off nine years ago in New York. I loved talking about our show, the book, and just where our lives had taken us. Since our get-together in Halifax, several other producers have joined our production team.

However, with only four chapters left to write for the book, I hit a wall. Between the blog and the chapters, I had written over one million, two hundred thousand words—or the equivalent of about twelve books, which I was making into one. I was feeling burned out.

"Go down to our house in Mexico," Sam said to me one day over the phone. "Sidney will be returning to Canada for Christmas, so you'll have the place to yourself. It will be a great place for you to finish your book."

"Thanks," I said. "But I can't really afford Mexico at the moment."

"I'll fly you down on my points," Sam said. "Everything is so cheap down there. It'll cost you next to nothing."

"I'll think about it, but thanks."

In the time I'd been working on the book, I was extremely disciplined—okay, I'll concede, OCD about my gym workouts and my regular visits to the renal clinic for my kidneys. The only thing I had really changed about my routine in years was drinking more water for my kidneys. Six glasses first thing in the morning. It paid off because almost three years after I was admitted to the renal clinic, they sent my doctor and I a letter stating my kidneys had improved moderately, but most importantly, the kidney disease was stable. I was to be discharged.

A few weeks after sharing this piece of good news with Sam and Sidney, I received a notification from Air Canada that Sam had purchased me a ticket down to their home in Cabo San Lucas, Mexico.

"Now you have to go," Sam said over the phone. "I've used my points, so it's paid for."

"Damn. Thank you. I guess I really do have to finish this book."

"Yep." Sam laughed.

A few days before I was due to leave for Mexico, the super in the building told me Ken had been taken to the hospital. A few years earlier, he had almost died during some sort of diabetic seizure. When he was released, I tried to help him, but he wasn't home an hour before he started smoking again and eating ice cream sandwiches. I liked Ken, but it was just too hard to watch him slowly commit suicide. From then on, I'd just drop by his apartment from time to time just to see how he was doing. The super told me gangrene had taken hold, and he had to go in to have his right leg amputated just below the knee. There was so much damage from smoking they literally had to gut the whole apartment and rebuild it. I made a point to see Ken in the hospital before I went to Mexico.

"You just had to give one away," I said to Ken, entering his hospital room.

"Well," Ken replied with a toothless grin, "I did have two. I guess I won't be going to the dance."

The nurse entered with a glucometer. "Sugars?"

"She's always calling me sugar," Ken said, winking.

The nurse took Ken's reading and offered him a pill with a small cup of water. Ken smelled the cup. "No rum," he said, frowning.

Ken explained to me he had nicked his toe cutting his toenails and that was how the infection started. I wanted to ask him, hadn't he noticed his foot turning black from the infection, but I already knew the answer to that. He saw it going black, but hating doctors, he chose to do nothing about it.

I started making a few notes in my small notebook while Ken was preoccupied with his dinner.

"Ya writin' a book?" Ken finally said, noticing.

"Yeah, actually, I am, and you're in it," I said.

"Not interested in a best seller, huh?" Ken replied. "Well, do I at least get the girl in the end?"

"It's not a work of fiction," I said. "But don't worry. No one is going to believe your character anyway. You're the only one who can out-idiot me."

"Goes without saying." Ken grinned.

I told Ken I was going to Mexico for a few months, and upon my return, I'd find out which government retirement home they'd sent him to. Besides his brothers who dropped by occasionally, the only other visitors Ken had were the medical staff. As I was leaving, Ken said, "Nicholas, have a good time." I looked back and just couldn't help feeling lonely for him.

Sam was right. Mexico was the right call. It didn't take me any time at all to adjust to palm trees and blue sky. After showing me around Cabo San Lucas, Sidney returned to Canada to spend the

An Orchestrated Mistake

Christmas holidays with her family, and I had the huge villa to myself.

Mary, the maid, came three times a week. She spoke very little English, and I spoke even less Spanish, but we got on very well, once even going shopping together at a local mall. I never did get used to the idea of having a maid, and I always found myself cleaning up before Mary would come over, but it was fun to have her around.

Sidney's good friend and neighbor, Wanda, an energetic seventy-seven-year-old from Canada, was also fun to hang out with. Wanda had lived in Mexico for almost twenty years and is fluent in English, Spanish, and French. Widowed, she's a take-charge kind of gal, and it was fun chatting by the pool and getting to know her. When my insulin-dispensing pen broke, it was Wanda who helped me communicate with the pharmacist, but in the end, I just used the backup syringes I had brought down from Canada.

The atmosphere was so conducive for writing I cranked out two chapters in two days. I only had a couple of chapters to go when Andre emailed me and said he wanted to arrange a phone call to discuss a contract with Three Walls for Sam and me.

A couple of days later, I was sitting in the backyard by the pool discussing our television contract. While Andre was talking, I felt I should throw a glass of water in my face just to prove I wasn't dreaming. It was almost sensory overload to be sitting in the tropical sun discussing our contract with a company I had worked for nine years previously. Andre and I agreed on the basic contract terms and briefly discussed the show, Mexico, and the new direction that life was taking.

Sam, back in Canada, was unable to sit in on the call, so I called him right away and briefed him with respect to our contract. Sam had more meetings to attend for his current job, so we agreed to speak in the morning to go over the details.

The next morning, and true to most of our calls, we ended up going down multiple rabbit holes relating to our story.

"Hey," Sam said, after about an hour of exploring the caverns of the show, "how's the book going?"

"What book?" I teased. "We just got a TV contract."

"Funny," Sam deadpanned.

"Nobody reads books anymore anyway."

"Finish the book, or I'm flying you home."

"I know, I'll finish. But just let me tell you this. I tweaked the pitch line for our show."

"The book," Sam said. "Finish the book."

"Okay. Okay. I just know this is show business. Everything can fly south in an hour, so for now, I'm just excited to be back."

"Great. Be excited about finishing the book."

****

The TV show would, in essence, mark my return to show business and provide the happy ending to my story. The reality was, however, writing begets rewriting, and life had one more curveball to throw at me.

EXT. MEXICAN VILLA – DAY

Across the street, an ambulance with flashing lights is parked in front of Sam and Sidney's villa. The large gates to the driveway are opened, and two PARAMEDICS wheel the patient through the gates towards the ambulance.

An Orchestrated Mistake

CUT TO:

A medium shot of the patient lying on the ambulance gurney. Wrapped in a blanket with an IV attached to a pole on the gurney is Nicholas Alexander (54). WANDA RUSSELL (77) walks quickly to keep up with the gurney. MARY SANCHEZ (32) stands watching from the front door in the background. Her hand covers her mouth.

> WANDA (Yelling)
>
> Nicholas, they're taking you to the hospital. You understand? You're going to the hospital. I'll see you there.

Nicholas gives a weak nod that he understands. The PARAMEDICS put Nicholas in the back of the ambulance. One PARAMEDIC gets in the back with Nicholas while the other runs to get behind the wheel.

INT. AMBULANCE – DAY

The PARAMEDIC attends to NICHOLAS, who just stares blankly around him.

EXT. HOSPITAL – DAY

The PARAMEDICS take Nicholas out of the back of the ambulance. He is then wheeled quickly through the emergency room doors.

INT. EMERGENCY ROOM – DAY

A team of doctors and nurses immediately get to work on NICHOLAS as he is taken off the gurney and placed on a bed. They speak to each other in Spanish and to NICHOLAS in broken English.

CUT TO:

An Orchestrated Mistake

WANDA enters the back of the emergency room. She begins speaking to one of the doctors in Spanish.

INT. EMERGENCY ROOM – DUSK

A few hours later, an English-speaking DR. RUIZ (40s) stands on one side of the bed while WANDA stands listening on the other. Nicholas's eyes open.

DR. RUIZ

How you feeling?

NICHOLAS

Good.

DR. RUIZ

You know what happened today, don't you?

NICHOLAS

Not really.

DR. RUIZ

We almost lost you today to a severe hypoglycemic episode. A mild episode is when your glucose

Drops to around seventy milligrams per deciliter. When the paramedics found you, you were forty-one.

NICHOLAS

Oh.

WANDA

Yeah, oh! You scared the hell out of us!

An Orchestrated Mistake

DR RUIZ

Do you remember anything?

NICHOLAS

Not really. I was talking to Sam on the phone. I hung up. Went over to my computer to work on the

book. Next thing I was on the floor surrounded by paramedics.

WANDA

And our neighbor Juan was there. Lucky he's a doctor and

was home. He rushed over.

DR. RUIZ

Any idea how your sugars got so low?

NICHOLAS

Not really. I mean, I've been giving myself insulin for decades.

DR. RUIZ

Anything like this ever happened before?

NICHOLAS

Never.

DR RUIZ nods but stares at NICHOLAS a moment.

DR RUIZ

Tell me, how are you feeling lately, Nicholas. I mean emotionally?

NICHOLAS just stares back at RUIZ

DR RUIZ (Cont)

An Orchestrated Mistake

Nothing bothering you?

WANDA

He feels great! He's almost finished his book! He and Sam may get their own TV show. Isn't that right, Nicholas?

NICHOLAS nods 'yes' as he stares out the hospital window before turning to RUIZ

NICHOLAS

Wanda's right. I feel fine.

DR RUIZ

I'm just asking. I'd like to know why this episode happened.

NICHOLAS

(Laughing)

What are you saying, Doctor? You think I tried to pull a Hemingway?

WANDA

Lucky that Mary found you when she did, otherwise you wouldn't be with us.

DR RUIZ

Pulled a what?

NICHOLAS

I'm fine, Doctor. I must have made a simple mistake.

DR RUIZ finally nods in agreement.

DR. RUIZ

An Orchestrated Mistake

I'd like to keep you here overnight, just to watch you. If everything looks good in the morning, we'll send you home. Fine with you?

WANDA

It's totally fine with him.

DR RUIZ

I'll see to it that a private room is prepared.

INT. HOSPITAL ROOM – NIGHT

WANDA sits in a chair beside NICHOLAS' hospital bed.

NICHOLAS

Mary really found me?

WANDA

Yes, you were slumped over at your desk. Scared the hell out of her. She ran over to get me. I got Juan and the ambulance.

NICHOLAS nods lost in thought.

WANDA

How do you think it happened?

NICHOLAS

(Shrugs his shoulders)

Someone once called me 'distracted.' Maybe I just got distracted by all the good news. I just don't know.

WANDA

Well, you better know. You're a diabetic. You have to know your sugars no matter how healthy you think you are.

An Orchestrated Mistake

NICHOLAS

Yeah. You know I had the stroke just days after I found out I made it to producer in New York. And now, with a TV contract and my book almost finished, I almost die from a hypoglycemic episode.

WANDA

Maybe it's good news that is your nemesis.

NICHOLAS

Seems like it.

WANDA

Well, let's pray your book and TV show are total flops.

NICHOLAS

(Chuckling)

You know what was funny? When I came to on the floor and saw the Mexican paramedics working on me, I had no idea what was going on. I didn't know if I was alive or dead. But you know what I did think? I honestly thought that if I'm dead, and this is Heaven, wait until Trump finds out that the Mexicans run Heaven.

They chuckle. WANDA gets up and walks to the door.

WANDA

I'm going to let you get some sleep. I feel like I could sleep for a month.

NICHOLAS

Wanda!

An Orchestrated Mistake

WANDA stops and turns.

NICHOLAS (CONT)

Thanks. And thank my guardian angel for me.

WANDA

You can thank Mary yourself when I take you home tomorrow.

NICHOLAS nods in agreement.

EXT. HOSPITAL – DAY

NICHOLAS is wheeled through the front doors in a wheelchair by a HOSPITAL ORDERLY. Once outside, NICHOLAS raises his hand for the ORDERLY to stop.

CUT TO:

CLOSE UP of NICHOLAS getting out of the wheelchair. He takes a deep breath, and turning, nods to the ORDERLY. He starts to walk towards WANDA'S car parked on the side of the road.

INT. WANDA'S CAR – DAY

Close up of WANDA watching NICHOLAS walking towards the car.

CUT TO:

From WANDA'S POV, we see NICHOLAS approach the car. He's admiring the blue sky and the sun.

CUT TO:

A TWO SHOT of NICHOLAS and WANDA. NICHOLAS leans in the passenger window.

NICHOLAS

An Orchestrated Mistake

Thanks for coming, Wanda, but I really think I want to walk home.

WANDA

You're kidding?

NICHOLAS

Na. It's a beautiful day.

NICHOLAS looks around at the morning sun. He takes a deep breath.

NICHOLAS (CONT)

I'll see ya later.

CUT TO:

NICHOLAS turns, taps the fender, and slowly walks away from the car. He looks up at the palm trees, the blue sky, and the warm Mexican sun. WANDA toots the horn as she drives by. NICHOLAS waves and his eyes begin to twinkle as he admires the day. A broad smile now breaks out across his face as he begins to run.

BLACK OUT

CUE MUSIC: JOURNEY "BE GOOD TO YOURSELF"

ROLL CREDITS.

An Orchestrated Mistake

About Shane O'Dell

Shane O'Dell has been in the entertainment industry in one capacity or another for the last thirty-five years. He was born in Eastern Canada, in Goose Bay, Newfoundland, but raised in Vancouver, British Columbia. He began his career in radio right out of high school, is a graduate of the American Academy of Dramatic Arts in Los Angeles, California, and performed for ten years before focusing his energies off stage and behind the camera. Shane wrote his first professional play at 28, and shortly after moved to New York to pursue his career in entertainment. In New York, Shane worked both in front and behind the camera in independent film before a health crisis sidelined his career. He currently is working on his second book and other writing projects in Halifax, Nova Scotia.

www.ingramcontent.com/pod-product-compliance
Lightning Source LLC
Chambersburg PA
CBHW020900080526
44589CB00011B/373